Keeping Hope Alive

D1103012

Keeping Hope Alive

How One Somali Woman Changed 90,000 Lives

Dr. Hawa Abdi

With Sarah J. Robbins

virago

VIRAGO

First published in Great Britain in 2013 by Virago Press
Reprinted 2013

First published in the United States of America in 2013 by
Grand Central Publishing, a division of Hachette Book Group, Inc.

Copyright © Hawa Abdi 2013

The moral right of the author has been asserted.

All rights reserved.
No part of this publication may be reproduced, stored in a
retrieval system, or transmitted in any form or by any means, without
the prior permission in writing of the publisher, nor be otherwise circulated
in any form of binding or cover other than that in which it is published
and without a similar condition including this condition being
imposed on the subsequent purchaser.

A CIP catalogue record for this book
is available from the British Library.

ISBN 978-1-84408-788-4

Printed and bound in Great Britain by
Clays Ltd, St Ives plc

Papers used by Virago are from well-managed forests
and other responsible sources.

MIX
Paper from
responsible sources
FSC® C104740

Virago Press
An imprint of
Little, Brown Book Group
100 Victoria Embankment
London EC4Y 0DY

An Hachette UK Company
www.hachette.co.uk

www.virago.co.uk

For Ahmed Aden Mohamed

BAINTE DEN STOC
WITHDRAWN FROM DLR LIBRARIES STOCK

Contents

Introduction: Keeping Hope Alive   *ix*

1. A Stranger in My Homeland   1
2. Gold Is Made Beautiful by Fire   13
3. To Stop the Bleeding   18
4. Paradise in the World   25
5. Friends and Enemies   31
6. Awaiting a Life, Awaiting a Death   39
7. Filling the Hole in My Heart   46
8. Losing My Past and My Future   56
9. Building My Practice   65
10. My Sisters Return   75
11. Necessity Is the Mother of Invention   82
12. Collapse   88
13. Why Do You Want to Do This?   96
14. Danger from Within   106
15. Today We Are Happy   115
16. Operation Restore Hope   125
17. One Wrong Decision   137
18. The Fourth Container   149

19. Vice Minister of Labor and Sports   160

20. We Can Remember   167

21. Ahmed   174

22. "A Doctor Bound by Humanity"   179

23. An Ocean of Need   189

24. A New Generation   197

25. The Attack   207

26. Women of the Year   219

27. Forgiveness   228

Glossary of Somali Terms   241

Hawa's Family   243

Acknowledgments   245

Introduction:
Keeping Hope Alive

She was twenty-two years old, with a bullet in her brain and another in her heart. I don't remember the day she was brought into our hospital, or even whether it was day—it was simply a clear moment in the dust-filled haze of a civil war that had, by then, long ripped our country apart. By 1995, in Somalia, young boys from different militias brandished machine guns looted from the former government and donated from God knows where else. This woman was one of hundreds of the war's victims—my patients—awaiting me at that very moment. But her story was different.

She was a young, strong Somali woman. I built my hospital to deliver her child—not to smooth my thumb and middle finger down her forehead in order to close her lifeless eyes. Before I asked my staff to search the bush for her family, I stopped and stood with her for a moment. As I turned away, I cried, not as a doctor, but as a mother. How will this girl's mother feel tonight, I asked myself, knowing that her daughter is dead?

Even in the most remote of places, even in times of chaos, bad news travels quickly. A woman came from the bush with information, and we walked together into the room where the dead body still lay. "The person who killed this girl was her mother," the woman told me. "Her mother killed her."

I was shocked, for I had never heard of such a thing! "How could it be?" I asked.

"The girl's father was from one clan, and her mother from another," the woman explained, shaking her head, as she looked at the dead young woman's calm face. She was still very beautiful—unaware, it seemed, of what had destroyed her. I was also unaware, until the woman continued: "When the girl and her mother went to the mother's family, the family said, 'This girl is from the wrong clan. We don't want you.'"

The woman looked up at me with sad eyes. "They say she killed her daughter so she could go home."

To this day, there is no way to know whether that terrible story is true. I never even learned the young woman's name. Her relatives from the area came to take her back to the bush, to bury her near her home, and I returned to my outpatient clinic, where a line of families waiting for me reached the trees outside. But that night and even to this day, I am haunted by a question that, at one time or another, every witness to war must ask: In a time of such darkness, if such a thing can happen, how will we survive?

When most people hear the word *Somalia*, they think of this, our tragic recent history—the deep divisions among our people, the droughts and the famines, the sea of sharks and pirates. Even the description of our land's geography—the Horn of Africa, splitting the Indian Ocean and the Gulf of Aden, pointing up toward the Middle East—is full of extremes. But it was not always this way.

In August 1983, when I began this hospital as just a one-room clinic 21 kilometers outside our capital, Mogadishu, life was peaceful. As one of Somalia's first female gynecologists, I was well known in the area, so when civil war broke out seven years later, my patients, my extended family and neighbors, and victims and survivors flooded the main road that led out of Mogadishu and passed right by the clinic. I took them in, and I gave them whatever I had—cool water, a place to sleep, a portion of our farm's harvest. Somali people have a tradition of hospitality: When a traveler comes to you, you have to give him the best of what you have; if you fill his stomach and tell him sweet words, God will bless you.

This is the story of how, after more than twenty years, these people have become my family, their huts stretching out forever, a sea of twisted branches and brightly woven mats, of unraveling rags and flapping plastic sheets: Hawa Abdi Village. Today, that one-room clinic is a 400-bed hospital, and the few families in need are now tens of thousands of people who live on that hospital's surrounding land. Beneath some of their homes lies a shadow village of 10,560 people—some who died by clan warfare or indiscriminate shelling, others by disease or by hunger. We buried them together in one place, never imagining that the war would continue for so long that the number of people seeking our help would grow to 90,000, and that a new generation would be forced by lack of land to build their huts atop a mass grave where, for so long, we have mourned.

We owe it to the dead and those who live among them to remember that our heritage is not one of violence and destruction. Centuries ago, in Somalia, our people lived in small settlements and coastal towns, lying like a jeweled necklace along the beautiful Indian Ocean. The rainy seasons were sometimes short, sometimes long; they gave the people green canopies from tall trees and the cleanest, sweetest air you can imagine. Even in the dry season of January, February, and March, the dead branches found new life by the riverside: They were bent into frames for makeshift huts, not unlike those that now crowd my land. There the families stayed until the rains blew in, the people returned home for the growing season, and the cycle repeated. While the weather patterns shift, the rhythm of the seasons forever guides our life; so, too, do so many Somali traditions, some beautiful, some damaging.

Like most Somali people, my mother's family were pastoralists. They reared animals for milk and for meat and cultivated maize and sorghum during the rainy season. During the dry season they wandered with their animals in search of water; they loaded their camels with their valuables, their dishes, and their carpets, as they searched for a place where their herds could graze.

The difficulty in Somalia can be explained by the fact that in every time of strife, as in every dry season, it is the same story: A gate opens, and all the animals run together after one patch of grass, trying to beat out the others. The herders follow. "This is our grass," says the strongest herder to the others, "so you find another spot." If the losers refuse to leave, they will fight the winners. The same is true if there is a group of people who live near one well; they will say to the thirsty people wandering, "You're not drinking this water." Years after, when the rain comes, the hunger and thirst are quenched. But the once-thirsty people remember, and the conflict remains.

As I've traveled all over the world to seek help for the displaced people living on my land, people have asked me, "How can it be?" How is it possible, they wonder, in the center of what has been called the world's most failed state, can there still be some safe haven, a refuge, a society living harmoniously in a village known simply by one woman's name?

In Hawa Abdi Village, I tell them, we treat all victims of the conflict equally—no matter what side they're on. I learned this lesson from my father, who had a wider worldview than his father or the generations who came before because tragedy had forced him onto a different path. Orphaned at age twelve, my father walked for ten days from his small village to Mogadishu, where he met a woman from the fishing community we call Jaaji. The woman took him in as her own son, giving him food, clothes, and even a job at the country's main port.

My father came of age during colonial times, but it was, for him, a peaceful time; he worked among ships arriving from every corner of the world. He befriended the Italians and the British, whose ancestors had each colonized different parts of Somalia, as well as the Indians and the Swahili speakers traveling up from the coast of what is now Kenya. These sailors and businessmen taught him their languages and about the history of their countries— lessons that he brought home to his four daughters. "You can change your life through hard work," my father told me. "You can make yourself indispensable if you understand the capacity of people to help each other."

I can still hear his voice and imagine myself as I was then, at age thirteen, in 1960—the year our country gained its independence from British and Italian rule. At that time, we Somalis believed that our future was bright. When the Italian flag was lowered officially, at midnight on July 1, I was with my father in front of the Hotel Shabelle. As the five-cornered white star of the Somali Republic came up, our national songs played over big loudspeakers. I will forever remember one, so clearly: *Tana Siib Tan Saar*, which means bring down the Italian one, and raise up the Somali flag.

We were told that some people died in those first days of independence because of the shock of happiness. I believe it, having seen the way my father embraced his friends in the streets as though they had survived a long war. "We had our difficult life, but today we are free," my father told us, his eyes shining, as we walked home that night on stiff legs. "Now we can pass through the center of our capital, where before we could not. We can go wherever we want."

In the beginning, the Somali people saw new opportunities from overseas—both from the countries that at one time colonized us and from newer, more trustworthy friends, and then, more and more, in our own neighborhoods. We worked hard, rising to the tops of our fields; we dreamed of changing our nation through education and hard work.

Just as violence is not our legacy, neither is clan division. Clans in Somalia arose from the tradition of *abtirsiinyo*, as we call it, or "counting ancestors," back and back one hundred generations.

From our earliest days, disputes between two families, or two clans, were settled peacefully, even harmoniously: Each clan sent a wise old man by camel, sometimes traveling a long distance— for days or even weeks—to discuss the matter under the shade of a big tree. In between each of the elders sat a mediator who would hear both positions, saying, "Yes, yes, yes." The elders analyzed the situation, talking until they agreed on the appropriate punishment, in which the offending clan would give some camels and some cows. After this was settled, the mediator turned to one side and said, "Bring twenty girls." The other side brought twenty boys, and then, as part of the reconciliation process, the young people from the two clans would marry. Interclan marriage built families to eradicate hate; in the future, the two sides, now related by blood, would not battle.

Our earliest days as a nation were glorious, but over time, corruption began to take hold. We lost all law and order in the early 1990s, when our government collapsed. This time, when the Somali people turned to their clans for protection, they regarded others with suspicion, or worse—even as their own veins ran with the blood of the other side. The only way that my work could survive was for me to remain neutral, giving all the war's victims, from every clan, my heart and my soul. So many times I thought I would give my life as well, during years of famine and senseless violence, as mortar shells fell, and still fall, from Somalia's brilliant blue sky.

What would my father say if he could see that beautiful girl, young and strong, killed by her mother because her father was from a different clan? If he could see the tens of thousands of people living on our family's land, where, for more than twenty years, we have been used as human shields for clashing warlords or rival militiamen seeking only to loot or to kill?

What would he say about the insurgent group Hizbul Islam, which came to my gate in May 2010, and about those who have followed in their footsteps, invading my home and hospital just as they have every other place Somalis once considered safe? These young men are our own sons as well—an entire generation that has grown up without law and order. They have clung to a fundamentalist, inaccurate version of Islam to give them a sense of power; as they try to destroy our society, they are also trying to destroy our religion. Now we are hostages to their ungodly belief that a woman is an object, an instrument, to be used only for their purposes.

"You are *old*, and we are stronger than you," said one of the young men who came to me in those terrible days of 2010. "You have to hand over the authority of the hospital and the management of your camp to us."

"That's impossible," I told him. "This is my property. I am the doctor here, and I have the knowledge for it. On what legal basis should I hand over a hospital to you?"

"You are a *woman*," said another. "You are not allowed to shoulder any responsibility and authority."

"We will protect you here," said the first.

"That's not your job," I said. Though the camp's elders quietly reminded me that the men could shoot me at a moment's notice, I refused to back down. "So they'll shoot me!" I told the elders. "At least I will die with dignity."

I remember so clearly my walk back to the hospital that day, to the sixty patients waiting in the outpatient clinic—and the additional hundred who had been admitted. I knew that these invaders, with their guns and their religion, were motivated solely by owning and taking, but in my anger, I would stand firm. My Islam sees women as valued members of society—as equals—so I never showed my despair.

I wish that were the end of the story, that the strength of my conviction was enough to change the minds of AK-47-clutching young men who have been raised to hate and to kill. But ignorance is the enemy of humanity: The same evil that killed the beautiful young girl in my hospital continues to threaten our lives, as it has for more than twenty years.

As I speak for millions of Somali women who have no voice, I also share their struggles in this complicated world we will forever insist on calling home. Like the women around me, I, too, have known unimaginable sorrow—I know, like them, what it is like to lose a mother, a sister, a child. The militants could have shot me— it's true. But I knew that if I died in the name of all I believed, it would have been no problem. Death, as you'll see, is not the end of our story, which continues to unfold against the most unimaginable odds.

Death is a part of life in Somalia, whether it comes to us through violence, through disease, or even through childbirth. We know the danger we face, and yet, we women still plan for the future. In some ways, maybe, we are moved to act by the fact of our mortality—knowing that like every other animal on God's earth, we, too, will die, but that somehow, what we leave behind will last.

This is why I must begin with the one thing that sustains us, the one answer to our question of survival—with hope. Hope is what remains, as we wait for peace, even as we bleed and we starve. Hope is also our practice, which is why the people living on my land use the same prayers, the same patience, that we have for generations. It may be that right now, we are living for hope— for a time when, we pray, the evil that has infected our society will be wiped out, and when the law will protect all human beings, rather than militias.

Like our ancestors, the leaders of my camp, women and men, come together in the shade—under the trees, just as we did in the old times. Near my hospital is a mango grove that I call my "Camp David." It is our retreat, not unlike the U.S. president's retreat of the same name, where we discuss the situation facing the camp or disputes happening within. Sometimes a group of displaced people will gather around there to lie on carpets at the end of a punishing day—to drink tea, to sing songs, or just to listen to the music of the rustling leaves.

These trees, which I planted myself, have witnessed drought and famine, disease and heavy shelling; they stand today because of their thick roots reaching down in every possible direction, finding water, holding on somehow. Their branches stretch out and out in the same way, shielding us from the afternoon sun as we tell stories, like those I will tell you now. We know that just doing so is an act of hope—that as we share our story with the world, we are inviting the truth to come out and to save us.

Keeping Hope Alive

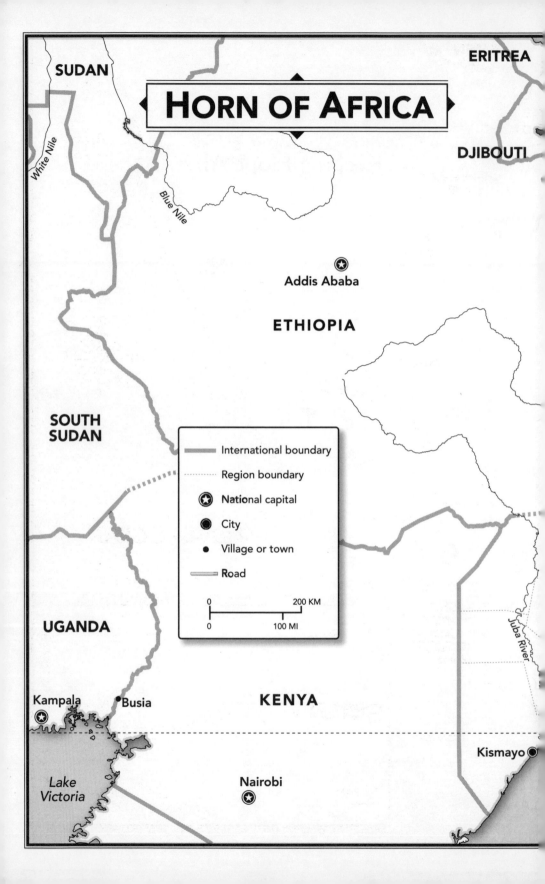

CHAPTER ONE

A Stranger in My Homeland

My career began in Mogadishu in 1971, in my country's prime and in my own. I was twenty-four years old and had just returned from medical school in Ukraine, where I'd studied on a Soviet Union–sponsored scholarship. When I presented my new diploma to Somalia's Ministry of Health, I immediately received a position at the European-built Digfer hospital. Somalia had only about sixty doctors at the time, and Digfer's 600-bed hospital was run by just thirty-five doctors—thirteen of them were Somali, and just one other was female. The rest of my colleagues were Italian men, for although we were newly independent, we were still emerging from the shadow of our colonial past.

On my first day of work, I put on a new outfit—white trousers and a white blouse, to match my brand-new white coat—and I went directly to the office of Digfer's medical director, Mohamed Ali Nur. Mohamed Ali Nur was also the country's first Somali pediatrician; he was trained in Italy and had returned five or six years ahead of me. Although I respected the work he had done to bring better medical care to the area, when we sat down to discuss my role at the hospital, we clashed immediately.

"You will start with a rotation in pediatrics," he said.

"I want the surgery department," I told him. "I have done rounds for two years, in medical school, and I am already a doctor." From the moment I participated in my first procedures, when I was a medical student in Odessa, I had dreamed of becoming a surgeon. I thought often of the cool-headed precision that I saw in one of my professors when, as a sixth-year student, I assisted him in a procedure to repair a woman's obstructed intestines. I had stood in awe with one of my classmates, holding the professor's instruments and staring down at the incision under the bright lights as he sewed them together with expert sutures. For every move that I could predict, there were at least two that surprised me. I'd decided then that to save a life like this, with such speed and confidence, was the most important thing anyone could do.

I told Mohamed Ali Nur that I loved the long, complicated process of surgery: consulting the patient, learning her history, settling on a diagnosis and a solution, and earning her trust. "Children can't talk with you," I said. "They can't answer questions about where they're feeling pain. They just cry."

"You will talk with the mothers," he said.

The mothers, I told him, were often the problem. Many didn't remember when their children's symptoms began or what food they had given them, so it was hard to know if the children had been poisoned or if they had been infected some other way. "I prefer working with people who I can ask questions, and who will answer me," I said.

"Throughout your career, you will see so many children in the most severe states of disease," he said calmly. "It's required."

"There are plenty of other doctors who want to be pediatricians," I said. "I know you are a pediatrician, but it's not my strength."

Mohamed Ali Nur was a kind man, but he was also very firm. "Protocol is protocol, and as a doctor, you will be required to follow it," he said, folding his hands on his desk and looking at me. "In this country, every doctor must understand how to treat children. If you don't choose to, you can leave." He stood, and in a quiet way forced me to follow him down the hall and into the pediatric ward. While he introduced me to my new colleagues, I thought only of how I would prove to him that I was a gifted surgeon.

Later that afternoon, my younger sister Amina met me at Digfer's gate. As we walked together to the center of town, I felt the sun warm my skin and the frustration leave me. I sighed loudly with relief, swinging my arms and breathing deeply.

Amina laughed to see me relax. "*Abayo*," she said, using the Somali term of endearment for a sister. "Up until now, you were waiting for your life to begin."

"You're right," I said, laughing at the strange idea of being reborn at age twenty-four. It was true, really. After seven long years in the Soviet Union, I had been delivered home, into the beauty that was five o'clock in Mogadishu—the best time of day, when the sun is lower and the salty breeze from the Indian Ocean feels cool on your skin.

That afternoon, Amina and I met friends for cappuccino at a place called Caffè Nazionale, which was popular on Thursdays and Fridays—our weekend. We went there often; if the Italian restaurant was full, we could also go to Hotel Savoia, a Western-style hotel and restaurant in the middle of the city, or down near the seaside for ice cream. When we headed back home that evening, some of the boys we went to school with stopped us on the street, flirting and joking: "Ah, Hawa, you need a ride? I'll give you a lift." Like the sun on my face, like the sweet Somali bananas and the grapefruit I had missed so much, I enjoyed the attention. Here, every person I saw was my brother, my sister.

In those days, everyone our age was feeling free and optimistic— eager to be a part of a country that was growing as fast and as strong as we ourselves were. All three of my younger sisters were still in school, for by this time, education was free on every level: Our president, Mohamed Siad Barre, had formed a medical school, a law school, and several other colleges in and around Mogadishu, so students came from other parts of the country to continue their studies, rather than going abroad, as I had done. Now, at age nineteen, Amina was pregnant: Our family was anxiously awaiting the birth of a new generation.

Amina had prepared for me a two-room apartment in a neighborhood called Hodan, near both the hospital and the villa that she shared with her husband, Sharif, and with our other sisters, Asha and Khadija. We still spent most nights together, as we had as children. We had grown up since the time when we ate rice from the same dish and slept in a pile together, our mother stretching her warm body around us and shushing us as we poked at one another. But some things had not changed: Amina and Asha still fell asleep easily, while I lay awake, long into the night, wondering about my future. To calm myself, I tried to remember what my mother once told me, on a walk to the seaside: "Listen to your inner voice," she had said. "When it comes time to make a decision, sit quietly until you can hear that voice—only then will you be able to find a solution to your problems." Only through quiet, through planning, through prayer, was I finally able to sleep.

In the region called *Lafole*, where the sandy roads of Mogadishu meet the soft, brown earth of the Shabelle River basin, my grandmother raised my mother. Together, they raised me. *Lafole* is Somali for "place of bones"—for the battles our people waged against the Italian colonists, who came to us more than a century ago. Even during the 1930s, when my mother was young, the Italian colonists who controlled the area kept Somali laborers like slaves in an area nearby the river. Those whose backs were not broken while cutting down trees or digging farms were struck down by deadly malaria.

Our mother's name was Dahabo, which means "golden"—describing the most precious of the metals. She was an only child, and as my grandmother was a widow, my mother was everything to her. In Somalia, there is no insurance; children are a family's investment and their retirement benefit. When my mother was a teenager, my grandmother heard that her cousin, a local businessman, wanted to take her to help dig the Italian farms, so she took my mother and walked out of their hut, into the night. They found their way by the half-moon, moving through the fog, and continued south along the curve of the river for 100 kilometers, where they reached a village near the coastal city of Merca.

There they stayed, counting two rainy seasons and the difficult dry times in between. To survive, my mother collected armfuls of firewood and kindling to sell at the market, earning enough coins during each trip to bring home a sack of crushed sesame seeds and a small packet of sugar, which would feed her and my grand-mother until she could gather enough wood to try again. When the second dry season came, they packed up their few belongings and came to Mogadishu to start a new life in the Abdul-Aziz dis-trict. My father lived there, among the fishing community, the Jaaji. He was a tall man, kind and soft-spoken, with a beautiful smile and a long neck. As is our habit, his first name, Abdi, is my last name now.

The Jaaji were a hardworking, honest people that came from many different clans originally—some from Hawiye, my father's clan; some from Dir, my mother's clan; and from many others. (The claim is that there are four major clans in Somalia—the two that I've just mentioned, as well as the Darod and the Issaq.) But the Italians condemned the fishing group, just as they had the ironworkers, shoemakers, and cotton weavers, as they felt this type of work was low-class. I was once told that the colonists would call the clan chiefs, saying, "Your people are the best—superior in this society. We will help you, but you should stay away from these four groups, which are the lowest." Living among a people who were mistreated for harvesting, selling, and eating the fruits of the sea, my father understood the benefit of living simply and the harm of dividing a society.

My parents' was a rare marriage of love. My father even sang to my mother, using lyrics he wrote himself, as was the way among romantics in our area, in our time: "*Sidii dayax iyo daruur u ekeey / Dahabooy ma ku daadaheeyaa.*" (O you, who is fair as the moon and the clouds / O Dahabo, should I hold your hand / And take a stroll with you?) I am their eldest child, born in 1947 and raised in a house with two rooms, a fence, and a door that closed to the outside world, protecting us. I awoke every morning to brilliant white light and salty air, and in the afternoons our neighbors came to sit around the fire, drinking tea until the sun dipped low.

Each time my mother became pregnant, everyone hoped for a boy. In Somalia, you see, the women cheer for the birth of a son. A boy is king, worth two girls—he increases the family's wealth and has the singular power to protect or to destroy. When I was five years old, I was desperate for a sister—a girl that we would call Amina. You know, sometimes children say something, and God accepts. My Amina was born strong and healthy. I loved her from the start.

In those days, we had no running water; the well filled our jugs, and the entire Indian Ocean was our bath and our Laundromat. We would walk with our mother down the alley behind our house at first light, dodging the stones, stray chickens, and animal waste until we reached the beach. On our journey, my mother would sing or tell stories about the ocean. I freely asked questions about her past or about our family, and just as freely, she declined to answer them. "I don't wish to talk about that," she would say as our feet fell at the same rhythm. When I pressed her, she said only that every woman should have secrets she keeps for herself.

My grandmother, whom we called Ayeyo, left Mogadishu soon after my parents married and returned to her cows and goats in the rural area of Lafole. As I grew, our family began to spend more time with Ayeyo, where the milk and meat were as fresh as the air, and we were free to run through the grass in our bare feet. Ayeyo taught me to make breakfast at four o'clock in the morning, before the cold left the earth and almost two hours before sunrise. I held a match to the firewood our cousins had brought the previous afternoon. When the fire was hot, I rested a pot of water on the wood until the water boiled. I added sugar—the most important ingredient—and a mix of tea, cloves, cinnamon, cardamom, and mint. In another bowl, I mixed sorghum flour, water, and oil into a thin batter, cooking it in a flat pan until it became a pancake—*injera*—to accompany the tea.

Ayeyo was a philosopher, and those mornings I sat with her, dunking my *injera*, she helped me understand the order of things. A curse was the worst thing possible, said Ayeyo; these ill wishes follow a man for fifty generations, as damaging as fire. This is an image, you see, that a child can understand: After a fire, you will walk around where the trees and the huts once stood, and you'll hardly be able to imagine anything but ashes. I had seen, after fire, just the bones of animals and small piles of charred sticks— evidence that the world cannot sustain life in the wake of a curse.

Blessing, said Ayeyo, is a heavy rain cloud hanging over a parched village after a season of harsh sun. From the first shower, the land awakens, the soil darkens, and tiny sprouts appear along the edges of the road. From there, greenery will spread, rising with the grasses, the maize, and sesame plants, and stretching up into lemon and mango trees that swell into fruits. From there, life continues, and only good things will come.

I questioned Ayeyo about the other facts of life—I thought I understood love, but marriage was a mystery. I knew only that when my mother was very young, just fourteen years old, she had been married to a different man—her first cousin. Some eve- nings, Ayeyo spoke into my mother's silences. She had promised my mother's hand, she said, because it was the way of our society, which believed that women who refused marriage were as good as in the grave. The men, who made the rules, could take as many as four wives so long as they provided for each one and for all the children. From the beginning of our history, said Ayeyo, women obeyed without question.

No one could explain to me how my mother could overcome the pain and fear of her first marriage. Her husband had beaten her, knocking out one of her teeth; she was so young when she gave birth to a daughter, Faduma Ali, that she left the child behind and ran back to Ayeyo, where she thought she'd be safe. Although the man who married my mother finally agreed to give her a divorce—something very rare for a Somali man of the time—he insisted on keeping Faduma Ali with his family in the rural area. Eventually, Ayeyo convinced the man's mother that they could raise the child together, which is why I grew up to call Faduma Ali *abayo*, sister, just as Amina called me.

Why didn't Faduma Ali live with us? "If your mother tells you not to ask, then do not ask," said Ayeyo. A Somali child's role was not to question her parents but simply to obey their wishes. "If you care for your parents," said Ayeyo, "you will get the world."

She also taught that discomfort was a part of life—something to be accepted, not questioned. "When your mother was a child, she never cried," she said by way of example. As I grew, I learned that memory can be short, especially memories of the most difficult times. New urgencies and new enemies arrive, demanding all our attention and intelligence.

The doctors of Digfer hospital were required to attend a physicians' meeting every morning at seven; before we discussed the events of the previous night, we began with a song about scientific socialism, singing that the way gave us prosperity and progress, that every one of us—even the young, the women, and the elders—was ready to support the cause, that President Siad Barre was the father of the Somali society. Only after we sang could the doctor who had been on duty inform us about what had happened the night before and what was now required—further examinations, Cesarean sections, other elective surgeries.

If any one of us didn't come at seven, or if he didn't want to sing, his name would be marked down for one of the members of the *komsomol*, the youth organization, and later he would be called into an office. "Why?" the representatives would ask him. "Don't you like your country? Don't you like scientific socialism? What would you want instead?" We heard rumors that if a person were called before the committee more than twice, he and his family would be seen as enemies, and arrested, imprisoned, or worse. I was uncomfortable about this pressure to say something good about the administration; I did sing, as was required, but I didn't go to meetings or participate in politics in any real way.

Our country's connection to scientific socialism had grown along with our friendship with the Soviet Union—a relationship that both sides had nurtured for years. You see, when Somalia achieved independence in 1960, we continued our relationship with Italy while also receiving investment from many new places. The United States provided grants and humanitarian aid for the big floods that had swept away homes and destroyed farmland in the early years; Arab states such as Egypt, Syria, and Iraq offered development help as well. The Soviet Union and China grew more involved as time went on; the Soviets provided training for our new military, prepared our land for agriculture, supported an iron company, and helped us establish milk and meat processing plants.

The Soviet Union also provided us with education. Back in 1963, when I was in secondary school, a friend told me about a free Russian cultural school that was held in a converted home with four classrooms. "They're giving scholarships to Somali students," she said. A few days later I was enrolled there and struggling with the Russian alphabet.

I'd always been an eager student. In primary school, when most of my classmates had emptied back onto the dusty road toward home, I would stay at my desk. Then I would get up, spin the globe at the front of the classroom, and discover the entire world. I had memorized the longest rivers—in Africa, the Nile; and in America, the Mississippi. I had learned the history of the African independent states and the Italian tenses. I had passed three grade levels in one year, catching up to my own age group, even though I had started school late. By secondary school, when we had competitions over who knew the most, in history or biology or another subject, I often won.

Although our government took a neutral position during the Cold War, we young people witnessed the East-West conflict first-hand, in our schools and on the streets. Most of our Italian school-teachers resented the Soviet presence. I remember one of them telling us in class that, "The Russian face is not aristocratic." Still, for us, it was simple: If actions speak louder than words, then at the time, the Soviets were people of action. We called my Russian teacher *maestro*, as we did the rest of our teachers, but he treated us very differently—as equals, almost.

In those days, my family was struggling to make ends meet, and my heart was wide and open, expecting that everyone I met would want to help me. One night after dinner, as I listened to the sound of the radio coming from our neighbor's home, I decided to write my Russian teacher a letter. I addressed him by name, Dimitri Stepanchecov, and asked him to find me work to support my family or a scholarship to continue my education.

There was no higher education in Somalia at the time, so I knew that any scholarship opportunity would mean a trip far away, to Italy or to the Soviet Union. I knew, too, that at that time, Somali society believed only in boys. Girls did not receive scholar-ships to study, and most families didn't want their daughters to go abroad, where they could become corrupted. But Dimitri Stepan-checov put my case forward to the Soviet Women's Commission in Moscow; he had my grades and his recommendation, and all he needed was my signature. I signed, not believing it was pos-sible, but less than two months later he told me that I had been accepted into a medical training program in the Soviet Union—one year of preparatory course, and six years of medical school.

Once I had my father's blessing to attend, the news spread quickly. My secondary school teacher, an older Italian woman, asked me to stay after anatomy class. "Hawa, the Soviet Union will spoil you," she said. "If you continue to study the Italian language, you can be a secretary in the Italian Embassy here."

"I plan to be a doctor," I told her.

"We believe that you will be a very good secretary," she said.

"A secretary and a doctor," I said, "are two different things."

When my father brought home my plane ticket from the Mogadishu post office, my sisters and I stared at it, turning it over in our
hands. I was seventeen years old, and with this one piece of paper,
I had passage to an entirely new place.

Then, on August 24, 1964, everyone I knew drove to the airport to wish me well on my journey: Mogadishu to Aden, Aden
to Cairo, Cairo to Moscow. My university classmates were from
Ghana, Tanzania, Ethiopia, and so many other countries; the
Soviet people, however, knew only one group with brown skin.
"Where did you come from?" they often asked as we passed them
on the streets. "Did you come from Cuba?"

"No," we would laugh. "We came from Africa!"

We represented many of the thirty-three African states that
became independent in the 1960s. In our orientation sessions,
some of our professors acknowledged the differences in our cul-
tures and urged us to form our own opinions. "Please, don't hate
us," said one professor. "Take the good things that you find in our
life, so you can strengthen your country. The bad things? Leave
them."

From Moscow I was transferred to Kiev, Ukraine, for a yearlong
Russian preparatory course in which we repeated every subject—
anatomy, biology, chemistry—in the Russian language. Although
I wasn't required to attend classes on atheism and scientific socialism, some of the national practices did get into my muscles and
my blood. At five o'clock each morning, when the booming loudspeaker signaled the beginning of calisthenics, my two Ukrainian
roommates groaned and pulled their blankets over their heads.
I, however, put my feet on the floor, splashed cold water on my
face, and followed the voice, which told me to, "Open the window. Take in a deep breath of cold air. Now march in place—one,
two, three, four." I will never forget those arm motions—straight
forward, out to the sides, up by the ears, down to the thighs, and

then back to the start. Even today, I move this way when I want to feel strength and focus.

Some of my fellow Somali students became involved in politics, making speeches, saying, "My brothers and sisters, we are here today, studying in the Soviet Union. Tomorrow, we will be the leaders of the continent." Still, I remembered what the professors told us from the beginning: I took what I wanted, and I left the rest. Of course I wanted our country to be built well, whether that was through democracy or socialism; what I most wanted to take with me from the Soviet Union was the work ethic and the respect for science.

CHAPTER TWO

Gold Is Made Beautiful by Fire

By the end of my first month in Digfer's pediatric department, I began to think that my problem was not with the children. They were very straightforward—if you joked with them while poking and examining them, they laughed; when something hurt, they cried. It was not with all of the parents, either—many were caring and careful, even when the situation was most difficult. My problem was with the privileged people in our society, who had the opportunity for the best medical treatment, but who didn't seem to have concern for their own sons and daughters. The attitude of a society changes every few years, and I had been away for almost eight. When I left, most of Somalia was in the rural area: When you have a small quantity of goats and cows and a small patch of land, you don't need anything—you live your life. Now, as more people moved to the urban area, it seemed that everyone wanted money and power.

When I was making rounds one day, I walked by a bodyguard standing outside one of the examining rooms. I entered the room later to find a two-year-old child who was convulsing, suffering from a fever of almost 104 degrees. I feared it was meningitis, or maybe another disease just as damaging.

The security guard, I learned, was for the child's mother—the wife of a Somali minister. She was dressed beautifully and expensively, and wearing heavy makeup. How could she take the time to dress like this, to make herself look so desirable, while her child suffered beside her? Had she dressed this way for her husband, whom she feared was out with his friends, or maybe another wife? Children without a parent's attention, I knew, were living in an empty vacuum. "You are doing your makeup when the child is in this situation?" I couldn't help shouting in disbelief. "You are not a responsible mother."

"Ha, what? What did you say?" She shouted back at me, not expecting such a reaction from a doctor.

I touched the child's hot skin again, feeling more anger coming up into my chest, from a place too deep to explain. What would become of the child, born to such a careless woman? "You don't want me to tell you these things?" I asked her, stepping back from the table. "This child is seriously ill. Why should I treat your child if you can't care for him yourself?"

"You cannot talk to me this way," she shouted back as the child wailed. I saw the bodyguard come into the room and walked by him; in the hallway I passed one of the pediatric nurses, who raised her eyebrows. "We need another doctor for the child in there," I told her on my way to the break room, where I poured myself a cup of tea. Mohamed Ali Nur appeared in the doorway a few minutes later. "You have to treat this child," he said. From the look on his face, he must have heard that his new doctor was trying to kick out the mother of a sick patient.

"Let someone else do it," I said. "That woman is irresponsible."

"You don't know anything about this woman," he said. "Your only job is to treat the patient that is in front of you." When I continued to argue, he pulled out a chair and sat down at the table, facing me. "Tell me your complaints," he said.

"Just because she's the wife of some high-level official man doesn't meant she can do whatever she wants," I said. "I want to teach her a lesson."

"When you wear a white coat, people appreciate you—they see that you are the highest class," Mohamed Ali Nur said. "They are seeking from you health—the most important thing that a human being can seek." It was not for me to say whether it was right for me to treat one child over thousands of others, he said.

Though I resisted, he finally convinced me to go back and treat the child. "Focus on him, so the mother will trust you again," he said. "But watch what you say to her: The right approach to a patient is as important as the medicine you use."

When I returned to the room, I did my best to treat the child as though he were my own and the mother as though she were a stranger. I admit that it was uncomfortable for me to work in this way, putting aside my own opinion and listening only to the needs of the body. The child eventually became healthy, but I believe that I was the one most changed by the experience. From that moment on, I would focus on the patient, rather than on the situation.

In medical school, our success or failure was entirely in our own hands: If I didn't go to my lesson, for example, I would be forced to repeat it. If I didn't clean my room, I would be judged using the same scale as the one that graded my aptitude for language and history. Everything that we students did or said was measured: A grade 5 was excellent. Good 4, satisfactory 3. We were told that a 3 meant that you didn't want to study, and if you didn't want to study, you would be sent back to your country.

One day, in my internal medicine class, I was asked a question, and I didn't know the answer. "You see Hawa before you? Her government sent her to study," said my professor, Petrov, as I stood awkwardly before the entire class. "Hawa, if you don't want to study, why did you come here?"

I went home that afternoon and cried, thinking of the hard road I had taken to get to medical school and the sacrifice I had made by leaving my family far behind. Petrov's harsh words echoed in my ears that night as I stayed up, bent over my textbook, reviewing the same lesson again.

"Why did you come here if you don't want to study?" My

reading lamp heated up my shoulder, burning down to my book as the clock read three, and then four. "Go back! Don't cheat your government, don't cheat us."

My eyes had not closed for a moment by the time calisthenics began. On my way back to class, I took a cardigan from my closet, buttoning it as I ran for the bus. A fat old Russian woman passed me on the street and yelled, "*Stoy!* Stop! Why are you doing these things?"

She poked her finger to my chest, and I saw that the pullover wasn't buttoned correctly—the top of the wool sweater flapped up on the right, while on the bottom, the left-hand side hung lower.

"Don't you have a mother?" the old woman asked me.

"My mother is dead," I told her.

"Oh my God," she said. "*Bo-zeh moy.* I'm sorry. Where did you come from?"

"I'm from Somalia," I said.

"Correct your buttons and go straight like that," said the old woman as I fumbled. "Not like this, no." Finally, after a struggle, I dropped my hands as she took the sides of the cardigan, correcting the buttons herself. Then I went on to class, where this time, Petrov was satisfied by my response.

Like Petrov, like the old woman, the people of Ukraine felt responsible for our well-being; they wanted to see us walking straight and performing well. Having lived through the World Wars, having seen so much trouble in their lives, they were unafraid to ask a harsh question of skinny young foreign students like me. Sometimes their words were like sticks, beating us— very difficult, very painful—but they wanted to understand our purpose and our hopes for visiting their country. At first, I hated Petrov, but now, looking back, I can see how I loved him.

Some of my colleagues in the hospital didn't appreciate the strict and honest philosophy I'd brought with me from the Soviet Union. "Hawa is very hot," they said. I didn't care that I wasn't liked then;

I only saw the goal in front of me. One day a very malnourished child was brought to the emergency room with severe dehydration from watery diarrhea. Although he was eighteen months old, he was so malnourished that he looked much younger. He was semi-conscious; his eyes were open and completely dry. I walked up to the examining table, but was stopped by the pediatric nurse who had been watching him. "*Dottoressa*, this child is dying," she said. "You should leave him with me and focus on a different case."

For the first time in my career, I made a decision alone—to stay. I worked swiftly, steadying the child in my hands, which seemed so strong compared to his tiny body. I examined his small arms for a place to put in an IV, but he was so dehydrated, it was impossible. I soothed the child as I made a small incision into his skin, found a small vein, made another incision, and inserted into the vein a small, small plastic tube. I made a few sutures around it, and put some plastic over his arm to protect it. I felt the eyes of the nurse and two other doctors, and the fears of the boy's parents, as a hydration solution flowed into his veins.

An hour later, the child's eyes became wet, and he became more active, crying and thrashing as his mother steadied him. She cried as well, and when I came back later to check on them, she thanked me for saving her son.

The Russians say that gold is made more beautiful by fire. Over time, I began to love pediatrics. You see a mother and a father, who are so sad when their child is sick. If you can help that child, you can feel the parents' happiness coming to you.

CHAPTER THREE

To Stop the Bleeding

After my three-month rotation in pediatrics, Dr. Mohamed Ali Nur assigned me to a rotation in the obstetrics and gynecology department. There, I discovered that I had to fight women's attitudes as much as I had to fight for their lives. Many women, after all, took their first breaths in the hands of their own mothers, who had been working when it became time to deliver and who came back from the pasture that night with the goats around them and an infant in their hands. These women waited too long before coming to us—some were already dying from labor complications by the time they were admitted. Many were carried in donkey carts. "The pain began two days ago," said one young boy as I examined his sister, "but we have no roads, no transportation."

Most Somali people trusted traditional healers more than doctors or hospitals; many insisted on waiting for a natural birth against all medical odds. "We cannot watch you and your child die," we would tell these women. "You have to have a Cesarean section, or you have to leave here." Many preferred to go, to read the Holy Qur'an at home; we had no choice but to wish them luck and to tell them that we would pray for them. Awaiting a life, says one of our proverbs, also means awaiting a death.

On my first day in the maternity ward, I was working alongside a young midwife who was planning to become a doctor. The midwife had just delivered a child when I turned my back for a moment and heard a loud noise, as if a pipe had burst. "Dr. Hawa!

Dr. Hawa! Look here!" she shouted. When I came over, I saw the young mother bleeding like a faucet, a brilliant red.

Some bleeding during and after childbirth is normal. If a tear happens somewhere away from the uterine artery, the blood is manageable; the body expels the placenta, and healing happens quickly. As I saw this rush of blood, however, I feared there was a tear in the uterine artery itself, which could mean heavy, even life-threatening bleeding. But I had no time to think about where the tear occurred; I had to do everything at once.

I called for the other doctors and ordered the midwife to inject the patient with medicine. Still I feared that if she continued bleeding for even a few minutes, she would die. I spoke with the woman and told her calmly that I would enter the vagina, to stop the bleeding. I put one hand inside and one on the top of her abdomen, to try to stop it mechanically. I stood there for a few minutes, reassuring her that she would be okay, pressing down as hard as I could. Finally, the danger subsided.

"You are lucky," I told the woman several hours later when I saw her resting comfortably with her baby girl.

"I know," she said, looking down at her daughter, not under-standing, most likely, how close she had come to death.

That midwife quit her job soon after, giving up her dream of becoming a doctor—the sight of that blood, the feeling of fear, was too much for her. But I was energized. While I had known that medicine is a fight against disease, against mortality, I learned in those days that you cannot always wait for a scientific or chemi-cal solution. Sometimes there is another way to stop the bleed-ing, to calm the body, to soothe the fever: A strong will and the weight of your hands can aid the body in times when chemistry is slow.

Sometimes medicine is also a fight against other doctors, but since I was the most inexperienced, I couldn't argue with my super-visors. One night I was called into a delivery room to examine the wife of an influential Somali man, a good friend of one of the highest-ranking doctors at the hospital. "What is the trouble?" I asked the doctor who had been on duty.

"There is heavy bleeding, but there is no laceration," he said. "I'm trying to stop it." He nodded to the bag of solution pouring into the woman's arm.

"May I see?" I examined the woman. "I see the place, the laceration," I told the doctor and the nurse-midwives. "Prepare sutures for me. Although—" I looked at my supervisor and the woman's husband. "May I continue?"

The two men looked at each other; as they walked into the hallway to talk, I tried to reassure the woman, to talk nicely to her. They returned ten minutes later, followed by a nurse with a different type of solution. "We will continue on with the plan we have discussed," said my supervisor, who thanked me for my time. While I knew I was expected to leave, I wanted to argue. I took a deep breath to talk but then stopped. Instead I continued with my rounds, to the surgical ward and then the pediatric ward, frustrated that I couldn't act on what I thought was best.

The woman died at four thirty that morning, in the best hospital, surrounded by the most highly qualified professionals. The nurse who had administered the solution told me the news and that I had been right in my diagnosis. She thought I'd be happy somehow.

I walked out of the hospital's main gate as the sun was rising, and I heard the sound of someone crying. It was the woman's daughter, about fourteen years old, whom I'd seen in the waiting room. I imagined that she was walking home to tell the rest of the family that her mother had already died. I fought the urge to go to her and comfort her, as I knew no words would help. If we'd saved that life, we would have saved the family. I continued on to my home, walked through my door, and slipped into bed with my clothes still on.

My mother became pregnant with her seventh child when I was eleven years old. By then she'd had Faduma Ali; then me; then a boy, Mohamed, who had immediately died; then she had my sister Amina, as you know; and then Asha and little Khadija, who was only two years old at the time. Somali families are often this large, you see, as many children do not survive.

This seventh time, as my mother's stomach swelled, she felt weakness and pain. Thinking the fresh food and fresh air would help her condition, my father sent a car to take her, my sisters, and me to Ayeyo's home in the rural area of Lafole. There my half sister Faduma Ali tried to distract me by teaching me to milk the goats, but I refused to leave my mother's side. Maybe Faduma Ali could sleep deeply in the room where my mother was suffering, but my mother and I were friends—I told her everything. Even then we talked late into the night while I stayed up, holding the place on her abdomen where she was feeling pain.

So many nights we sat that way together; I cried to see her turn her head from side to side, saying *ah-ah-ah-ah*. We tried to bring her under the trees in the afternoons, and one day, at about two o'clock in the afternoon, she lost consciousness. Amina ran to get water, to splash it on her face, but while she was gone, we could see heavy blood spreading from under my mother's robes. Ayeyo tried to keep us away, but we saw that she held in her two palms a small, small child, dead, the size of just one of her hands.

This was my brother; he had been in my mother's womb for just a few months. My grandmother sent me to find a white shroud, or *karfan*, to cover him in the Muslim burial tradition. Then I dug a grave somewhere, where we would put his small body.

My mother's pain continued after the burial, and we all sat inside for the rest of the day, sobbing as she moaned and cried. Listening to Ayeyo's orders, Amina and I carried the blood-soaked cloths out to scrub; by the time we hung them and returned, there were more. That night I lay on the ground next to my sisters, hoping to hear the steady breath of their dreams, praying that my mother wouldn't die in the night.

The next day a group of my strong, young cousins came to

our place with a stretcher made from big sticks. They carried my mother, and Ayeyo and I followed behind them along the dirt paths out to the main road. There my father was waiting for us with a car, to take us to Mogadishu's biggest hospital, Martini. My younger sisters remained in Lafole with Faduma Ali.

I cried on the road to Martini hospital, remembering that one of our neighbors in Mogadishu had died there, while her family was asleep at home. "Hawa, you must believe in these doctors," said my father, after my mother was placed in a ward of forty-five beds. "They are trained to help."

I defied their orders immediately, crawling into bed with my mother. "I will stay with you," I promised, and for the three months she was there, I did. Every morning at seven o'clock, I would bring her some tea before I went off to school, updating my friends on her condition before losing myself to the lessons of the day. I would come back after school, around 4 p.m., and stay as long as I could. Since she loved films, I saved my small spending money to buy her magazines—beautiful photos of Italian and French women; from her pillow, she had fantasies of a glamorous faraway life.

Sometimes the Italian doctors tried to explain to me that they were going to give my mother injections or draw her blood; otherwise they ignored me unless they were asking me to leave— my least favorite time of the day. I earned the pity of two Somali nurses whose eyes looked past my small body, hidden under my mother's blanket, as they continued their rounds. These women, I discovered, knew everything—how to measure blood and medicine, to listen to the heart or hold the abdomen in order to identify where my mother's problems lay. Though there was no pain medication at the time to help, they seemed pleased when they could tell us something to comfort us.

When the hospital staff finally cast me out each evening around nine o'clock, I scooped up the tea containers and began my walk home through the quiet streets, searching and searching my mind for some small way to help. I could think of none.

When my mother didn't seem to improve, the doctor discharged her. "Take her to your house, read some Qur'an to her, get her to eat more," he said. "When she gains weight, you can bring her back here, and we will try to treat her again."

The neighbors and relatives came to our home from all over, bringing food and incense, reading the Qur'an around the clock, and separating into small groups in our courtyard to talk or to pray. Without my sisters, I was alone, forced to make one pot of tea after another, and to listen to my family's false reassurances.

Although I prayed always, always asking for an answer from my God, God was not hearing me. Ayeyo prayed as well, crying, "Leave this daughter, God, I want that she will bury me!"

One early morning, a week after we returned, I crawled onto my mother's bed and touched the part of her stomach she had been rubbing. I knew she had been growing weaker; I gripped on to the place she felt pain and pressed down, hard, which had worked in the past. "Oh Ma," I said, realizing that my best efforts did not make any difference. "I'm afraid I won't be able to sleep even one more night with you."

Our cousins came into the bedroom around eleven o'clock that morning, to read the Qur'an. "I'm not going to die in this room," my mother said weakly, "I want out."

"Dahabo," said an uncle, "you have to stay in your place." As I was a child, I couldn't say anything.

"Please bring me outside to the courtyard, where people can sit." So a group of my cousins, strong and young, prepared some kind of bed and carried my mother through the door.

"Where is Hawa today?" my mother asked when she was first set down. I was beside her, but I could not answer, *I am here, Mama.* I began to cry, but my voice made no sound. She looked up to one side, and I ran around her bed, to stand between the wall where she was looking and her eyes. But she immediately closed them, and without opening her mouth, she took her last breath.

There is some part of the Holy Qur'an, when a person is dying, that is read; they say it helps people pass away. My voice returned in a big cry—*waaaaaaah!*—and the uncle reading the scripture slapped me hard across the face. I saw a bright light and fell down. "Don't cry," he said to me while Ayeyo cried with a loud voice. Still I remember that voice.

We didn't have a telephone, but the news of my mother's death traveled fast on the wind of a dozen gossiping aunties. Six people held my mother's body as we walked to the gravesite, an hour away from our home in Mogadishu.

On the way, we passed an old woman of Ayeyo's age, who stopped us on the road. "Who are you carrying?" she asked.

"Dahabo," said my cousin.

"You are carrying Dahabo, and Salaho is left alive?"

Hearing her given name, Ayeyo spoke up for the first time. "God is deciding who will die first," she said, "and who will die after."

I did not return to school for some time after that, but when it was finally time, I arrived very early, holding a few coins for my breakfast and waiting for the gates to open. My teacher at the time was young and active; before I'd left, we had begun to study biology. "I want to study the human body," I told him when he finally opened the door. "I want to find out what killed my mother."

CHAPTER FOUR

Paradise in the World

More than a decade later, I moved from my small apartment in Hodan to a big new villa in the same neighborhood, so we could all be together. One early morning, when I was reading a *Cosmopolitan* magazine and drinking juice, Amina came out into the sitting room. She'd just finished bathing; her skin gleamed and she'd woven her wet hair into braids. "I'm feeling pain now," she said calmly, smiling, while the rest of us scrambled to take her to the maternity ward at Digfer.

The most qualified midwives welcomed us, but I still paced the halls, thinking of every possible complication, every bit of pain that I had witnessed with my own eyes. God is great: At four o'clock, the child was born—a strong baby boy they named Kahiye. We returned home, and for the next forty days we observed the *umul*, the traditional rest period following the birth of a child. There, in the beautiful villa's rooms, which were full of light all day, we gave Amina nutritious food like soup made from the head of the goat, and we offered her new clothes and henna for her hands and feet.

One afternoon soon after, I was making rounds in the hospital when a laboring woman from the rural area was brought in with what we call prolapse: One of the baby's hands had come down first, instead of his head. I felt panic as I examined her, for the hand had fallen on the sand somehow, and everywhere was very dirty. When I touched the hand, though, I could see that the child was alive—he took my hand.

What to do? The woman's family had come from 200 kilometers, in a rented car, from a place where there was no telephone or no other means of communication. To try to bring the hand back into the uterus somehow, to turn the child for a proper delivery, would risk sepsis, which could be fatal. For more than thirty minutes I sat quietly, trying to carefully disinfect the hand. Then I guided the hand back into the birth canal, so we could deliver the child through a Cesarean section. We were successful: The child was born healthy! I prescribed an antibiotic, so his mother would recover as well.

That night, I shared the story with my sisters; we all shook our heads, amazed by what was possible. Celebration surrounded us those days, after Kahiye's birth, for we were also preparing to celebrate my wedding. Those evenings after dinner, we discussed the plans, selecting a Western-style white dress and veil like the one Amina had worn, renting the same hall, and choosing a big cake for us to cut.

I knew it was the right time for me. I'd met my future husband, Aden Mohamed, as a student in the Soviet Union, and I'd accepted his marriage proposal with a full heart. While many marriages in Somalia were arranged, Mogadishu was becoming a modern city, and like Amina before me, I had made my own choice. In the last days of February 1973, when it was time to make the marriage contract, I stood up to give my consent; the only tears that would be shed that day were tears of joy.

We were married that March, during one of the hottest dry seasons on record, in a hall filled with 120 people who had come to wish us well. Amina was so happy that day, running to make sure that we slaughtered enough sheep and goats to feed everyone, while young Khadija's only concern was putting down one record after the other—the tango, and rock and roll, especially the "Hippy Hippy Shake."

After the party, one of my girlfriends from university and her husband drove us in the direction of Lafole to an open-air restaurant called Bar Ismail, owned by a Somali man who had lived in

America for many years. He set up a beautiful table in the garden for us, under the trees. He served *pollo al diavolo*, some fried potatoes, and champagne and beer for all, although my girlfriend and I declined. When we finished our meal, he came to sit and toast us. "It's their wedding night," said my girlfriend. "Give them some advice!"

The man looked at Aden with a smile. "Try to give her what she wants," he said, "and try to avoid what she doesn't want."

"And for Hawa?" asked my friend's husband.

"My advice is for her to give the guy what he wants, and to avoid what he doesn't." We laughed at the simplicity of the statement, and by the time we got back in the car later, all the tension and worry of the event fell away. The next thing I felt was a slap on the knee. "It's your wedding night!" my friend shouted. "Wake up!" But I was too happy in my new life, too comfortable in the bouncing backseat, to open my eyes.

It wasn't until I met Aden that I finally understood what my father had meant when he'd talked about loving my mother. He'd refused to marry after she died, even though my sisters and I had begged him to do so: "Please, give us a brother," we'd said, eager for another man in our family to support and protect us.

"I have had, in my life, the most beautiful horse," my father had said. "I would never accept a donkey."

Just four years earlier, Aden was also a Somali student like me. He had lived in Odessa, Ukraine, near my medical school, and had studied engineering at a nearby military academy. He and two of his friends came one day to visit my cousin Asli, who lived in the dormitory room next to mine. I was with her, studying. And although they stayed in the room for only a half hour—long enough to invite us to the wedding of two fellow Somali students—I could not stop staring at Aden. He was quieter than the others, with kind eyes and a welcoming face. He was tall and handsome, and unlike so many Somali boys I had met at university, he was shy and respectful: He didn't try to shake my hand or talk with me aggressively.

He didn't ask any questions of Asli or of me, other than a simple, "How are you?"

When they left, I asked Asli about him.

"Ah!" Asli said. "That one? He just sits there without doing anything—one day, I think, you will regret it." But many of my other girlfriends sympathized with him, so I decided that maybe Asli was contrary—Aden was handsomer and calmer than her husband.

Three days later, at the wedding of the two students, I walked over to Aden and his friends without thinking twice. We spoke easily. He told me about his family, who was from the north of the country. His parents had divorced before he was born, and his mother died when he was young, like mine. I told him about my family, and about my wish to return to Somalia. That was his wish, too, he said.

Until then, I knew love only through the memory of my parents' relationship and the stories from my roommate Lena, a beautiful Ukrainian girl who spent an hour each day in front of the mirror instead of doing calisthenics. I suppose I also had the role model of a very outspoken Asli, who, even as a married woman herself, was so much freer than me. "Should I be like you, kissing your husband openly in public?" I asked her once when she was teasing me about being reserved. "Should I walk up to these boys and say, 'I'm attracted to you, I love you,' as you would?"

"Should you stay closed in this room, thinking and studying?" she asked. "You are just wasting your time."

"I have responsibilities," I said.

"I am a wife and a mother," she said, "but still, I do everything I want. That way, when I am older, I will have no regrets."

With Aden, though, I began to understand that when love is shared, it is a bit of paradise in the world. Though we were reserved in public, we were always together on Saturdays and Sundays, talking, talking, talking, wherever we went. As we got to know each other at the restaurants in Odessa or at the cinema, in a group of friends, I allowed myself to imagine a future in Mogadishu with him. I didn't say anything, though, for fear of getting hurt.

On our way back from seeing a film one afternoon, we stopped in a public garden to talk. "I don't want to bother you," he said, taking my hand. "I want to marry you."

I was so happy to hear his words, but I knew that I had to be honest with him if our relationship was going to work. In our day, engagement and marriage were close to the same thing: It meant that you found one room and lived together. I knew I loved Aden, but I'd made the decision long before that I would become a doctor before I would become a wife. "I don't want to believe any man until I have my own credentials and my own money in my hand," I told him.

Aden knew this about me, like he knew so many things; he knew that my father's small salary was not enough to support our family, and that I saved as much money from my three-ruble daily allowance as I could, to send back home.

"Okay," he said. "I will wait for you."

We continued on together in the same way, growing closer and stronger, until he graduated. At dinner the night before he left, I gave him some money I'd saved, which I asked him to take back to Amina. We said a tearful good-bye outside my door, but when I sat down on my bed, I knew that I needed to see him again. So I bought a big flower from a local shop and went to find him at the airport.

He was surprised to see me there. "I love you," I said when I gave him the flower. "I couldn't see another man in front of me if there were thousands." I knew we were close when we were in the same place; I needed to test to be sure that the feelings would stay when we were far away. According to the Holy Qur'an, men can have up to four wives, but for me it was different. When people had told me that Aden had the right to marry four, I always told them that he had the right to marry only me—no other woman.

"You can't have anyone else," I told him that night. "If you become different, I will stop loving you."

"As long as you're alive," he said, "I will never go to another woman."

I returned to my dormitory that night with perfect faith that, even with distance and time between us, he would keep his word.

CHAPTER FIVE

Friends and Enemies

When we were first married, Aden worked as an officer in the Somali Marines, and we were given free housing in an area called Secondo Lido, right by the seaside. Our villa was old, built by Italian engineers with quality stone, a charcoal stove, and a chimney. Because of Aden's position, we had amenities that were uncommon at the time, including two indoor toilets and a telephone. It was a very beautiful place; instead of the sound of traffic, we listened to the waves.

Since Amina and Sharif's family was growing, Asha and Khadija came to live with us; the nation's best schools were in Mogadishu, so Aden's brother and sister came as well, from the north. We hired a cook to help with meals and divided everyone into two rooms—one for girls and one for boys. I knew Aden's family didn't approve of the way the boys did housework alongside the girls, but it was my decision. We had come from the Soviet Union, where everyone was equal.

Aden and I usually ate on our own, after the others, and then we'd walk down to the beach for a bit of privacy. As we sat, watching the moonlight dance off the whitecaps and light up the white buildings stretching out along the coast, we talked about our family—Asha was studying biology at the university and Khadija was quickly becoming a headstrong teenager with a rebellious streak. We'd caught her dressing up and going to the nightclubs, and while I tried to stop her, it was no use. Once, out of frustration,

I'd locked her out, refusing to respond even as she'd banged on the door and cried.

Some evenings I told Aden about the internal politics at the hospital. "Doctors are like roosters," I said one night, laughing. "They get jealous when they see another one." If you were not well liked by the senior doctors, if you didn't go along with what they said, exactly as they said it, they could transfer you to an external district in one of the rural areas with nothing but forceps and a prescription pad. While I was still technically a resident, I was determined to fight to stay in Mogadishu, with the specialists and the international visitors. I knew that if I was sent to the rural area, where I could not perform any complicated procedures, I would return knowing nothing.

We discussed national politics as well, our concerns and criticisms drowned out by the crashing waves. We knew that speaking ill of the government meant a risk of jail or other punishments. Some of our colleagues were party leaders, carefully watching how the staff was talking, how they were working. It was hard sometimes, living with the idea that there were people going after you, to see what you are doing, with whom you'll talk.

A few months before we married, I was on duty one day when an American Embassy car hit a frail old Somali woman. They brought her to us when I was in the emergency room, so I treated her wounds, which were not serious. Later, during my break, a tall, well-dressed, middle-aged man with brown hair walked up to me. "How's the patient?" he asked me. He was American. I became filled with panic, realizing that he was talking about the old woman.

"She's okay," I said, wondering who the man was and how he had known that I had treated her. An unsettled feeling started in my head and moved down to my stomach.

At the time I was enrolled in an after-work English class at the John F. Kennedy English Language Center in Mogadishu. I went to class as usual that night, but when a group of us walked out afterward, we discovered that a huge line of military men holding guns blocked us in. Beyond them sat a row of police cars, sirens blaring and lights flashing. As we waited for information, I ran through the day's events in my head, convinced that something had happened to the woman hit by the American car and that the police had come for me.

"Hawa, do you see that house?" one of my friends asked. I'd never noticed, but it was modern, very beautiful, with an open first floor of only pillars and two other stories above. The front gate had been broken. "That house belongs to Salad Gabeyre," she said.

As I understood the reality, I felt first relief, and then dread. When Mohamed Siad Barre had seized control of Somalia in 1969, the high-ranking army official Salad Gabeyre Kediye had been the operations chief of the coup. Aden and I had just met at the time; we'd heard on the radio from the Soviet Union that our president, Abdirashid Ali Shermarke, had been assassinated by one of his own bodyguards, and that the military had taken full control of the parliament and the territory.

In the few years since Siad Barre had declared himself our president, a vicious power struggle had arisen among the leaders of the revolution. Now, in 1972, Siad Barre had sentenced Salad Gabeyre and two others to death for conspiring to overthrow the regime. The time had come: The radio had been calling on all Somali people to come out at eight o'clock the next morning to watch the execution. What we witnessed was not my arrest for malpractice; it was government troops invading the homes of their former comrades.

Many people attended the execution, although Aden and I refused. After the physicians' meeting that morning, I looked out the window at the rain. Maybe the sky was crying for those very active, very educated men, I thought. Although for a while I expected that the strongest people of their clans would stand up in revenge, no one moved—no one even talked.

Soon after, a paper pinned to the gate of the John F. Kennedy school notified students that classes had been suspended by the order of the Somali government. It was a decree echoed across the country at the time, as citizens were required to use the newly established written Somali language. While we had spoken our mother tongue for centuries and still used it in our homes, we'd relied on the colonial Italian or English as a common written language for our schools and our businesses. Now, the nation's educators were required to go to the rural areas to teach the people there how to write and read in Somali. One of our fellow doctors at Digfer became our language teacher, and we in the hospital also began writing that way. While the transition was at first difficult, the Somali language also uses the Latin alphabet; with a bit of practice, writing became no problem.

Years later, some people suggested that Siad Barre benefited from the language program by empowering uneducated members of his clan to run the government. It's true that in those years, more and more people from the president's clan rose to power, many of them without much education. I heard story after story of people imprisoned for suspicious activities, people beaten, even killed. It was hard not to intervene somehow, to say to some of the people I knew, "You are not right—why are you doing these things?"

Around the typical home in Somalia is a type of protection we call a *dugaal*, shielding our open courtyards from the threats of wind or wild animals. I always say that when you have your parents, you have your *dugaal*. But in Odessa in 1969, just a few months after we Somali students heard the news that our government had been overthrown, Asli brought a letter into my room, and that shelter disappeared.

"Guess what I have?" Asli asked, holding out a letter and teasing me with it. We students lived so simply in those days that the mail was one of our most precious commodities. Whoever picked up the mail for the group played this game with each recipient, making her guess who sent a letter and then pulling her onto their feet to dance and sing before the mail was handed over. "Get up!" she said. "If you want to get it, you have to get up!"

It had been almost two months since I'd heard anything from my family, and I had been worrying every day about my father's health. When I'd returned to Mogadishu for Amina and Sharif's wedding the year before, I was far enough along in my studies to recognize the symptoms of tuberculosis, which was common in our area, and very serious.

"You have a fever!" I'd shouted. He was also thin and pale, and he was trying to hide his coughing.

"*Dottoressa* Hawa," he'd joked, "you come home and immediately make a diagnosis?"

We'd taken him to a hospital that specialized in tuberculosis. The examination was free, although the medication to treat his condition was not. For that, we'd used the $300 I had saved from my allowance and some small summer jobs. We hadn't talked about what would happen when the medicine ran out.

I'd brought my student identification card to the Mogadishu hospitals, begging the doctors I saw for any sort of help. "Please, can you help me bring my father to the tuberculosis hospital in the Soviet Union?" I'd asked. They'd all advised me to go to back to school and to search for some help there.

The letter was from Amina. I begged Asli to read it.

"Sister," read Asli, and then she stopped. I sat up and faced her, and she continued. "I haven't gotten any answer from you after our father died."

As she continued to read, the news flooded my body. The only thing I could understand is that Amina had sent other letters, and none of them had arrived. I wrestled the blankets out from under Asli, flipped onto my stomach, and stayed that way, heaving and crying, until I fell asleep somehow. Though she tried for a while to comfort me, I could not even feel her hands on my shoulders, her voice in my ears. I had failed my father, and still, my sisters were alone.

"Father, wait for me," I'd cried at the airport as I'd hugged him, my cheek against his chest. "Wait for me! I will come back to you."

I slept through the loud announcements the next morning and ignored the knocks on my door. "Tell them I'm sick," I told Asli, who had brought me dinner that next evening. "Do not tell anyone what happened." Maybe I would wake up from the dream, some-how, and my father wouldn't be dead.

As the news of my loss spread, friends slid notes under the door, which my roommates piled up on the dresser next to Amina's let-ter. When I was finally able to stand up, I threw away Amina's letter and returned to bed, exhausted from the effort. Now there was no one. "We are waiting for you, *Dottoressa* Hawa," my father had written to me, as a letter of thanks for a watch I'd mailed him from school the year before. But I had not been able to reach him in time.

My desire to protect my family had only grown as I returned to Mog-adishu, and as I saw the way that our country's politics were affect-ing the rights of our people, I became desperate to do something. A few months after the John F. Kennedy school closed in 1972, I decided to enroll in the law school, following in the footsteps of Amina's husband, Sharif, who had begun a few years before. As I registered, I remembered what Sharif had told me when I'd returned to Mogadishu after my father's death and told him about Aden. "Okay," Sharif had said, "but if you want to marry, you should marry and live abroad. Things in Somalia have changed." He hadn't approved of the military rule, preferring to be free, independent, with the right to say whatever you wanted. "Finish your studies, search for work outside, and then, if you can help, send for us."

I'd told him that I loved my country and my sisters, and I approved of the Soviet Union's rule that when you finished uni-versity, you had to go back home. "I know what it's like to live abroad," I'd said, "but my life is here."

Now, when I expressed my fears about the changing times, Sharif was already fed up. "I told you this would happen," he said, "so now you can't say anything."

My law school classes met in the afternoons, so I was able to go to school after work: Most days, I came home from the hospital for lunch around 1:30 or 2 p.m., and then I would go to class from 3:30 until 7 p.m.. We were introduced to every type of law: international law, public law, private law, administrative law, as well as Sharia, or Islamic law. While I appreciated many aspects of Sharia—the business and commercial provisions are similar to modern law—I always argued with my professor over women's rights.

According to Sharia, the groom's family pays the bride's family before marriage. Since she receives her portion this way, she is not entitled to the same rights as her husband. That is why, if you are a woman and you are killed, your murderer would pay your family fifty camels, unlike the one hundred camels that would be owed for a man's head. My professor tried to make this sound straightforward in class, but my personal experience had taught me otherwise.

As he lectured, I remembered the pain on my father's face in 1962 after I returned to Mogadishu, after some time away, to learn that Ayeyo had died of a sudden infection. "Your uncles didn't come for the burial," my father had said. "They came the day after and took all the cows, all the goats."

At the time I was so shocked by the sudden loss of my beloved grandmother that I hadn't understood the significance of my father's words; then, slowly, with his arms wrapped around his chest, he'd struggled to explain what my professor taught us so simply. In death, Ayeyo's male relatives, no matter how distant, were entitled to more than we were, as her granddaughters. My mother had not left a will to defend the livestock she and my father had bought to raise on Ayeyo's farm. "All our cows are for my mother," she'd said. "She has nothing, except my children."

So while my father had prepared Ayeyo's grave, her nephews had arranged to sell her beloved herd. Just like that, my family's small security, our hope to survive, was gone. In its place remained only one small wood-chewing goat, my half sister Faduma Ali's, which my father had insisted be spared.

"Why don't you do something?" I'd asked my father at the time. He had told me simply that he could not take back what had already been sold.

"Professor, how can I be half?" I argued now. "Fifty? Why? Why can't I be one hundred?"

CHAPTER SIX

Awaiting a Life, Awaiting a Death

In May 1975, I gave birth to my Deqo—a quiet baby, as she is quiet now, with eyes just like Aden's. I had been hoping to get pregnant for years, and when I finally held her in my arms, I understood what it meant to be a mother. Aden was a proud papa—some afternoons we would all go together to the market, where the women among the stalls would look at Deqo, look at Aden, and tell him, "No one can ask whether she is your daughter or not!"

At the time, the government granted working women four months of maternity leave—two months before the birth and another two months after the birth. It was one example of the way our government supported us, even though, in other ways, they constricted us. Siad Barre was a big supporter of women's rights; under his leadership, Somali women were teachers and police officers and even construction workers, carrying iron and stone to transform our rapidly growing city. The year Deqo was born we saw the passage of the Family Law of 1975, which gave women equality in property rights and established that no man can divorce a woman without her consent. It was a revelation: For so many years, women were treated as subjects, as property that a man could throw out the door. Now a woman could report the action to the town's orientation center, and a committee would come to defend her position.

Our government had also provided essential assistance during the long drought that began years earlier in Somalia and neighboring

Ethiopia, and that became a devastating famine. In order to save thousands of people from starvation, our government took over portions of the rural area near the Shabelle and Juba Rivers, establishing refugee centers and cooperative farms. More than a hundred thousand people were resettled, transferred from the less-developed northeast part of the country to the south, where they received food and agricultural or fishing training.

Despite these successes, our international reputation hung in the balance as our association with the Soviet Union began to change. In 1974, after a revolution in Ethiopia, the Soviet Union began to support their new leader, Mengistu Haile Mariam. We'd long had a complicated relationship with Ethiopia, as their eastern region, the Ogaden, was once a part of Somalia. After the Soviets accused Siad Barre of backing a liberation movement inside the Ogaden in 1977, we went to war.

I cried when I heard the news about the war, knowing that the men on the front lines were my brothers—our friends from university. At first we feared that Aden would be sent to the battle, but he was allowed to continue working for a government transportation company inside Mogadishu. We came home every night to hear the news on the radio, as Somali soldiers, armed with heavy Russian artillery and tanks, pushed toward Ethiopia's capital city, Addis Ababa.

At that time, my Deqo was a small child; I was newly pregnant again and worried about our future. We were at war with a nation that had built our very army; now, they were bringing troops from across the world—from Cuba to Yemen—to support the Ethiopian regime. As the fighting worsened toward the end of the year, Siad Barre issued an ultimatum to all of the Soviets living in Somalia: "Leave within twenty-four hours." How we cried at Digfer, talking with our Soviet colleagues, who had worked by our sides for so many years. Though we tried to express our sorrow, it didn't matter. Politics is a death game—after seventeen years, our best friends became our worst enemies.

One of our classmates sent to war was a man named Yusuf, who'd gone on to study logic and philosophy in Moscow and to work for Siad Barre's regime. Yusuf was called to the front lines in Ethiopia, in what we came to call the Ogaden War, but one night he went out on his own, maybe to the bathroom, and he was shot. "We thought he was the enemy," said one Somali man later. They called it an accident, but we all had our suspicions. There will always be part of a society that hates a tough and talented man; those who don't have the power become jealous, and they will do everything they can to destroy him.

We had always known Yusuf would be successful. I remember him barging into my medical school dormitory room one day. "Hawa, what are you doing?" he'd asked when he saw I wasn't dressed.

"I'm getting my breakfast in bed," I'd told him, annoyed that this younger boy would challenge me, a medical student. "I want to relax today."

"That is bourgeois," he said. "You should get up, get dressed, and do your duty." I'd laughed as he closed the door, but he'd inspired me to get up and work. That was Yusuf: He loved his country and spent his life searching for the thing to do immediately; he also pushed others, believing that people can do anything they put their minds to.

In 1978, when Ethiopia's Soviet-backed military launched a surprise attack against the Somali troops, the teachers defeated the students, and Somalia lost the war. Thousands of people died, and the men who came back were physically and emotionally destroyed. Some of the members of the regime began to act as bandits—using their authority to steal from the poor, rural people, or favoring their own clan over another, more vulnerable group. We heard, time and again, of Siad Barre's relatives guaranteeing their own private property over the national interest.

You know that from our earliest history, Somali society respected most the man who was able to mediate conflict between two groups. The more our president supported his own clan, the more deeply he destroyed his power and his reputation among his own people. This marked the beginning of our troubles, as the men who had been sent to war returned with only frustration and hatred. In time they would use that anger as a weapon, destroying everything that they had once fought to protect.

There is a shared understanding in my profession that doctors should not treat members of their own families, but when Amina became sick that year, soon after the birth of her third child, I forgot every rule I'd ever learned. For days, she'd felt pain in her right side that was becoming worse and worse. When her skin began to turn yellow, we feared it was hepatitis.

"I should be caring for you!" Amina wailed, gesturing to my growing belly, as Aden and I drove her to the hospital. I was due to deliver in a few weeks.

"Just rest," I said. "There will be time yet for you to care for me." Then, while she slept, I ran through the corridors, trying to find the internist on duty, knowing that when acute hepatitis got a hold of a person, they had little chance to survive. The diagnosis was confirmed, and for the next seven days I was in hell, my world becoming smaller and smaller. We brought her to a different hospital, Medina, to consult with one of our best hepatologists, but she continued to suffer, refusing all the food we brought her.

In well-developed countries, doctors have different ways of treating liver failure; they can even put in a new liver sometimes. It was not the case in our time. My heart tore open again as I watched my sister suffer, and for those seven dark days, that hole got bigger and bigger. As a doctor, I knew that her condition was deteriorating, but when I sat down with her children at night, I could not tell them the truth.

As the yellow color moved into the whites of my sister's eyes, I asked my colleagues to help me with my rounds. I sat with her day and night as she began to lose consciousness; I called for more opinions, more specialists. I stood with them as they nodded slowly to one another, regret in their faces. She died as we surrounded her, looking on helplessly.

Sharif was inconsolable about his wife's death. Aden had to return to work, but I stayed in bed for days, relying on our helper to care for the children. None of us could find the right words, so a silence grew up around all of our family. At night, I would lie awake and say to myself: "What is your destiny? From your mother, you raised three children; now, from your sister, you will raise three more—two boys and a girl."

I still mourn Amina, who was the sweetest, the calmest among us. She was the only one who truly understood me, and the only one who always believed that we could hold our family together. Asha and Khadija were like Sharif—digesting the news in their own way, and not coming to me for consolation. So as the first months passed, I was with the children alone, confined to our sitting room and a few small bedrooms.

I tried to remember what Ayeyo had told me in the first awful days after my mother's death. "Even though you are upset, life is continuing," she'd said. "You have to care for me, to care for your father and your sisters."

I had been just thirteen years old then, a skinny child, helpless to comfort Ayeyo as she cried. I had tried my best, pounding the sorghum with a mortar and pestle and shaking the milk until it became butter. I dug the farm myself, and I planted the seeds for more sorghum, maize, beans, and watermelon. While we were still in Lafole, I rose at four; when we returned to Mogadishu, I rose at three. It was the only way I could study before I had to prepare breakfast, wake my father, and then feed and bathe my sisters. I had tried to do everything, but in the end, I could not protect them.

I was in our sitting room just a few weeks after Amina died when I heard a series of explosions. I was confused at first, but as I continued to listen, I began to understand: It was gunfire, but also something louder—explosions from mortar shells, maybe, something I'd heard before on the radio. Terrified, I kept quiet. How do you explain this to your small children? We sat together in one of the bedrooms and sang songs. I would start, and Amina's two oldest would take over.

The explosions could come and take us, I imagined, but my feeling of grief was so strong that I didn't feel any fear. When the city finally fell silent, I checked that the door was locked, and then I went to sleep with all the children. When we awoke, I learned that a group of antigovernment militants had attacked one of Siad Barre's houses, but it was not a well-organized coup. The fire had been returned by the government troops, who later arrested eleven men, sentencing them to death.

A few days later, I gave birth to another baby girl, and I called her Amina, so I could remember my sister all the days of my life. "You will cover the hole in my heart," I told her when she was just seven days old. "You will care for me as Amina cared for me."

An old tradition says that if a woman dies and she has an unmarried sister, her family may give the sister's hand to the woman's husband. I refused to listen when people began to talk about our family, thinking of my younger sisters, Asha and Khadija. I knew that Sharif was mad with grief, but his love for Amina had been true. The fact was, though, that without her, our family was ripping apart.

Asha came home very late one night, while I was sleeping outside, where it was cooler than inside the house. "I was in Lafole," she said before going into her room. "I had to take some papers to the university there." A few days later, a family we knew came to me to apologize. "We are sorry that things did not happen in a traditional Somali way," they said. Asha, suspicious that she would be forced to marry Sharif, had married another instead.

Not long after that, Sharif's cousin came to me. "We want that you will give us Khadija," he said.

"Khadija is just seventeen years old," I told him. We made small talk for a little while, and then he wished me well and left.

I didn't see Khadija that night or the next day. When I returned from the market the following afternoon, one of my relatives came through my door. "You have refused," he said, "but Sharif has won."

"What do you mean?" I asked.

"He took his wife, and now they are together." While Sharif had been away, grieving, he was preparing another apartment, far from his house. That afternoon, he had married Khadija, without our blessing or our presence.

Since Asha was already gone, I told Aden the news. I didn't tell the children, who had been staying with us, without their father, for weeks. We simply tried to continue on as we had, until one evening Sharif returned to our house to take his children back.

"Why?" I cried. "They are happy here. How will you raise them?"

"These are my children," he told me firmly. "I'll do what I want."

No matter how I protested, I knew that it was true. I walked into the bedroom. "Your father has come," I told Amina's children, and they all ran out to him, jumping and hugging him. "He will give you everything you need," I tried to tell them, though they were too excited to listen to me.

Sharif came back again, a few months later, this time with Khadija. They both said hello to me, but after that, Khadija kept quiet. "Excuse me, sister, what has happened has happened," said Sharif. "We want now that you will forgive us."

To hear this request, so direct, so unashamed, was shocking to me, and when I saw them there together, all of the sadness I'd felt turned to hot, white anger. "I don't want to see your face," I told him. "Go away."

CHAPTER SEVEN

Filling the Hole in My Heart

When I returned to work after Amina's birth, I transferred from the Ministry of Health to the Ministry of Higher Education, where I would work as an assistant professor of obstetrics and gynecology at Somali National University. I had grown tired of the complicated internal politics of the Ministry of Health; I wanted a change and an opportunity to teach. Now, a few mornings a week, I gave two hour and forty-five minute lectures; when I did my hospital rounds in the early afternoons, I was often trailed by a group of fourth- and fifth-year students.

I loved giving these students the hands-on experience, for I knew from my own education that a thousand books could not equal a few hours of observation. I gained a reputation as a harsh teacher, however. "If you don't know this subject, I will not give you a grade," I told my students, echoing my own professors in Ukraine. "I don't want to cheat my people, to say that you are a doctor when you don't know anything." While they feared me, I also think they respected me. I enjoyed walking the hospital halls with the young, eager students, remembering my school days.

I finally finished my law degree the next year, but still, my days were just as busy. Many nights Aden was out with his friends, drinking tea, chewing *qat*—a popular stimulant made out of leaves from a native shrub—and discussing politics and business late into the evenings. Without my sisters to talk with, I moved from the breakfast table to the hospital to the classroom to the dinner table, or sometimes, when I was late, right into the girls' beds, to hug them and bless them. Sometimes I would sleep there until the morning, when it was time to return to work.

I became friendly with a clever, confident doctor named Fido, who worked in Mogadishu but lived on a big farm in Lafole, near where I grew up. Sometimes, in the break room, we discussed the beauty of that area, with the big trees and the clean, sweet air. Fido told me what it was like, being both a doctor and a farmer. He would wake up early every morning to make sure that the crops had water and that his workers were doing their jobs. He would be at the hospital by seven o'clock for the morning meeting, but instead of returning home to eat his lunch and relax, he'd change back into his work clothes and walk back to the fields.

Through Fido's stories, I began to remember what life had been like in the rural area, when I was a child. We were healthier than the city children were, since we were raised on fresh, nutritious food. The families there were also more unified: The parents and children brought their animals back home around six in the evening, and while the mother prepared food by the fire, the family sat together, each person talking about what he or she had seen that day. I began to see a new future for my family in the shape of our own farm, where my daughters could have the childhood that my sisters and I had, before everything changed.

On my next day off I returned to Lafole, to visit my half sister, Faduma Ali. As the driver sped along the Afgoye Road, I closed my eyes, felt the warm wind on my face, and remembered the last time my sisters and I had left Ayeyo's home, which for so long had been our home as well. By then we had lost our mother and our grandmother, our cows and our goats; we could only bring what we could carry. I'd taken Ayeyo's teakettle, which I'd put in a basket on my back, and we'd walked together toward Mogadishu. I'd turned to look back only once, when we reached the top of the first big hill, thinking that I would never return.

Now fifteen years had passed, and from that one goat my father had saved, Faduma Ali had raised many more on a small portion of our family's land. She was living alone in those days—her daughter had gone to live with her ex-husband's mother—and so was grateful for my company. She led me along the paths, to see the bush and the open fields that were once our playground; over lunch, we laughed about how life had changed since we were children. The drive was short, I told her, remembering our two-hour-long camel caravans and the donkeys loaded up with goods. Now people had pickup trucks, eager to offer their neighbors a quick lift back to the city.

When we had finished our food, I took a sip of my tea and told my sister that I wanted to come back. "Mogadishu is different now," I said. "I'm fed up already."

"I would be happy to have you," she said, "but your job is in the city."

"The road is nice; by car, only about fifteen minutes," I said, thinking of Fido. "I would much prefer that drive to having my children playing only in a small, dark bedroom." The girls would get to know our relatives, many of whom still lived deep in the bush, far from the main road. They would grow strong in the fresh air, with fresh milk and meat; when they were old enough, they would also have the benefit of going to Mogadishu for school, and someday, maybe, for work, like their mother.

Mine was a dream unlike most Somalis' at the time. Much of the land around us lay fallow, while people flocked to Mogadishu in search of work and an urban life. The property in and around Mogadishu was in demand, especially by the seaside. That included a small piece of land I'd bought years earlier, before Deqo was born. One of my father's relatives had been living there when, in the early 1970s, the Somali government bought up 2,000 square meters of property near the American Embassy in Mogadishu. Although the government had offered to sell him 100 square meters to stay on, he did not have the money to buy it. "Sister," he'd told me, "you should take this land." I'd gone to the Banco di Napoli for a small loan, and I'd bought the land for about $425 U.S., using the rest of the money to make a border of stones around the property.

Aden and I had begun to save, and even to buy gold. In the meantime, we'd understood that real estate had been the best investment. Just after Amina's birth, a man had come to me, wishing to buy my 100 meters by the sea. "How much?" he'd asked me.

"Four hundred fifty thousand Somali shillings," I told him— about $75,000 U.S. He agreed immediately.

As I sat with Faduma Ali, I told her this story, and I asked her to tell her neighbors of my intentions to buy land in Lafole. Since so many people had abandoned the area for the city, the price was cheap—just a little more than $200 for one hectare, or about two and a half acres.

"We'll have the best of everything," I told Aden, but he wasn't sure about my plan. For him, life in the rural area meant not only a distance between his home and his job but a separation from his friends.

"The lady has run mad!" one had told him. "Why doesn't she put her money in the bank?"

One day, as I was walking into the hospital, I saw one of my mother's cousins, who had also heard the news. "You—your bank refused you?" he joked. "Why are you buying this empty land far from the city?"

"I like that place," I said. For me, it was that simple.

Aden slowly accepted the idea, and we began to dream together. We sat up at night, discussing the animals that we'd rear and the trees that we'd plant—mango, papaya, lemon, and grapefruit. I came back to Lafole one day to meet with three brothers who owned the land nearest to my family's area, serving the men *bun*, green coffee beans cooked in oil, as we talked about my family, and my interest in the land. Since they knew my father, they were gracious; as they'd accepted my food, they accepted my offer to buy: First one hectare, then another two, then six.

In those days, in Somalia, labor was cheap, but the building materials were very expensive. Since the local city council dictated that construction had to begin on land within two months of purchase, I began buying and storing stone, concrete, and iron sheets in a shed we built on the property. One of Aden's colleagues, an American-educated Somali engineer, agreed to help us realize our plan: First, there would be a new house for Faduma Ali, closer to the main road, so she could set up some kind of shop to earn an income. Next to her new home would be a small shack for chickens; we brought two hundred for her, from a local poultry farm, and a small white cow, which gave us 4 liters of milk each day.

In 1981, construction began on our family compound: two apartments, each with two bedrooms, two toilets, a kitchen, and a small veranda where people could sit. As I was inspecting the progress one day, a representative of the Afgoye mayor came to me.

"You cannot build here," he said.

"Why?" I asked, waving my deed at him. "It says here that I'm required to do so."

"You have to pay an additional fee," he said. "You need a building permit."

"I heard there were bandits in the region, but I didn't think they would come from the mayor's office," I said.

The man left without a problem, but while I acted innocent, I knew that corruption had infected every level of government. Our family was more concerned about Siad Barre's special militia, the Red Berets, who had begun targeting people from the north—including Aden's clan, the Issaq—under suspicion that they were plotting to overthrow the government. I decided that we'd build more slowly, and only at night, when no one could see. I hired a guard to keep watch over our project and over Faduma Ali's house, and I told the contractor that our concrete floors would have to wait, as the process demanded too many people, too much equipment.

The short rainy season arrived, and one Thursday evening, when the moon was full and white as a big light, we drove to Lafole with the children, to sleep on the dirt floor of our new home. My sister Amina's eldest son, Kahiye, was with us, and he begged us to let him sleep in Aden's car, which was parked near where three workmen were assembling Faduma Ali's chicken coop. Aden wished him good night and then went to walk the grounds and enjoy the cool mist; I fell asleep on a pile of blankets inside, next to Amina and Deqo.

I felt a hand grip my shoulder and awoke trembling. When I sat up, Aden stepped back and turned off his flashlight. "I just saw a military car," he whispered. "You say that we will live here? They'll throw us in jail first!" We sat for several minutes, holding our breath and thinking of our nephew in the car. "You are putting us in a terrible situation," Aden said. "You are responsible if something happens today. You brought us here."

He decided to go out to get Kahiye, and I prayed and listened. After a few minutes, I came outside as well. "What happened?" I asked Aden. He stood alone next to the car, where Kahiye slept as though nothing had happened. There were no workers, no guard. He threw up his hands.

"I haven't heard anything," said Faduma Ali as we carried the sleepy children inside her place. It was three o'clock in the morning, but Aden and I drove into the center of Afgoye, to report the incident to the police.

"You are from the Hawa Abdi place?" asked the policeman. "We had some disobedient people there."

"What do you mean?" asked Aden.

"It's illegal to build on that property," he said. They had arrested the workers and were holding them in their jail. When Aden and I were finally able to see our men, and we learned that twelve armed soldiers had forced them into their cars, we apologized. As relieved as we were to know that they were safe, we did not give the money for their bail. These police tactics were Mafia tactics, Aden and I explained; we wouldn't fall for them and beg for forgiveness. Instead we stayed at our place in Lafole for seven days, bringing breakfast, lunch, and dinner to the men. After a week, my friend brought me to the mayor of Afgoye.

"If there is something you need, I am ready," I told the mayor. All that they wanted, he said, was the fee for the building permit. We talked for a while, until I felt that he understood me. Finally I gave them the money to release the men, and I knew our family would be safe. We could pour the concrete floors, finally, and in the earliest days of 1983, my family moved to the rural area to begin our new life.

The first residents on our farm were ten cows and another five hundred chickens, which we kept in a large coop that looked like the one we built for Faduma Ali. At the time, Aden's father owned a place in Mogadishu called the Sarar Hotel; he bought the milk from our farm, 60 liters at a time, and another friend who worked for the American Embassy bought two hundred eggs each week. We hired a few men to work with us and began living as Fido had, going to Mogadishu each morning by about seven o'clock—I by bus and Aden by company car—and returning around 2 p.m., to spend the rest of the day in our place.

Farming is the same all over the world: You have short-term yields and long-term yields, and each step forward gives you more confidence to try something new. The animals thrived, and we turned our attention toward the crops we'd discussed. One of our neighbors made a very good living irrigating farms; I invited him to lunch one day to ask him how my cows could graze during the dry season. "Do you know a place where I can irrigate?" I asked.

"Yes, I know," he said. The land was owned by one of his uncles. He told me that he would try to impress his uncle with the fact that one of Aden's relatives belonged to Siad Barre's clan, which had big money in those days.

Before our meeting, I lay down our finest carpets under the

trees and prepared a big container of water, so the man could wash before we sat down to talk. When he finally came, escorted by my neighbor, I saw that he was an older man. "What is your name, my daughter?" he asked as he settled down for the food that we'd offered.

"My name is Hawa Abdi Diblawe," I said.

"Abdi Diblawe is your father?" He took his cane and hit my neighbor, who jumped. "Then why did you say she belongs to Siad Barre?" His wrinkled face cracked as he smiled. "I know Abdi Diblawe—he helped me in his time. He is my brother. Let's go."

Together we walked down to his place, nearby my great-great-grandfather's farm, and he showed me every corner—sandy roads and trees we call *garas*, with wide branches. He stopped under the trees. "Your grandfather had a son, by his other wife," he said. "When he was young, I sat with him right here." Later, near a field of sorghum, he leaned on his cane and leaned so deeply, I thought he might fall. "When I was a child," he said, "I chased away the birds that came down to steal the green seeds."

I saw his memories, my own memories, too. And I saw my future. "I am pregnant," I told him—a secret that Aden and I had not yet shared with many of our friends. "If it is God's will, our children will sit under these trees with your great-grandchildren."

"From now on, you and my daughter Nuune Ahmed, you are the same," said the old man. We bought 50 hectares from him and immediately began clearing the bush. Since the place was just a kilometer from the river, my friend's husband, the Somali Minister of the Interior, helped us with irrigation. We planned for sorghum, beans, maize, sesame, spinach; together Aden and I planted an entire orchard of fruit trees: four hundred mango trees, a thousand grapefruit trees, and some lemon and papaya trees besides.

We put so much of our hearts into the farm that I began discussing our progress with my patients at the hospital. Some of the women who lived in the rural area began coming to see me at home, rather than in Mogadishu. They told their sisters and daughters and friends about me; so I began to schedule appointments on Friday afternoons, when I was home with my children. While I performed examinations in one of our bedrooms, other women sat on our veranda, waiting to talk with me. Though I had little equipment, I tried to help them in whatever way I could. Some mornings, the only way to help was for Aden to drive his Land Cruiser into Mogadishu with a crying woman and her children in the back.

The women told me about their friends and neighbors—people who had never seen a doctor—so I began going to the villages to see them. By then, Deqo and Amina, who were eight years old and three years old, came with me. As I became more heavily pregnant, they proudly carried some of the equipment; we sang as we walked. Even though many children ran away when they saw my white coat, we tried to talk nicely to them, to reassure them.

Sometimes, at the suggestion of a village elder, we would go inside one of the families' homes. "How are you?" I would say, entering the small hut slowly. "Are you okay?" I would introduce myself and explain how I had known that there was a problem, and who had told me. "Show me the child, please? I want to see." I would try to examine him, listening to his lungs and heart and looking at his face to see if he was very anemic. If a woman was pregnant, or if she had just delivered, I would do an examination, and if a child had malaria, I would give an injection or some tablets. We would pray that the next time we came to the village, the same boy would run to us; many times, he did.

When I visited these rural areas, I was not just a doctor—I was a lawyer, trying to convince the women to trust me, as I could help them in a way that their own families could not. It was hard not to become very frustrated with the women who resisted me because they didn't have an education. "I am a mother and I am Muslim," I said. Science and health were gifts from God, I explained—like our own innate intelligence.

One afternoon Siad Barre called a meeting of all the doctors. After we filed into a big hall, one of the senior doctors stood up to address the issue of private practice, which, at the time, was against the law. "Mr. President, we receive a small salary, but some of our patients, when they become healthy, want to bring us money and other gifts," he said. "To refuse compensation is no way to live." A few months later, Siad Barre issued a letter giving permission for doctors working within the government system to establish private clinics.

One day shortly thereafter, after a long afternoon in one of the villages, I brought the girls back home so they could get their lunch. I remained outside, to have some quiet time to think. That day I had seen a young girl nearing her last month of pregnancy; if she delivered at night, and a complication arose, she wouldn't be able to get the help she needed. I looked out at a group of trees, my mind full of worries for her. She needed to deliver in a hospital, with a doctor who understood the danger she faced. Would she go? I had seen a few other women that day who hadn't needed a hospital, but just another woman who could support them, who could offer advice. I wished they could come to me somehow.

What if, in the clearing near our home, I built a one-room clinic? Many pregnant women from the villages could travel the few kilometers to our place in the middle of the night. Behind it, where a thick thatch of trees stood, we could build a small corridor, where patients could sit and wait for me. I couldn't save them all, but I could do something.

CHAPTER EIGHT

Losing My Past and My Future

When I was still in medical school, my father once told me how he'd bragged to his friends: "They celebrated when they got their sons," he'd said. "I told them, 'When Hawa was born, no one celebrated, but look at her now. How are your sons, and how is my daughter?'" Although my father did not live to see me become a doctor, he knew that I would succeed. "You are now tougher than their sons," he'd said.

It's painful for me to remember this, for when my mother was dying, my parents imagined a very different life for me. "There is a man who has asked for your hand in marriage," my mother said one afternoon in 1959, in the same soft, even voice she had used to introduce me to distant family members that were now lying outside on our carpets.

"I don't want that," I said. I was just twelve years old. "I am studying. I want to go to secondary school. I want to stay with you."

Her head never left the pillow as she told me about the man. "We gave you a very good boy," she'd said. "I liked him as soon as I saw him." His father and my father had known each other— they had both come from the same part of Somalia, far away from Mogadishu. To me, that meant that we were living where the sun rose, and this man was living where the sun set. "His family came this morning, to talk to me and your father," my mother said. "We have accepted."

"I don't want to leave you!" I cried.

"You must marry," my mother told me. "Then, if I die, I will have a clean heart."

A few weeks after we buried my mother, I learned that the man's family was ready to make a wedding. It was worse than if I'd learned that I would go to the grave. I know that my father felt sorry to see me cry, but since he had not needed my consent, he hadn't asked me for it.

My mother's cousins wanted the wedding to be in Mogadishu. "No, no, no," I said. "I have no mother, but I have a grandmother. The wedding will be in Lafole." So Ayeyo called all the people of her generation, all the women and men, and they came to her side, bringing camels, cows, and goats for a feast.

I cried as they wrapped me in a new *guntiino*, the traditional one-shouldered Somali dress. It was bright red, my favorite color. "Oh, she is crying for her mother," said some of the older women softly, but my friends knew the truth.

My father also cried as he hugged me. I know he felt sorry. "Your mother wanted it this way," he told me, so there was nothing else to do.

In that time it was traditional for the young people, girls and boys, to accompany the bride to her husband's house. So around eleven o'clock that evening my friends gathered in front of Ayeyo's home to bring me to Mogadishu. During the hour-long walk, they sang a popular song—words I knew were meant to comfort me. "Run away from that guy," they sang. "You are so beautiful, you are the queen of the society, and you are going to marry that man? No, no."

I was a child then; I didn't know the expectations of a bride on her wedding night. But as my friends sang—"We will wait for you at the market!"—I became less fearful. I even began to laugh a bit, as they put their arms around my waist and we walked together. After a while, the friendly faces all around me distracted me from my sadness and fear.

When we arrived at the man's home, one of Ayeyo's relatives bent down and took me up, like a child, onto her back. I entered into the courtyard this way, with a person on all sides of me, right and left. I squeezed my eyes shut, listening only for a familiar voice, and when I opened them, I was in a room filled with strangers, all surrounding a bed made up to be very beautiful, with orange and red blossoms on top. On the cement floor I saw a mat that Ayeyo had been weaving since the day I first spoke with my mother about marriage. As is the tradition, the woman carrying me said, "I am not putting her down until I am given my money."

The man's parents were in the room. They gave the money, and the woman put me on the bed, my bare feet touching the flowers first. I sank down. There were big containers everywhere, filled with milk, sugar, and sesame oil. Everyone began drinking fresh camel milk from a cup, but when it was handed to me, I was crying too hard to drink.

My girlfriends came around the bed, whispering the same song, "We will wait for you in the market, don't remain here with this guy." But almost immediately they left, and only my husband's family remained.

They held out tea for me, and cool water. "We are your family now," one woman said. "You have nothing to cry for. Stay calm, and everything will be just as it should be."

"But I love those people," I cried, my face in my hands. "I grew up with them. I do not know you." But to go with them was impossible. Another woman in the room, who had never known divorce, gave me a beautiful new headscarf and a blessing to accompany it. I sat still as it was tied tightly around my hair. "We give this to you so you will never fall down," she said.

The man walked into the room by himself. He sat down on the bed and took my hand. "Don't cry," he said.

I could not obey. Even after all I've seen over the years, the seven days to follow I still count as some of the worst in my life.

My first husband's name was Mohamed Hussein. He worked as an officer of the Somali military police, and he smoked so much that when he smiled, you could see that his tobacco-stained teeth were red. He tried to reach out to me, to console me, but I was scared and in pain; whenever he came close to me, I felt a chill. This was not love, preparing food for him, cleaning and washing; the beautiful headscarf I'd been given felt more like a mourning veil, an *asaay*.

Just a few weeks after the wedding, Mohamed Hussein's position was transferred to Kismayo, a city about 500 kilometers south of Mogadishu—farther from my family than I had ever been. I didn't want to go, and the night before we left, I stayed with a friend. She agreed to go with me, so I wouldn't be alone, and in the morning, she and I went together to the big military car waiting for us and sat together in one seat, holding hands.

Mohamed Hussein was surprised to find both of us there. "Who are you?" he asked my friend, "and where are you going?"

When I tried to explain, he threw his cigarette down. "You are a stupid child," he said to my friend. "Why would you think that you could come with me and my wife?" As we pulled away, I could see her running home from the open-top military car.

In Kismayo, we lived in military housing—each family had one big, open room divided into a kitchen and a bedroom, and a walkway passed between the rooms, which meant the neighbors could see what was happening inside. I tried to talk with the other wives, but they were so much older than I was. I walked into town by myself, visiting my favorite shops for some oil and sugar.

Some afternoons I lay on the floor, feeling as though I'd been infected with a horrible disease. The bright sun and salty air that I loved in Mogadishu seemed suddenly harsh; Mohamed Hussein's hands on my body remained those of a stranger. Even the smell of cooking food made me vomit. When he was sent north, on a mission to the border of Kenya, I remained alone for ten days, too sick to go to the market for my daily needs.

I could hear the voices of some of the women, looking in: "Oh, you see how she's lying there? She's a child, and inside her is another child."

When Mohamed Hussein came back, he saw how I was sick. I told him that I wanted to go to see my father and Ayeyo. At first, he tried to refuse—his friends feared that I might miscarry—but after several arguments, he bought me my bus ticket. I stepped into the car with excitement, hoping the pang of homesickness would go away, hoping, also, that I would never return.

I arrived in Mogadishu early in the morning and went straight to my father's stall in the market. When I saw him, I began to cry uncontrollably, falling into his arms. "Calm down, my child," he said as he stepped back to look at me. "I am happy you are pregnant—I will have a grandchild!" I stayed with my family for the rest of the pregnancy. My father took me to see a doctor and then to Lafole, where, from the comfort of Ayeyo's old mat, I breathed in the clean air. She washed my face and gave me cool water, sweet bananas, and papaya.

The night my water broke, Amina ran for my father. Together we waited and waited for a car to bring us to Martini hospital. I cried, not wanting to return to the hospital that had failed my mother, but my father insisted. In the waiting room, as we waited for a midwife to come talk with us, he gripped my hand and told me to remain calm. I tried, although I felt pain—so much sharp pain.

Morning had come by the time a midwife finally examined me. "This area is totally closed!" she wailed. "What have they done to you?"

I did not understand. I knew that I had been closed—it was a memory so painful, from when I was just seven years old, that I do not speak of it. It was the reason why a woman had to stay with me on my wedding night and the days after—to care for me as I healed, and to reassure me, as my mother once had, that every woman goes through the same thing. I didn't understand the implication of being cut and stitched together; I didn't know what it took to deliver a child. While I would later learn the term *female genital cutting*, the frustrated midwife had a simple explanation.

"If the child comes, I can't do anything," she said. She steadied me on the table and began to cut.

Oh, it was painful, painful, painful! It's natural to jump when you feel pain; when I moved, she cut into my muscles, some other places too. But still the child did not come, not for hours, until the afternoon. When I finally saw the baby girl, she was not crying, not moving. "She's alive," said the midwife as she slapped her back. "It's no problem."

"Oh!" my father said, looking at the child, and then at me. "I think they are the same weight!" He named my daughter Faduma, a common name for a family's oldest girl—like my half sister, Faduma Ali. When we were discharged, we stayed for forty days in the home of Mohamed Hussein's parents, but they did not follow the Somali customs of the *umul*. They fed me only small portions. I gave Faduma my breast, but I didn't have enough milk for her. I struggled, and when my father came to visit and saw that I was still so thin, he brought me back to our family's home, to care for me properly.

Faduma could not move her head as a baby should, and when I saw some swelling around her scalp, I showed it to my father. Early the next morning Amina and I walked together to an outpatient clinic, standing in a long, long line of patients until the afternoon, when we finally heard "Faduma Mohamed Hussein."

An Italian doctor, probably forty years old, came to talk with us. "Did she fall?" he asked, holding Faduma's head in his hands and looking closely.

"No," I said.

He asked many questions: How old I was, and how long I'd been in labor. When I told him, he said that he thought something could have happened to the child during her birth. "You are so small," he told me. "Her brain may have been damaged during delivery." He wrote for us a prescription for some medicine, but the problems continued. We brought her back to the doctor, but there was nothing he could do.

The Holy Qur'an says that a husband must care for his wife and his children, to feed and clothe them, but Mohamed Hussein hadn't cared for me at all as I'd suffered. He had seen his daughter only once, when he and a few of his relatives had come into the sitting room in my father's house. He didn't say anything—he just looked at the child, for five or ten minutes, as I breast-fed her.

"Your father with the red teeth came," I sang to my daughter, so Mohamed Hussein could hear, "and he doesn't love you, because you are a girl. Ah . . . you don't know that he's sad, because of you. You're a daughter, so he won't get any satisfaction."

One of his relatives overheard and shouted, "Do you know that this is your husband? How can you address him that way?"

About two months after Faduma's birth, Mohamed Hussein's position was transferred to the city of Beledweyne, closer to the Ethiopian highlands. My father and Ayeyo insisted that I live with him there. We had been there just a short time when, one afternoon, I came home from the market to find him in our small sitting room, still dressed in his work uniform. He stood. "I have come to tell you I'm sorry that your grandmother died," he said, reaching for my hand; he'd bought my bus ticket for the dusty journey back to Mogadishu, without him.

On the road, Faduma and I became sick. I pulled a shawl over my head and face; she lay, hot, against my chest as I shivered. When the road ended, I went the rest of the way by foot, passing the tall weeds and the now-empty fences until I saw my sister Asha in the distance. I called to her, walking faster, and we came together, holding each other and crying. Later I left the baby sleeping in Amina's arms and went to the place where a small stone marked Ayeyo's grave.

There I stood, first without motion and then swinging my head and my arms, twisting in the wind. I felt my eyes sting and hot tears on my face. I bent forward, put my hands and knees onto the ground, and then I lay on my side, my cheek to the patch of sand under which Ayeyo lay.

Faduma was still sleeping when I came back; when we all

awoke the next morning, her fever had returned, her small breaths shallow. I rubbed her back and gave her my breast, but she wouldn't take it. I asked Amina to tell our cousin that something was wrong. "Can we call my father?" I asked him when he came. "My daughter is sick—we need a doctor."

"This child is going to die," he said sternly, "so you must keep quiet."

We didn't believe him, but as we sent a young neighbor boy to tell my father, we waited and prayed.

Death has a different plan for each of us. When my mother passed away, it felt like death took years; her soul fought so hard as her body became weaker and weaker. But for the old and the young, for Ayeyo and for my Faduma, God had a different idea. My cousin was right—she was gone in just a few hours, although I sat holding her until my father came, at about three that after-noon. He turned her tiny face toward him, and I saw tears in his eyes. By then, my cousin had already dug a tiny grave near Ayeyo's, so we prepared the body, washing and dressing it in a tiny *karfan* and then reading those familiar passages of the Holy Qu'ran.

When my mother died, I lost my identity; now, without Ayeyo and Faduma, I had lost my past and my future. I was restless for three days, unable to sleep or to eat. When my father prepared to leave, I told him that my sisters and I would follow.

"No," he said, "you must go back to your husband."

"I can't just relax by myself, knowing how you are suffering," I told my father, but I could not disobey him. On the bus back to Beledweyne, as I thought about my sisters alone, I tried to listen to my mother's advice, to silence the voices of others, to listen to my inner voice in order to reach a solution. "I cannot leave my sisters," I told Mohamed Hussein when I arrived. "If you don't want my sisters, then I don't want you."

"You belong to me, Hawa," said Mohamed Hussein. "I love you. I am not contrary to raise your sisters, but my father doesn't accept that."

"I asked you to help, and you won't, so we have to stop," I said. "You are just a police officer, with a small salary. You should find a girl who doesn't have heavy problems like mine." Our relations never should have happened, and now, I wanted to go back.

"You have suffered a hard loss," he said, but he agreed to let me return to Mogadishu, to school and to the home that my sisters and my father shared.

And so I did. Around that time, Somali radio was talking about liberation day and night. On June 26, 1960, the northern region of Somalia got their independence from the British; less than a week later, the Italian part would get their freedom as well. A neighbor gave our family a message that Mohamed Hussein was called to Mogadishu for a twenty-day security patrol, but I didn't even think of him.

I came home from school one afternoon and was surprised to see Mohamed Hussein in our home, drinking tea with my father, as any other visiting neighbor might. I didn't feel anything when I saw him. When he saw me, he stood, wished my father well, and said good-bye.

"Mohamed told me, 'I don't want to disturb Hawa, and she has told me many bad things,'" my father said, his shoulders stooped forward. "He said, 'Here is her paper. I divorce her.'"

He showed it to me: There was no going back. I began to cry, because I was still a child maybe, or because I felt Ayeyo would have disapproved. "Don't be upset, my child," said my father, and I felt his hand on my head. "I bless you, and your mother and your grandmother blessed you. You will find everything you want." Though I slept that night with a numb mind and a tired body, when I awoke, I, too, was free.

CHAPTER NINE

Building My Practice

For three months, I set aside as much of my salary as I could for materials—mostly cement and iron sheets, which, as our engineer friend and I discussed, would become a one-room clinic that could hold twenty-three beds. I assembled a small staff as well. One of my relatives brought me a midwife who still works with me, and from a new women's and children's hospital called Banadir, which was started by the Chinese government in 1977, I hired two nurses and a very nice cleaner. The cleaner, I knew, had the most important job—in a delivery room, there is a lot of blood, and a lot of bedding to wash.

At the same time, Aden and I built up the farm. We went together to the development bank, bringing with us our deeds in order to guarantee a loan, and then Aden went to the Department of Agriculture, returning with a tractor. It was hard work, but we were rewarded: The crops were growing well, and each morning at sunrise my cousin drove our loaded pickup truck to Mogadishu's main market, Bakara. He'd return with our money and the meat and sugar and tea I'd requested, and then he'd get his breakfast with our family and drive Deqo to school.

In May, I gave birth to a strong baby boy, Ahmed, who had a long neck, just like my father's. Faduma Ali helped to care for me, as did my young daughters, and I regained my strength walking among our crops. We opened the clinic's doors later that year, on August 15, 1983.

In the beginning, we had very few patients—sometimes five, sometimes ten. But since we were on the main road, and since news spreads quickly, I soon found lines of women awaiting me when I returned from work in Mogadishu. Most of my patients who delivered without any complications stayed with us for only one night. In exchange, they would pay the equivalent of about 35 cents—a low amount, but not unheard of at the time. This was not true for people who had the means; when I treated businessmen's wives or the wives of Siad Barre's cabinet ministers in my clinic, they paid more. If I knew someone couldn't afford treatment, I worked for free.

If you think such a thing seems generous, you must understand that when Somali people want something, they will persist. Even if you go out, they won't leave you; they'll follow, saying, "We pray for you! We don't want to curse you! Please, treat our daughter!" I couldn't resist seeing someone in pain—I had to do something! If someone had a severe complication and needed to be referred to a hospital, I sent her to a group of Chinese doctors I'd befriended at Banadir—an OB/GYN, a general surgeon, an internist, and a pediatrician. When they weren't working, they drove out to our farm to get fresh fruits and vegetables.

One afternoon, I came back from a lecture to find a woman sitting on the bench in our waiting area. "Hello," I said. "Are you sick?"

"No," she said. "My cousin brought me here. I want a job." Her name was Faduma Duale, and her only experience was a Red Cross and Red Crescent emergency first-aid course. I told her to return at four o'clock, and as soon as I'd looked after our most urgent cases, I explained how to welcome the patients, to show them the toilet, to register them. She began working immediately, and from then on, Faduma Duale was my right hand.

By the time the clinic had been open for about two months, we were receiving about a hundred patients each day, and the line of women sitting with their parents or their children stretched long past the corridor we built. In order to finish around 10 p.m., I tried to visit each patient for about ten minutes—just long enough to examine her, to say that all was okay or to make a diagnosis, and if necessary, to give some kind of prescription or topical treatment. Over time we learned that while patients in the rural area were often less informed about health and basic hygiene than my patients at the hospital, they also hadn't built up the same type of resistance to certain antibiotics and other medications. That meant that they often returned to health more quickly.

But despite my independence and growing confidence at my clinic, I still needed approval to perform any kind of surgery in Mogadishu—even in the most urgent situations. The power struggles there continued, for as people struggled for prestige, they used science and knowledge as weapons. I remember one prominent doctor who was so eager to publish new research that he sometimes would try a high dose of medicine or give an unnecessary injection, as an experiment. Some of the midwives and I talked together, worrying about what would happen when those patients left us. Even if the mother seemed okay while in the hospital, you never knew what would happen to the child.

As my rural practice grew, and referring my patients to other doctors became more difficult, I began to dream of my own operating room. A surgery department turned a practice into a hospital, however; Siad Barre had given us permission only to open and run small clinics. I stored away more and more materials nonetheless, talking with the engineer about my idea and about other new additions. "Hawa, when will you stop?" said Aden, "Do you want to build from here to Mogadishu?"

Amina was still just a child, but Deqo could understand and support me. "Mama, you have to build!" she said.

In those days I treated Siad Barre's personal secretary, Halawe, who supported my plans to expand the clinic. One day, a man came to me in Digfer while I was making rounds with the students. "Tonight at eleven," he said, "you will meet with the president."

"Tonight?" I asked, surprised.

"Go to the gates of the State House. His secretary will meet you there."

I was not surprised that Siad Barre would have me at his office so late. He received visitors from around 11 p.m. until 3 a.m., subsisting on black coffee, and then slept from 4 a.m. to 11 a.m. I returned home that afternoon, did my rounds in the clinic, and changed my clothes—not to be very formal, but enough to show respect. The car came to our place and drove quickly down the Afgoye Road, while I wondered if the president would refuse my request.

Halawe hugged me when she met me at the gate, and she led me through the courtyard, lit up by beautiful colored lights that stretched along the big driveway and up to the building itself. About thirty guards stood outside, while around them other people, in uniform and in plain clothes, sat, talking in small groups and drinking coffee and tea. As we walked into the office, we passed the president himself, playing Ping-Pong in the open air. He looked happy, like he felt young; he didn't look up as we continued on. We passed through a dimly lit hallway into his office, where I sat down in an easy chair. Halawe brought me a bottle of orange Fanta to drink as I waited.

I sat there like that for more than forty-five minutes, while Siad Barre met with one of his wives. Finally Halawe came out and said, "Come with me."

The first thing I noticed about the president was his face— I could tell by his skin that he lived well, and his eyes were lively, smiling at me from the top of his light khaki-colored uniform. "Sir, Mr. President, thank you for receiving me, for allowing me to meet with you," I said. He motioned for me to sit, and I did so, straightening my trousers and crossing one leg over the other. "My name is Dr. Hawa Abdi Diblawe. I am living between Mogadishu and Afgoye, in a rural place. There are many people who are suffering, and they don't have the transportation to come to our hospitals in Mogadishu."

"You want to build a hospital," he said.

"Yes," I said.

"Do you know how difficult it is to build a hospital?" he asked. He listed many complications of building and the need to maintain high standards of cleanliness and to follow the national protocols. "This isn't an easy thing," he said.

"Sir, Mr. President, I want to make this hospital," I said. "The women are suffering."

He interrupted to tell me his position on the rights of women, whom he called the backbone of Somali society. When he finished talking, he dismissed me. "Maybe you will go back and have a meeting with the Minister of Health," he said. Since I hadn't expected an answer, I simply thanked him for his time and left. In the car, I tried to remind myself of the good the president had brought to our country—even if it felt like all of Somalia hated him, there were certain things that I did agree with.

The next time Halawe came to me, she was carrying a pink envelope from the president's office, which contained a letter that authorized me to build a surgical ward and another twenty beds: Hawa Abdi hospital. An international organization called Church World Service sent an American company to do an assessment on the project. They gave us enough concrete for a good roof and strong pillars to support it, and we set aside the leftovers for future building. Meanwhile Aden assembled more and more farm equipment, including a big East German–made engine to power a water pump that would serve our house, the farm, and eventually the clinic.

We built and built, only stopping if the money was not there or on Fridays, when no one worked. Then we would take our pickup truck and drive to the edge of the farm, where the breeze was the best. We would pack a big picnic lunch—camel meat, pasta, rice, sugar—and prepare it under the trees, inviting our staff to come. Amina loved to look at the young bananas, still green and beautiful on the trees.

Years later, my son Ahmed would tell me that he remembered those days as some of the happiest in his life. Memory is complicated. I can't go back to the past—to a day in 1986, when I walked out onto our veranda and saw a sea of green in the distance. Sometimes I wonder how I would have felt if I could see into the future. But that is as impossible as the idea that I can step onto that same veranda today and picture young Deqo running fearlessly out to the farm to find Aden.

I thrived on my routine: Leave early for Mogadishu, come back to rest, go to the clinic, come back to sleep. Our children grew strong and healthy, eating the freshest food and running in the bush. A cousin brought us one of the first Panasonic televisions that had a videocassette recorder. The television programming, which came from Kuwait, ran from 6 p.m. to 10 p.m. on the weekdays, and on Thursday afternoons, Aden took the children to rent videos. They brought home three each week: a Bollywood film, a Western, and a martial arts film—movies that Aden knew didn't have a threat of a sex scene. While the television was not allowed during the day, Deqo figured out how to rig up the small generator, so they could watch even more before Aden and I came home. Eventually we caught on, and Aden started bringing one of the connecting cables to work each day.

Aden and I had little time alone together; we began to disagree from time to time. The Somali way, as you know, is for the man to work and give orders, and the woman to raise the children and obey him. Since I had bought the land and built the home, I made many of the household decisions, even if Aden disapproved. The stress of the political situation and the growing tension at Aden's office did not help matters. Ah, some days I remember that Ayeyo blessed me for a happy life; she didn't say anything about a happy marriage.

Our disagreements became arguments, and I insisted that we speak in low voices so long as the children were awake. Sometimes, by the time I came home after my rounds, he was already out of the house—in Mogadishu on business, or out on the farm with the workers, to ensure that the irrigation system wouldn't flood our fields overnight. I thought, in those moments, of the advice that my sister Amina gave me, a week before Aden and I married. "You know, Abayo, there is something I learned about love," she said. "After marriage, fifteen percent of love, it goes out."

One night while Aden and I were watching the ten o'clock news, we saw a friend of ours—the husband of one of Siad Barre's daughters. He was near Hargeisa, the biggest city in the north, which was a base for the Somali National Movement, an opposition group founded by the members of the Issaq clan. As the camera pulled back, it showed him next to a dead body, burned beyond recognition. To our shock, our friend looked directly into the camera, into our own eyes, his left hand pointed down to the body. "Anyone who is contrary to the blessed revolution, we will make like *this*," he said.

As Aden was Issaq, we feared for his safety; all we could do was continue to live our lives in the right way. That meant, for Aden, saying nothing when he saw colleagues stealing government money or cars. We took solace in our own immobile capital—big land, a clinic, a farm—but we still had to smile and sing for a government that was killing its own people.

In May 1986, Siad Barre was seriously wounded in a car accident and sent to Saudi Arabia for medical treatment. While many people hoped that a new leader would emerge, we kept quiet, as we had since the earliest days. He returned to health, running, unopposed, in a rigged presidential election that December. "What is another seven years?" sighed the husband of one of my patients.

In those days, Somalia's head pharmacist was a very wise man, who helped bridge the gap between modern and traditional medicines. Under his leadership, Somali researchers traveled to the rural area to collect samples, hoping to investigate the remedies that had long been contained in the leaves, flowers, and roots. Unfortunately, we didn't have the right laboratory equipment to conduct many of the experiments, so the material was sent to Italy. I visited his office regularly, hoping for news of the latest research results.

When I was in the rural area on my days off, I began talking with the traditional healers, some of whom had been elders of their small villages for as many as fifty years. While they were surprised that a young, Soviet-educated doctor would want to learn from them, they were generous with their stories, opening their work to me.

The first treatment I witnessed was for a man who had a big, swollen sore filled with pus on his foot—something that, in our hospital, we would puncture and drain. The healer brought a mixture of leaves and spread it on the foot. I was doubtful, but after a few hours, the sore opened and drained on its own. I noted the leaves in my book with disbelief, asking too many questions as he showed me a combination of seven different types of plants— two from the sea, and five from the bush—known to treat major infections.

From then on, whenever I had patients suffering from difficult problems, I would stay up at night to make notes about their cases. Then, on Fridays, when I went to talk with the healers, I would ask their opinion.

One young woman came to my clinic from the bush, feeling deep pain. Though I didn't have the resources for a biopsy, I guessed, from her symptoms, that it was cervical cancer. I explained what that meant, and what she could do, but she did not want to go to the hospital, which her family feared. So I admitted her and followed the advice of the traditional healers, mixing together a combination of plants and applying the paste to the affected area, bit by bit, week after week. Over the next three months, the affected area shrank, until it became the size of the head of a pin.

I did not talk publicly about my patients, but I also didn't work in secret, which is a dangerous habit for any doctor. One day, when I walked out of the outpatient clinic to get some air, a man approached me. "Dr. Hawa," he said, "I want to tell you something."

Since he had been there all day, I had assumed that he had been waiting for one of the women inside. I asked him to take a walk with me around the back of the clinic, toward the bush. "You're being watched," he said. "The police know that you are using this traditional medicine." He looked very serious, pressing his lips together in between sentences. "Your situation is in danger."

Unsure of what to say to the man, I told him that I followed all government protocol in my work. Then I said, "Thank you," and he left.

The next morning, before my lecture at the university, I stopped in the office of the head pharmacist, shut the door behind me, and began to shout. "I'm using these trees, in the way that you're encouraging, and someone came to me and told me I was in danger," I said. "What is this supposed to mean?"

The pharmacist had also been educated in the Soviet Union; he understood the implications of what I was saying, but still, he was passionate about his work. "You continue your job," he told me. "Let them accuse us—we know how to defend ourselves." I thought he was right. This research, these discoveries, gave me confidence. I began to document my work, dreaming of a new treatment for cancer out of those very trees.

A few months later, I was doing rounds in Banadir hospital when I examined a woman who had a dangerous-looking growth on her vulva. When the biopsy came back, we saw that it was cancer, already in the second stage. Oh, I was sorry to deliver that news. A few weeks later, she came to me in the clinic, searching for some small hope. "We have a good treatment for you here," I told her. That woman stayed with us for three months, and every day, I applied a bit more of the mixture to the infected area. With her permission, I took photos as her situation progressed, and slowly by slowly, the growth began to reduce in size.

Aden's friend invited our family to camp under the stars near a big meteorite, which was a major attraction in the area. By then, Faduma Duale had enough experience to take care of the clinic in my absence, and to call on one of my colleagues in Mogadishu in case of an emergency. For three days, our family was together, laughing and playing. Amina delighted in cooking over an open fire, while Deqo sulked to be the oldest, left with most of the hard work. "I can understand," I told her gently, "but this is your job."

When we returned on Saturday, I went immediately to the clinic to check on the patients. But the woman I'd been treating was gone. "I didn't see her leave," said Faduma Duale. We relied on our patients to check themselves in and out; it was easy for something to happen without being noticed.

"She wasn't finished with her treatment," I said.

We never found out what happened to that woman, but that day I stopped all use of traditional medicine. Its benefits were not worth the danger that I was bringing to myself, or to my patients.

CHAPTER TEN

My Sisters Return

One afternoon when the clinic was slow, I sat on our veranda and saw in the distance two veiled women walking toward me. Behind them followed a line of children, going by three by three by two. Assuming they had come for medical help, I stood up to return to work. As they got closer, though, I could see that it was Asha and Khadija. Behind them ran their children, and my sister Amina's, who all ran to hug their long lost Mama Hawa.

"Hello!" shouted Asha.

Aden heard the noise and came out; so did Deqo and Amina, who carried Ahmed in a sling on her back. My sisters had come from Mogadishu, walking from the bus stop along the Afgoye Road, about fifty meters away. "Please, brother, we have nothing to eat, no place to go," Asha told Aden. As we talked, we learned what had happened in the time since we'd spoken: Asha had divorced, and Khadija was alone. A few months earlier, Sharif had gone on hajj, the pilgrimage to Mecca, after a popular sheikh. He was still there, somehow, so they hadn't paid their rent.

There were some among us who, for generations, believed that sheikhs had extra powers—that they could support you with health and riches and send you to paradise when you die. Sharif had been running after the same family of sheikhs for as long as I'd known him. A few times a year, he and his friends would go to the rural areas, where the sheikh held big meetings in honor of the birth of the Prophet Muhammad or some other prominent sheikh. Families would travel from far and wide, bringing camels, goats, and cows, rice, oil, and sugar, money, or gold to offer the man, as a way to get closer to God.

"Hawa, you have to believe in this sheikh," Sharif had told me years ago. "He will bless you, and you will get everything in this world!"

"How?" I'd asked. It was as difficult for me to accept that this man was a small god as it had been to believe the Gypsies we used to see as students, who said that reading our palms would tell our fortunes. But Sharif believed; even Aden, who had been in the Soviet Union with me, seemed to accept it.

The children ran after Deqo and Amina to see the television inside, and I kept quiet for a few minutes, listening to Aden and Khadija talk. Then I shouted to one of the boys working with us, asking him to call the woman who helped with the cooking and cleaning. "These are my sisters," I said to the boy. "Clean the extra apartment; it will be for them." I excused myself and walked into the kitchen to instruct the woman working there to prepare an additional ten portions—eight children and two adults.

I returned to Asha and Khadija and pointed to the other building. "We'll prepare dinner and bring you a carpet to sleep on," I said. "In the morning, we will talk."

That night, as Aden slept, I lay awake, wondering if they knew how much they'd hurt me. *Raalli gelin*, they'd told me—"I apologize." I had given up so much of my life for them, putting their needs ahead of my own. After our mother died, I began a competition with my mother's friends and neighbors, who had daughters that were around our age. Whatever their daughters did, my sisters had to be at the same level—with education, with behavior. I had succeeded, with the help of my sister Amina. But after we lost our beloved Amina, Asha and Khadija had left me while my pillow was still wet with tears.

Like so many women, my sisters had believed in their husbands above all else. I had seen so many women make this mistake, throwing away their fathers and mothers, their brothers; in the end, there was no way for them to go back. Seeing my sisters return to me with no money, no hope, I grieved again for my mother, my father, and for Amina, who were no longer there to help me find a solution. One part of me did not believe that my sisters could change. But the other part thought of their children—the eight voices that crowded into our sitting room, cousins that my children barely knew. Maybe they will be good people, I thought. As it was almost dawn, I stood up to begin the day, having made my decision. I found the energy to raise their children as my own. We had everything to offer them— a well-running farm with many cows and chickens, a big area in which to play, and a family that would finally be together.

The arrival of more adults who thought they could act as boss was not an easy thing for the farm and hospital staff, or for my children. Our home became more crowded, and more complicated. One day Deqo ran to me while I was in the clinic. "Mama! I don't want the workers to leave us!"

"Why? What has happened?" I asked.

"Mama Asha told them to," said Deqo. I asked her to tell whoever was upset to wait for me, and when I finally came out I saw a group of my staff standing there, furious and insulted.

"She told us, 'This is my sister's place, so I am also the owner,'" said one of the men. "She said, 'I don't like the way you address me, so you must go.'"

Asha didn't understand that if you are leading a group of people, you have to administer instructions, and punishments, equally.

One night, when one of Aden's relatives' boys started some trouble among the camp's children, one of the youngest got caught in the scuffle and began to cry. Asha came out of her room and said to Deqo in an angry voice, "Did you hurt this little boy?"

"No, Mama Asha," said Deqo, but Asha didn't believe her. The fighting escalated between Deqo and Asha until I ran out and got between them.

"You stupids!" I said, raising my voice against my sister for the first time in a long time. The little boy ran into the bush. "You are paranoid," I said to Asha, while holding Deqo's shoulder still. "You're starting trouble with my daughter, while I'm protecting you? Don't do these things again."

Khadija needed some medical treatment, so we paid her way to Saudi Arabia, to stay with one of our cousins, who lived in the city of Riyadh. She hoped to reunite with Sharif there. Asha decided that she wanted to go to Saudi Arabia as well; she came to me one day and asked me for 60,000 Somali shillings, so she could follow the sheikh.

Politicians, doctors, businessmen—they all believed in the power of these men: *Oh, Sheikh so-and-so says that! We have to go! We have to pay!*

"These people are lying to you, Asha," I said. "They are cheating people—God will punish them."

"You are Russian now," she said, accusing me of being without religion. "You cannot understand how powerful they are."

"So take it," I said when I returned with a handful of bills. "Then, when you get all your power, you can divide it and give me some." She went but returned soon after, horrified by the way that Saudi men touched her and propositioned her. "Do you know why so many people come back from Saudi Arabia so rich?" she said. "They are practicing prostitution, and I don't want that."

The children all remained with us, eating well and growing to be good friends, chasing one another outside all afternoon. They came into my room one day to tell me that they all wanted to be doctors—Deqo a gynecologist; my sister Amina's eldest girl, Su'ado, a pediatrician; and her youngest son, Abdi Karim, a surgeon.

"What kind of doctor will you be?" I asked my Amina.

"Any kind I want," she said.

I dug a new garden near the clinic; the plants sprouted quickly, just like my practice, which had grown from a single room with twenty-three beds into a building that could house sixty-two and accommodate surgical procedures. With further help from Church World Service, we had built a second floor above the clinic and replaced our iron roof with a concrete one. Now with our new operating room, we had the ability to perform Cesarean sections on our own. While I could now save so many girls and women who could not deliver normally, I still had the challenge of explaining why surgery was necessary.

"To just cut open her stomach like that," said one woman's mother, "are you sure she will be alive?"

"Yes!" I insisted. "The biggest way that we doctors show we care is to take a knife and cut someone open."

I worked with two other well-qualified doctors in those days. Our surgeries were elective, and since we didn't have an anesthetist on staff, we often had to wait for one to arrive so we could perform an operation. There were times, of course, when I wanted to intervene immediately, but as was the case in the Mogadishu hospitals, we had the rule that no doctor should operate alone. I'm grateful, for there have been times over the years when I've fainted or have had to leave a surgery unexpectedly. But never, in all forty years of being a doctor, have I ever lost a patient on my operating table.

Our brand-new surgical suite, the first of its kind outside Mogadishu, was for me an oasis, free of the politics and the oversight that had held me back. I could not foresee at the time, of course, how important the room would be in twenty years, when the city's hospitals would be overrun by squatters and militiamen. Then, some of the senior doctors who had challenged me in Digfer would come to my place. "Hawa," they would say, "we need someplace to operate, someplace to admit our patients."

"Okay," I would say. "You are welcome."

During the first few weeks others would use our operating room, I'd hear of tragic mistakes—first one patient died on the table, and then two. Finally, I would tell them to stop: "This is my hospital, and we will be damaged if people begin talking and hearing, 'We brought her to Hawa Abdi hospital, and she died there.'"

Somali people say that life is like a day—in the early morning, you see a dark shadow falling on one side of the tree. But then the situation changes; by the late afternoon, the shadow is on the opposite side. Today you are powerful, and maybe tomorrow you will become weak. Your responsibility is to try to do right by everyone.

In those days, we made international phone calls at the Mogadishu post office. One afternoon I received a message from one of Sharif's friends, so I went to place a call to him in Saudi Arabia. As I stood waiting, I feared that something had happened to Khadija. She'd been searching for Sharif for weeks, hoping that the sheikh could help make peace between them.

After several tries, the connection came through. "How are you?" I asked Sharif's friend.

"We found Sharif dead in his hotel room," he said. "He was in Riyadh."

I held my breath while, in an even tone, he explained how such a thing had happened. Sharif accompanied the sheikh back from *hajj*, but when they tried to enter Riyadh, the military did not allow the sheikh to enter. I don't know why: Perhaps they had a problem, or perhaps he tried to enter in a wrong way. Thinking only that his sheikh was sacred, Sharif argued with the soldiers, striking one. They turned around and beat him well.

Soldiers, you know, are well trained in violent tactics; they know how to beat someone so that the trouble in their body grows slowly, doing lasting damage. Sharif got up from the fight and walked back to his hotel, but his friends did not hear from him for days. The hotel staff finally called the police, who broke down the door to find Sharif lying on the bed, with blood in his nose, his mouth, and his ears.

My cousin arranged a phone call with Khadija, who was shocked. "I'm going there to see if it's true," she told me. She later called me from Riyadh, where authorities had put his body in refrigeration. She'd insisted on seeing her husband, and although the hospital officials at first refused, they finally agreed to let her into the morgue. When they brought his body, she ran away. "I could not see his face," she cried to me. "I only saw his hair."

Khadija had hoped they would reunite in Saudi Arabia. "Sharif, he ran away when I was in Somalia," she cried into the phone, "and when I came to Saudi Arabia, he left me here." The authorities listed the cause of death as a heart problem, and they buried him in Riyadh.

I tried to console her, although I didn't know the words she needed. "That is God's decision," I said. "We cannot change anything. You are strong and well now. You need to come back to your children."

When a Somali person dies, his family slaughters some animals for the guests who will come. Since Khadija was still in Saudi Arabia, I took a big bull from among our forty cows to give to Sharif's mother. "Kahiye," I said to his oldest son, the child of my beloved Amina. "You will sit in the front of the pickup, with the driver, and bring it to your grandma."

Kahiye, by this time, had grown into a strong, handsome boy. While he tried to remain calm, I could tell he was crying. He needs his father, I thought, as I hugged him. His mother was dead, and even his stepmother, Khadija, was still in Saudi Arabia. What could we do to protect him?

"Ayeyo, this is my cow," he told his grandmother when we arrived. "I want to help you to bury my father. This is a little thing that I can do." They slaughtered the animal, she blessed him, and together, Kahiye, Asha, and I came back to our farm.

CHAPTER ELEVEN

Necessity Is the Mother of Invention

In 1988, government forces sent airplanes to the north of Somalia to attack the Somali National Movement rebel group, dropping bombs around the city of Hargeisa, killing as many as 5,000 people. It was a massacre. The terror and outrage spread across the country as government troops rounded up members of Aden's clan, the Issaq—officers, professors, lawyers—beating them and killing them. Another strong clan to the south, the Hawiye, formed their own resistance group, the United Somali Congress, and they, too, became government targets. Countless men were under suspicion, targets of the military police, which monitored people's conversations and often came into homes at night, terrorizing everyone inside. At one point, a group of prominent Somali people signed a petition that called for elections and for human rights. To Siad Barre, the message could not have been clearer: The society doesn't want you. But those people were threatened with death.

Some of the tension exploded into clashes on the city streets, while government soldiers—stern, young men—stood at the gates of Mogadishu at so-called checkpoints, holding Russian machine guns and interrogating every person trying to flee. "What is your clan?" they would ask. If they heard what they considered to be the wrong response, or even the wrong tone, they would shoot. Some people died immediately; others, wounded, staggered down the Afgoye Road in search of help.

Necessity, they say, is the mother of invention. We had studied emergency medicine in the Soviet Union, learning from veterans of World Wars I and II, who told us what would happen if a bullet went into an abdomen and how to treat a stab wound to prevent internal bleeding. The Soviet Union was peaceful at that time, however; so we never had a case to treat. Now, we had to do what we could with what we had, and we also had to work in secret— if government soldiers saw that their victims were being treated by us, they could shell or shoot up the hospital. When wounded people came to us, I often administered first aid quickly and sent them into the bush to recover.

One day we received a young boy who had been shot at one of these checkpoints. He'd run away when the soldiers pulled their guns, but they'd shot him in the back anyhow, a bullet ripping through his intestines and forcing him to walk on his hands and knees. Somehow, with his intestines hanging out, he made it down the Afgoye Road to us. We don't know how long it took him to travel the 24 kilometers, although we do know that sometimes he hid in the bush from the soldiers; other times he fell unconscious, onto the sand.

How that boy wanted to live! He asked us for help, crying softly. I gave him some antipain and antishock medication and cleaned his wound as best I could, but the bullet had damaged so much. While I sat with him and asked him questions, to understand what had happened, his brothers and friends were searching the countryside for him, carrying his photo. We stood together while he screamed. "Don't cry—if you die, die normally," someone said to him. "It is no problem to die."

I stepped outside for a moment, worried about what I could do. We couldn't operate: We had no blood bank and no one on duty, and without anesthesia, the boy would die of shock. We sat together with him until his cries stopped and his breathing became ragged. When the time came, we took his photo, in the hopes that we could find his family and tell them the news. Then we dressed him in the *karfan* and buried him in our place, just 300 meters away from the hospital. He was our first casualty.

When his desperate friends finally came to our place, Deqo brought them tea and showed them our photo. They cried when they saw it, and we took them to visit the small grave. A short time after, we would bury beside him another young, wounded boy, whose mother had carried him to us on her back.

My regular patients no longer came to me; they stayed home, hoping to resist the heavy shelling in the Mogadishu streets or the unpredictable violence in the bush. Late one night, government troops invaded a home about 3 kilometers from our place. The family came to me the next morning, around eight o'clock, pushing a young woman in a donkey cart. "Mama Hawa, help me!" she cried when I saw them out front. We brought her inside, and I gently pulled away the blanket that covered her.

Since the other doctors were on duty, I called them to see the wounds. A gunshot to her stomach had shattered her pelvic bone; half of her bladder was gone, and somehow her intestines had come out through the wounds, like a flower. One of the doctors ran away, and the other turned to me and said, "Hawa, we'll have to send her to Mogadishu, and the road is blocked by checkpoints." We argued for a while, but he was right; I went back to talk with the family.

The woman's sister told me what had happened. "Lie down," said one of the stupid soldiers when he walked into her room. She refused, knowing he'd rape her, and she threw sand in his face. He shot her in the stomach and ran out of the home, back into the bush. The family waited all night, praying, as they tried to stop the bleeding themselves. When they believed they would be safe, they came to me.

I explained the situation, and the mother and father, who were listening with the sisters and brother, all fell to the floor, crying for me to help them. Finally, they decided to go back to their home. My eyes ached as I told them that I was sorry.

Mortality is a cup of juice that every person in the world will drink. Sometimes, I know, the best you can hope for is to die without begging someone, without saying to him, "No, don't do that, please, I will do whatever you want." That young woman did not accept being made into a victim by the soldiers. She died with dignity.

The people fleeing the violence came to us with nowhere else to go and nowhere they could return, so we cleared out the beds from the empty hospital wards, so more people could stay. When that space became full, we cleared out our small café and other rooms, and finally families began sleeping under the trees. These were not poor families—some were dressed well, carrying food and money. All they were missing was peace. Since Ethiopia, Uganda, Djibouti, and several European states opened their borders to Somali refugees, many people stayed with us for just a few weeks. Those who had no money or no transportation remained.

It was a difficult, tense time. The light to our corridor was always on, and every time we heard a rumor, we prayed it was wrong. One night, the government collected forty-three Issaq men, dug a big hole near the seaside, and then buried all of the men in it. They shot some men before they buried them, but most were still alive. One of the men did not die of suffocation; he crawled out of the dirt and found his way to us, and that's how we know what happened.

I came home after work one day to see a strange car parked outside, among some of my patients'. I assumed it belonged to one of their relatives, and I went inside to see Aden and to get our lunch. When we had finished eating and I was preparing to go back to the clinic, we heard a sharp knock—*goa-goa-goa*—at our door. "Open!" we heard, and Aden jumped up from his chair and headed toward the back of the apartment.

I opened the door. "Aden Mohamed?" A government soldier pushed past me, two others behind him, and he kicked Aden's empty chair. "Come out," he said. "Get your car keys. You are coming with us." I looked in the doorway to see Deqo, Amina, and little Ahmed staring with shocked eyes, unable to understand that their father was being targeted because of his clan. It was the first time a gun had been brought into our home; as my eyes gravitated to the AK-47, Aden walked back out of our bedroom, gasping.

Deqo ran for his asthma medicine and Amina caught Aden's leg: "Father!" One of the soldiers kicked her sharply in the side, and she fell down, crying. She scrambled back near Ahmed as the soldier pushed Aden through the door. "Drive it," said one of the soldiers, pointing to our car. "We will go together."

We were helpless as they left us, Aden grinding the gears of the car. They sped off toward Mogadishu, and we walked into the clinic to search for some help.

Since it was a Thursday afternoon and few people were working, I didn't know how we would find someone to help us. One of my patients offered to drive me to find him, and before I left, I went into the bedroom and grabbed a suitcase full of money from patient fees. I feared that those corrupt soldiers would return to our house, looking for money and valuables. I had no choice but to leave the children behind with the other adults. We stopped at the post office, where I called a friend who was a member of Siad Barre's clan.

He agreed to meet us at the police station, and we spoke to the authorities together. Before I left them to continue the conversation privately, I asked for their help. "Please," I said, "my husband was put here, and he has done nothing wrong." We sat in a waiting room, wondering if they would keep him, release him, or kill him, and finally, at eight o'clock, Aden came walking out the front door, looking shocked but unharmed.

We gave the suitcase to our friend for safekeeping and returned home to find all the children in the sitting room, crying. It was impossible to understand what had happened, let alone to explain it. "The car is still gone," I said, "but we don't need a car. We need your father with us, alive, and here he is—he is fine!"

"We don't need a car!" shouted Amina. She was still rubbing her left side, which would bother her all her life.

While the children slept, Aden and I sat up all that night, worried that the men would come back for us. In the morning Aden went to his friends, searching for the car, I know, and searching for a reason why the men had bothered him. "Do they have any concrete evidence that I committed a crime?" he asked me later that night, pacing.

While we were not disturbed again, in some significant ways, our life changed after that: Aden never returned to work, which meant, for the children, more time to spend with their father on the farm. Deqo, who was closest to Aden, was especially glad. There is sometimes no clear distinction between peace and war. Deqo, Amina, Ahmed, and their cousins still studied and they still played, chasing one another into the bush and drawing huge circles, with sticks, in the sand. We still had our cows in those days, which meant that mealtimes were still crowded and chaotic as the children sat, five of them hovered over each plate, scooping up the stewed meat and porridge and giggling and swatting when their hands touched. Next door, in the hospital, the expectant and new mothers were not thinking of clan division and violence— just of the pain and effort of childbirth, and the relief and delight of motherhood.

CHAPTER TWELVE

Collapse

On January 26, 1991, the United Somali Congress invaded the state house, driving Siad Barre and his men into the streets. We listened to the radio in disbelief, hearing that government soldiers had raided the national bank, killing the guards who tried to refuse them entry and loading the contents of the vaults into trucks waiting outside. Would Siad Barre be killed? Who would take his place? As we sat, asking questions, our cousin drove Amina and Ahmed, who were just ten and eight years old, to their primary school in Afgoye—even farther from the fighting. Everyone had an opinion about what would happen, but I tried to speak calmly for the sake of the children.

"I have school, too," said sixteen-year-old Deqo, who'd been studying for weeks in preparation for her final exams that day.

"Today," I said, "Mogadishu is fighting."

"I've been working too hard to stay! I'm going!"

Though I forbade her, she ignored me and walked out the door, as hotheaded as I am and as hardheaded as her father. I returned to the hospital for a while, but sometime after she left, the radio was reporting heavy shelling near Villa Somalia, which was also near Deqo's school. "God help her!" I cried. Two of our cousins took our pickup and went to find her. Right after they left, one patient came to me to say, "Siad Barre collected all his soldiers and gave them all the government weapons. He only said to use them against the Hawiye and the Issaq."

"Oh," I said. "If these clans fight, Somalia will be destroyed."

Though the streets were chaotic, they were open; our cousins drove to Deqo's usual bus stop and found Deqo standing, shaken, waiting for a bus that did not come. On the way back out to our place, they passed many of Deqo's schoolmates, who recognized our pickup and ran toward it. They took everyone it could hold and brought them all back to our place.

A crowd had gathered under the trees, and our helpers brought lunch outside, so we could try to make sense of the situation. "Let's go to Siad Barre," I proposed to some of the people who were gathered with us.

"No, Hawa, it is too late," said one. "We already tried, and he's refused us. If one of us comes to him to reason with him, he will immediately kill us."

The Afgoye Road was so crowded with cars and people fleeing the city that Amina and Ahmed waited for hours to be picked up from school. They finally joined us, sitting cross-legged on the carpets with some of their friends, listening to adults and asking too many questions.

"There are some people who don't believe in the government, and that has made a problem," I explained. "That's why there is fighting."

"Are we going to school tomorrow?" asked Ahmed.

"No," I said.

"Will we have school next week?"

"*Insha'allah*," I said. God willing. How could we have seen the future? Aden climbed up on our roof to shout "Get out!" to Siad Barre's men—his government officials, his relatives, and members of his clan—as a huge line of cars and pickup trucks traveled west up the Afgoye Road and away to Nairobi, the capital city of neighboring Kenya. He waved his hands as the trucks, filled with government money, passed him by. "Get out!" he yelled. "Get out!"

By 2 p.m., when a group of us joined him on the roof, it was a different scene. Driving in the opposite direction, toward Mogadishu, were big buses filled with the clans that had long been persecuted by Siad Barre's regime. Young boys hung out the windows, gleefully waving green leaves and Somali flags. "Come back!" they yelled, and my children waved down to them. "Come back to Mogadishu! Come back!"

"God is great," I said, looking at Aden. "Maybe there will be peace."

While we waited for peace, while we prayed for it, the sound of the shelling continued day after day, along with the rattle of machine gun fire. As people streamed down the roads away from the city, many stopped in our place, asking for water or for treatment. Many were Darod, members of Siad Barre's clan, coming to us on their way south to cities such as Merca, Brava, Kismayo, anywhere. We began giving the families our just-harvested maize, sorghum, and sesame to cook for themselves. Some began building makeshift homes from the sticks in the area, the way their parents and grandparents had done. By the middle of 1991, we had 800 families living with us—more than 4,000 people.

The stories they brought into our lives shook the children, who imagined mortars crashing through metal roofs, killing sleeping families beneath. "I will never go to Mogadishu again," declared Deqo one day as I was worrying about one of the workers we'd sent into the city to try to find more supplies. "You should never go again either."

The violence began during the long, dry season, so as Mogadishu emptied of resources, its people fled. When a woman became sick, she came to us not just with her small children but with her whole family—elders and cousins. We knew that the number of people wounded by the senseless violence was going up and up; it seemed only natural that the problems we could solve—like giving someone a place to stay and some small feeling of safety—should be solved.

I shook Deqo from bed every morning at three, when she

joined her cousins in an assembly line to make *chapati*, a type of bread, for all the needy families. They were the chefs! Amina and Ahmed watched as the older children prepared the charcoal and put down the baskets, one, two, three, and then took them out, one, two, three. Then they'd do it again and again, until seven in the morning, when I came to distribute the breakfast.

"How many people do you have in your family?" I'd ask each person. She'd tell me, or sometimes she'd try to cheat me. "We are six," the mother of one, or two, would say. Sometimes, if we refused them, they argued, their eyes narrow, their hands clawing.

Food prices were high, the market stalls bare; people still trapped or waiting inside the city became desperate. When you are hungry, you have nothing to lose: Mothers walking slowly down the Afgoye Road stopped holding their children's hands or looking for oncoming traffic. Entire families were killed this way, hit by cars driven wildly by the bush people who had stolen them. Still, they continued. "Better we die walking than collapse of hunger," one mother told me.

Our farm staff had stored our sorghum in 50-kilogram sacks, and with so many hungry people to feed, we went through about twenty sacks each day. We also began rationing our meat very carefully, trying, always, to make it through until things improved. We gave food first to the children and then to the weakest adults. We boiled the bones twice, sometimes three times, but even so, our store was finished earlier than we'd planned.

One morning, during food distribution, I left Deqo and the other children and walked straight out to the edge of my land, far from the shouting and fighting. I looked back at this distance, to see what I had created. I forced myself to look: my hospital, with its pink walls; my small café made of sticks. Why had God given me such riches in a place where nothing could grow? I leaned back against a tree, feeling the tree bark digging through my white coat to my spine as I cried.

✻   ✻   ✻

When I was eight years old, I used to walk 4 kilometers to the river every morning and afternoon to collect water in a canister, which I strapped to my back. Although the village girls often walked down in a group, I liked making the journey alone, so I could day-dream along the way. Pulling water from a river is not as easy as it seems—when the dry season comes, the only way to get what you need is to dig for it, your knees sinking down into the muck, your bottom raised, your fingernails full of sand. The groundwater will then pool up into the canister, you will shake the canister so that the dirt falls to the bottom, and you will return home with enough water to fill the teakettle and the cooking pot.

I remember jabbing into the riverbed with my fingers, building a small mound of sopping sand next to me, and hearing a man's sharp voice above me. "Get up! Get up!" I couldn't see him, so at first I thought that someone else was in danger. "Get up! Get up!" came the voice again, closer, closer, and I stood up and looked around, seeing no one. Then a pair of strange, rough hands were on me, tossing my small body up onto the bank like a sack of maize.

Since my eyes were fixed on the man who had scrambled up the riverbank after me, I heard the roar of the water before I saw it: a wall of white water swallowing the sand pile I'd created.

"You could have been killed!" said the man, his hot breath in my face. "What are you doing here? Where is your home?" The rains had come early from the Ethiopian highlands, he said.

Looking down at the churning river, seeing big branches, some taller than I, snap like twigs, I began to cry. "Lafole," I said.

"It is a miracle that I was sent for you here," said the man, still gasping from his effort of throwing me up the bank. Though he was stern, he took pity on me, helping me fill my jug at a well I hadn't known about. Then he walked past me and back toward the bush. "God is great!" said Ayeyo when I finally returned home. "This man has saved your life!"

I still felt the danger in my eardrums and my cheeks as she spoke. Afterward, each time I made my way back to the river, I carried a sharp stone of fear close to my heart. My eyes moved across the sand with new suspicion, and even the birds seemed menacing. For months, I would return home, place the water at Ayeyo's feet, sit down next to the canister, and cry.

"A woman's work," Ayeyo had said, "cannot be done by anyone else." I had tasted life's first bitterness, she said, a sign of wisdom. But in 1991, when the rush of people came to us, there was no salvation in sight.

We were lucky, I suppose, that we had little money to steal. While people who had put their money in the bank now had nothing, all our money had been put into materials for the hospital or the farm. We still had some gold, however: some that my mother had given me before she died and some that I bought when my children were young. I gave 150 grams to one of my cousins, who took it to Mogadishu to sell. He brought back the money in a bucket, covered with a layer of plastic wrap and a pile of bananas and mangos from Bakara Market. We spent that money on sorghum, which we struggled to find in the empty markets, and which would last us another forty days.

When that, too, dwindled, we were forced to divide the camp into two groups. One morning, we gave group A the *chapati*—three for every person—and the next morning, group B got their portion. For about three months, it was the best we could do to ward off starvation, as the families were still coming, by ten, by twenty—sometimes as many as sixty people in a day. Most of them were from the Darod clan—Siad Barre's relatives, fleeing the violent backlash from the other groups like the Hawiye, who had been persecuted by the regime and now sought revenge.

Since it was no longer safe to drive to Mogadishu, where a car could be stolen or one could be shot, I took a bus to the UNICEF office, to ask for help. The representative that I met wrote a letter, and soon after, their white trucks showed up with sacks of a nutritious porridge. Since we had run out of sorghum for *chapati*, we began to distribute dry portions of the cereal. Every child came, bringing his round cup, to get his part, and when the families saw what we were able to provide, they blessed us. They could divide a kilo of porridge into several sections, and then water it down further, so they had twice as much to eat.

While porridge, rice, beans, and oil filled bellies, those who had been starving for weeks could not be saved. When the sickest people tried to eat, they suffered from debilitating, bloody diarrhea, and we had no hydration solution to give them to restore their health. At the height of the crisis, we were losing fifty people per day. Unlike natural disasters that hit without warning, famine crawls up onto a society in the same way that a single person starves: It starts with the body, and then it gets into the mind. Then, as bones dig into skin and weak muscles droop, the body turns against itself and everything shuts down.

We needed to bury the dead as quickly as we could. An Arabic organization donated cases of *karfan* to cover the bodies. Near the place where we buried our first few patients, our farm workers and some of the other young, strong men in the camp began digging a big grave. We had no money to pay them, but an extra portion of porridge gave them the strength to continue.

As the world heard of the disaster in Somalia, many international aid organizations sent in ships full of food, medical supplies, and plastic sheets for shelter. Most were blocked by the warlords who had laid claim to the airports, seaports, and roads, capturing the food aid that managed to come in, selling it in the market at a much higher rate, and using the money to buy more weapons or *qat*. In the countryside, we waited, shaking our heads and apologizing for having nothing to give.

We sent our tractor to a local water catchment tank three times a day, carrying back, each time, eighteen drums of water to distribute. The children set up a kind of roadside stand, and they brought with them whatever supplies we could afford to give the displaced people—milk or water, sometimes one of their *chapati*.

One afternoon, when a man walking in our direction fell into the road, Amina and some of the other children tried to help, fetching some milk from our home to bring out to him. But by the time they came back, the man was already dead.

"You have to get up and help someone else who needs you," I told Amina as she cried. I could offer little comfort, little explanation. Sometimes I turned to the Holy Qur'an, which teaches that if you are poor, God is testing your perseverance, and that if you have something, God is testing your generosity. While we cannot shield our children from everything, I did insist they stay away from the grave diggers, at least while they were eating or working. Since children are curious, wanting to help—wanting, at least, to see—Deqo and Amina had to chase Ahmed away from the growing graveyard.

The fighting continued, and by November 1991, civil war broke out between the followers of two warlords controlling Mogadishu, both from Hawiye sub-clans: the Habr Gidir, led by Mohamed Farrah Aidid; and the Abgal, led by Ali Mahdi Mohamed. Mogadishu was divided into two, with a Green Line splitting the city into north and south. Everyone had a gun, openly taking whatever he wanted. Terrified people fled the explosions, running out of the city gates in big crowds until it seemed there could be no one left. For a while, the popular joke was that only the dogs and cats remained in Mogadishu—food for the uneducated people who now ruled the city alongside the mental patients, who had been turned loose when their hospitals had been shut down. "They are in charge now," we said, shaking our heads at the endless violence.

While the Habr Gidir and the Abgal warlords hated each other, they shared the common goal of wanting to profit from the international aid groups. Years later, one of my security guards would tell me that with bribes of money and qat, he was recruited to defend Mogadishu port. "Our mission was: Shoot down every ship coming in with donations," he said. The ships and their precious food turned around, back toward safety, while hundreds of thousands of our people starved to death. These warlords are responsible. Criminals.

CHAPTER THIRTEEN

Why Do You Want to Do This?

Talk among the village elders turned to AK-47s and "technicals," which were pickup trucks with heavy machine guns bolted to the top. It was another new language for Somalia. Still, the deadliest weapon in those days was the car, barreling through the Mogadishu streets with punctured tires, or screeching along on iron rims. One of these cars hit a young Darod girl and shattered the bones of her leg. Afraid that the Hawiye militiamen would kill her for belonging to Siad Barre's clan, she limped along the road and hid in the bush near our place for weeks, eating grass and growing thin and hysterical. Someone told us what had happened, and for days, hospital volunteers tried to convince her to come for treatment. Finally, they brought her in, and we gave her a bed and medicine for her pain. I couldn't promise to fix her bones, which had already begun to fuse together in a very crooked way, but I said that I would try.

Representatives from the International Committee of the Red Cross (ICRC), who had been working on relief efforts since the start of the conflict, had begun visiting me in my camp in early 1991. I admired their commitment, struggling to deliver food and medicine to us at a time when militiamen were sending heavy mortars out to the ocean, sinking some ships and sending so many back. In our camp, ICRC built Somalia's eighty-eighth feeding kitchen; they drove to me a few times a week on their tours of the other refugee camps in the area. As busy as we were, I always made time for their team, which included a Somali man named Hussein Salad, who worked at the side of a tall Belgian man named Wim Van Boxelaere.

We often had long talks—about the state of the world, travel, philosophy—as I showed them our work and the people we were helping. One day, Hussein Salad asked me a question that was hard to answer. "Why do you want to do this, to collect people like this in your place?"

As a means of explanation, I led them into the hospital. As the number of the starving people had grown, surpassing the number of the wounded people, we'd had no choice but to lay patients on cheap mattresses or blankets along the hospital corridors. We walked past suffering children whose anxious loved ones swatted flies from their faces, and into the room where the girl with the broken leg lay. Wim was shocked to see how a leg could heal like that, so crooked, the bone jutting out somehow unnaturally, covered in skin. He cried when he saw how the girl's life had been crushed by violence and fear, and then, turning his big, kind face to me, he took out a paper and wrote an immediate donation— rice, oil, and beans. He hugged me when he left, calling me Mama Hawa, promising that he would return.

Wim was true to his word. In the weeks that followed, ICRC gave us a standing weekly donation of fifty sacks of maize, twenty cartons of oil, and twenty sacks of beans; they began to give us medicine as well. Often he and Hussein came to deliver the goods themselves, along with a woman named Dahabo who was the head of all the feeding centers in the area. While they worked hard, sometimes they also just came to relax and to visit. Wim especially loved to see the families and the children in our makeshift orphanage; he often sat down to talk with them. He never seemed as big as he did when he was crouched down next to these small, small children; somehow, in those moments, he became one of them.

The ICRC delegation told us, time and again, that they liked our place because it seemed calm. While it was sometimes hard for me to look beyond the chaos to what they saw, I was happy to think that, with us, they could relax. When they came, I welcomed them into our hospital's meeting room, trying to offer the best we had: fresh fish from the seaside, coffee and tea, and after the harvest, slices of watermelon—juicy and sweet. Wim found a big shell while walking along the beach, and he brought it back to the meeting room, to use as an ashtray for the afternoons when, for a few minutes, we were friends talking about our families, our countries, and the politics of the area. We would all admit that we talked too much about politics, but it was hard to escape. Whenever ICRC traveled in our area, they were accompanied by heavy security, and Wim worried about what would happen in the night.

"If people come to loot this food, you give it to them," he told me. "We will give you more." At that time, in the camp, we had our own two, very good guards, who helped with security in the clinic and with water distribution. Sometimes they tried to negotiate with the local warlords, but Wim didn't like to hear that. "If they want to loot your food, don't fight with them," he said. "Even if the rice is stolen, it will go into the market, which will lower its price."

One day, when the fighting was especially bad in Mogadishu, a group of ICRC staff came to us. "There are two hundred more people who came to me today," I told Wim, shaking my head, "and many of them are wounded." There was nothing more to say about the situation, which every day became worse and worse. The only way Wim knew how to respond was to give more—two hundred sacks of rice, one hundred jerrycans of oil. I remember that day well. It was a Monday.

That Wednesday afternoon, after I'd finished my rounds in the clinic, I took the bus to Mogadishu to pick up some supplies for the camp. I got off at my typical bus stop, and as I was walking toward the market, I saw two ambulances, with flashing lights and honking horns, going straight to Medina hospital. I didn't think anything of it. At the market I greeted the shopkeeper, who knew people in my camp. "Oh!" he shouted. "Did you hear about your friend?"

"What friend?"

"Those ICRC people. Hey!" The man nudged his neighbor. "Who was it?"

"The Belgian man," the other man said. Wim. I worried all that afternoon, as I walked through the market, buying the medicine and the supplies that I could take by the Afgoye-bound bus before evening fell. I sat on the bus, among the slumping mothers and the nervous young men squirming in their seats, thinking of Wim turning away from the girl with the broken leg with tears in his eyes. The war had brought people from across the world to help us, but we could not shield them from the violence.

The news was on the radio by the time I came home; before evening prayers, the children and some of our staff came in to listen. That morning, Wim had been working at Martini hospital, where the biggest stockpile of ICRC food was located. A man came into the storehouse with a gun, pulling it on Wim. A Somali elder jumped in front of him, hoping to shield him, but was killed instantly. The same bullet had seriously wounded Wim as well.

That night, we couldn't sleep. We made a big postcard: *Don't give up. Come back. Mogadishu is crying for you. Everyone is praying for you.* The next morning I was back on the bus with the postcard. I went straight to Medina hospital, where I knew one doctor working in the surgery department. "What has happened?" I asked when I walked in. "Where is Wim?"

"Oh," he said sadly. He showed me back to a room where a man lay under a white sheet, covered totally. "You see? That is Wim. His brother has come to get him—they're bringing him to Belgium." I held my breath, wanting to reach out to him, to know if he was conscious or unconscious, but I didn't want to disturb him. Next to us, my colleague said, was the dead body of the man who had given his life to save Wim.

As Wim flew over Italy on his way home, he passed away. When we heard the news, we cried, knowing that this kind man, supporting Somalia in so many ways, was killed by those he was trying to save. We could not see then how we would mourn the tragedy of Wim's death and the death of so many like him, but we knew it was a heavy blow to the confidence of the international community, and a sign of the danger for foreigners who came to Somalia as friends. How would people want to help us when we killed the best people who were brave enough to try, and in the process, we killed our own people as well?

"Don't give up on us," I told Hussein Salad when he came back to the camp.

"This is our job," he insisted.

Many months later, Wim's mother and father came to Somalia, to see the work that their son had done for us. Hussein Salad brought them to us, wearing a black suit, as Europeans do. We offered them juice and sat under the trees together, and Aden stood up to make a speech. "Wim was one of our men," he said. "He was a part of our body. What has happened, we are all sorry." We brought them to the meeting room where we used to sit, and I gave his mother the big shell that he used as an ashtray. Together we visited the orphan children, who had worked with a few of our volunteers to make a sign: WIM DEDICATED HIS LIFE FOR OUR WELFARE, it said, and when his mother saw it, she turned around, looking for her husband, saying, "Come see what they wrote, these children!"

Before she left, we embraced, and we cried together. "Wim always said he had very good relations with Dr. Hawa," she said. "You were, for him, a calm place." Years later, when we received more funding, I created a small nursing school inside the hospital: The Wim Van Boxelaere Nursing School. It still exists today.

For us, the days were the easiest because we had expectations: rounds and scheduled surgeries and meetings and feedings and visits from international delegations. We feared the quiet nights, after the aid workers and their bodyguards returned to their compounds in Mogadishu and armed boys and men ran up and down the Afgoye Road like ants: swarming the checkpoints and then scattering into the bush to attack defenseless families, raping the women and tying up the animals to take them away.

A group of Hawiye militiamen lived near our place—some of the boys had visited our farm as children; Aden had given them rides on our tractor. They came one night like ghosts and stole all fifteen of our cows—the only livestock remaining on our farm at the time. Aden, who had many friends in their clan, made a few phone calls and tracked down twelve of the cows before they reached Bakara Market for sale. "These are mine," Aden told the boys, hoping to shame them. Though it took us another two months to find the other three cows, those eventually returned to us as well. At night, some of our older boys began sleeping by the pen for security purposes.

We were so vulnerable—a village of persecuted minority groups and women, wondering whether the people from the surrounding area would attack us. Our only security was the two guards and our band of boys—eight, ten, twelve years old—some of whom kept watch on our verandas. While they had no weapons, they were able to stay up all night, huddled in packs. They were the first ones to hear the crackle of gunfire in the distance or the sound of a car cascading into the area, its lights and motor off, as a way to be undetected: someone coming to us in search of money, of food, of children to rape.

We heard about rape almost every day; we did everything possible to protect Deqo and Amina, just seventeen and thirteen, and all their friends. For five months I slept in the hospital every night; our guests brought their girls to us so they, too, could sleep under lock and key. Some nights, we had as many as fifty girls sleeping in a spare room in the hospital, almost shoulder to shoulder, and another fifty in our bedroom. During Ramadan, they ate a small meal together after dark and then huddled up in their blankets, gossiping and teasing one another in hushed voices as they tried to sleep. It was too dangerous for them to go outside to the toilet, and Deqo was so afraid that she slept with her shoes on, so she could run faster if she had to.

"Nothing bad will happen to us here," I told her one night, sitting on her pile of blankets. While it was a hollow promise, it sometimes helped her sleep.

Amina never slept. If I sat down to get some air on an outside bench, in between late-night rounds in the hospital, I saw her small shadow in the distance moments later. "Go back," I told her as she ran out to meet me. "I'll be in soon."

Late one night I treated a man who belonged to a clan called Galgale that had been especially persecuted in our area. I gave the man food and a bed, and I discharged him in the early, early morning, before dawn. "Don't go through the main road, go this way, through the bush," I told him. "Save your life."

By eleven o'clock that morning, thirty-five young men carrying heavy guns were standing outside our hospital; they'd heard about the Galgale man. They tried to enter, but one of my nurses struggled against them, insisting that guns were not allowed in our place. I heard the noise, came out of an examining room, and met them outside. "We don't have anyone here," I told them. "This is a hospital. We have only two mothers who are delivering babies."

Trying to reason with a starving, *qat*-fueled boy holding an AK-47 is impossible. "You lie," he said, his shoulders twitching up and down. "We'll search room by room, so we know you're telling the truth."

"Those people, you killed most of them already, and the remaining, they fled," I said. "They are not here. They aren't staying with me."

"Let us in," he said, shaking his gun on his shoulder. One of our midwives walked out of the hospital and, seeing what was happening, darted quickly back inside.

If we let these men into the hospital, they would start raping our girls. I looked into the boy's wild, red eyes and tried to reason with him as I would with any of my children. "The people who are here are my guests. Do you see?" I stopped and sighed. "I am treating your people. How can you come to me to think that I would keep your enemy? We're not living together? We're not the same people?"

"Let us in!" he shouted, moving closer.

"The only way you can enter is if you kill me first," I said.

One of the other men spoke up. "She is right," he said. He held out his AK-47 to me as a gesture of apology. "Please excuse us," he said. The boy stepped back but kept the same stare.

"You're mistaken," I said, holding up my hand. "I don't know how to use this. Take it back, but don't come another time to my place."

Sometimes when I remember this time, I remember a conversation I had with a journalist, who had asked me the same question that Hussein Salad had asked: "Why do you want to do this?"

I tried to explain, but the journalist had her own theory. "I think you are a little bit crazy," she said. I can see that talking directly to these young men was practically asking them to kill me. But if the poor people I protected died in front of me for no reason, I could not live anyhow.

We received word that an organization called Swedish Church Relief would make a huge donation to our camp—100 tons, enough rice to fill fifteen trucks. As we waited, I imagined the heavy, heavy sacks of rice coming from across the ocean. One day a man who was helping me with security came to discuss the matter. "We will handle the transportation contract," he said.

"It's not my choice—if someone is donating, it's their job," I said. "If you want the business, it's up to you to go to them and ask."

But he did not want to ask. "If you don't give us the contract now, we'll loot all this rice," he said. "It will never go to your place."

"Ask or not—it's up to you," I told him. Although I acted as if I didn't care about his threats, I worried that we would be victim to the violence that had stopped so many other aid organizations. I went to the port in our white Toyota Corolla, a driver and two security guards to accompany me, to oversee our food's arrival and to make sure that it was loaded properly onto our trucks. We passed through the city unquestioned, though we could hear some gunfire once we passed through the port's gate and into the warehouse. Still, everything went smoothly, and we followed the caravan heading out of the city and along the Afgoye Road.

Along the way, 100 meters in front of us, a big ball of light flashed, shaking the earth with explosions. Our driver jerked the wheel back and forth, trying to pull beside the truck in front of us to see what had happened. We continued this way for about 2 kilometers, weaving, until someone ahead sent one salvo as a sign to turn around, and the entire convoy stopped. Still jittery, my driver stepped on the gas, passing the trucks to get us back to the camp, to safety. But as we passed the front of the line, I saw a technical car (an improvised fighting vehicle) stopped on the road next to a truck swarmed by militiamen. When they saw us go past them, they turned their guns on us.

"Run! Run!" I slouched down in the middle of the backseat, my heart pounding. It was a car chase like those I had seen in films, although I closed my eyes.

"We can shoot back!" shouted the security guards.

"No!" I screamed, as I heard *pah-pah-pah-pah-pah*.

We pulled into the local office of Swedish Church Relief, and the technical kept driving. Finally, we were safe. "I'm sorry, what has happened?" asked one of their employees, who came to greet us at the car. "We heard that Mogadishu is under fire."

I received a phone call at their compound: It was from my own security man, who had threatened to loot me. "How are you?" he asked. "Are you safe?"

"Yes," I said in disbelief. Was he responsible for the attack? And if so, how could he lie to me this way, pretending to care about my well-being? When we finally returned to the camp, we passed along the way one of the trucks, which had skidded to the side of the road. When we looked back and saw that the food inside was gone, we feared that other trucks had met a similar fate. Still, we counted thirteen trucks when we arrived, and as we stood outside, talking, the security guy came to me. "How are you?" he asked again. This time, I ignored him.

Growing up in the bush, I learned that hungry animals ran and fought without any care for their children or the other wild animals that might eat them. War changes people's logic in the same way, sending them after the food that belonged to needy people. I had not changed my own logic, so I did not expect that the people who knew me, whom I helped and who were working by my side, could steal from me. Sometimes, though, I was wrong, and the wartime logic prevailed.

Seventy tons of food remained: by far, the biggest donation we had ever received. Was it enough to risk my life? What about the lives of my children, who were living among the people fighting over such things? What if they were kidnapped? I had no money to buy their safety—only a parched farm scattered with people in need.

The next day, Aden and I began sawing oil drums in two; each half became a cooking pot, which sat on the fire. We cooked twenty 50-kilogram sacks of rice a day, so that donation, our biggest, lasted us seventy days. Two months and ten days.

CHAPTER FOURTEEN

Danger from Within

One night, while I was making final rounds in the hospital and Aden was out with his friends, Ahmed heard a group of cars roll into the camp. He ran to Deqo, pushing her awake. "They're here," he said. "What do we do?"

They came to me together in their bare feet. I heard Ahmed's small voice first. "They're here," he told me. "They're here."

Shaking, Deqo stood behind Ahmed with her hands on his shoulders. "We're going to run," she said.

"No one can move," I told her firmly. "You have to stay here and wait with me."

"I'm taking my brother," she said, and pulled him away, out the door, and into the night. I turned around to the next patient, who was resting comfortably. If Ahmed was right, I thought, I should not run after them. I had to trust that Deqo knew the way in the bush. As I walked up to the second floor to check on the other girls, I prayed that Ahmed had imagined the noise.

I heard the door downstairs open and slam; from the window I could see men standing outside their still-running cars, guns pulled. Then I heard shrieks inside the hospital—it was one of our nurses, calling for help. By this time Amina had pulled on her shoes; so had her cousins. "Stay here," I told them. "But if you hear shooting, take Mama Asha and run for the bush."

I took the back stairs down to the outpatient clinic, and when I entered, I saw one man standing guard while, out of sight, I could hear at least two others beating that crying nurse in an examining room. "Don't beat me, my brother!" she wailed. "I am your sister! I am of the same clan!" Another nurse told me that she had been captured while walking through the surgery department with a box of injections.

I ran into the hallway. "Don't beat my daughter! I am Dr. Hawa! What do you want?"

One of the men walked up to me, holding his gun. "You are not Dr. Hawa—there is a fat, old woman who owns this place."

"It is mine," I said, glaring at him, and when I did, he took the handle of his rifle and slammed the back of the gun into my side. I didn't feel the first blow, but I was doubled over by the second one.

"You have some *fakash*," he said, using a pejorative word for a rival clan. "Open this door." I jiggled the handle on the glass door to our washroom, where doctors scrubbed their hands before surgery. It was locked, and I didn't have the key. Panicked, I tried to break the glass with my hand. The man stopped me. "You will hurt yourself," he said.

At that moment, the sound of gunfire outside sent the men running out through the doors to meet the others. "Mama Hawa," screamed the nurse who had been beaten, "They want to kill you! We have to run!" One of patients crawled out of a fuel drum that she'd been hiding in since the men came in. "They asked me to show them where you stored the money and food," she cried, shaking her head. "I told them I was only a patient!"

We assumed they would come back to kill us, but before we could run, I first had to search the hospital, to make sure that there was no one around—I ran through the rooms, trying not to stop at each place where they had broken down doors. I called out, but there was no one else hiding—just two patients who were of the Hawiye clan, like the men, and who preferred to stay in their hospital beds.

We left around midnight, but with no moon, it was too dark to know exactly where we were, other than under rustling trees. The gunfire was still continuing as we crept silently into the bush, wondering if another group of men had come to the area, to attack the men who had attacked us. We finally sat, my mind numb as I prayed to God to save my children. The rattling finally stopped, and we could hear the cars pull away. Only then did I begin to feel the sharp pain in my side, but I stood up anyway, holding the nurse's hand as we walked.

"Deqo! Amina! Ahmed! Kahiye! Su'ado! Dahabo! Abdi Karim!" I called the children's names, one by one, and again, but I got no answer. Again I called, faster, my voice growing louder as my fear for their safety overtook my fear of being discovered. Could it have been possible that some of the men came during the gunfight to take the children? We waited for hours, suffering this way. Then the sky lightened, and I heard a small voice.

"Hey, did they leave?" It was Deqo.

"*Hooyo, hooyo,* come out," I said, using the Somali term of endearment that we all use so often. "It's safe, *hooyo.*" Shouting was difficult, my entire side tight with pain, but I couldn't stop as I heard the rustling and saw the children, one by one. They'd been afraid that I had been held hostage, calling out to them with a gun to my head, one of the boys explained. But that all was forgotten, and they were giddy, breathless, even laughing—big, gulping laughs.

"Can we go home?" asked Amina, but I was too afraid that the men were still in the area. "No," I said. "We'll wait for a while." So we sat together in the dirt, the youngest children lying on my lap, and they told me their story:

They waited in the bush for what felt like forever, trembling and hushing one another, whispering about what could happen. First, one girl wanted to use the toilet, and within the next hour, they all had to go, squirming as they felt their bladders throb. Finally, they decided that they'd go at once, crouching down under a group of low bushes. But the sound of the splash on the ground was loud, and the boys came out, yelling at them to stop. We all laughed, and when they told the story again, we laughed again. Then we fell quiet for a while, and some of them fell asleep. Deqo told me softly that she'd cried out when she heard the explosions, sure that I had been killed. "I'm here, *hooyo*," I said.

When the sun was high enough, we stood up together, although my body was so stiff I could barely walk. I pulled away my clothes to see that my side had bruised from the blow. I showed the place to Ahmed. "My son, you see how they hit me yesterday?"

He began to cry, and I cursed myself for saying that. I, too, was in shock. I was trying so hard to amuse the children that I ignored what they really needed, which was to be far away from the danger. I consoled Ahmed for a moment and then made him laugh by showing him the stiff way I walked. After a few minutes of effort, we both felt better.

When we reached our place, we saw several donkey carts outside the front door: One family from the neighborhood had heard the gunfight, thought that we were gone, and began going through our things. Some had even climbed up the outside of our apartment, hoping to steal our roof.

When they saw us, they spoke quickly. "How are you?" one of the men asked. "Are you safe?"

"Yes, we are safe," I told him. He hid his face, and along with the rest of his family, he left. I walked into each of the rooms ahead of the children, picking up the first precious things that I saw and setting them, as best I could, in their right places—on shelves and tables, or inside the pocket of my filthy white jacket. In my bedroom, I saw that our pillowcases had been split open. I fumbled around until, on the floor, I found two untouched pillows, and in one, the 500,000 Somali shillings I'd stuffed inside months earlier. In their haste, they had forgotten to look behind the bed.

I asked the cook to make some tea, and as she lit the fire outside, I washed my face and hands. I came back to the veranda, but before I could sit down to drink, I saw some of the men who had attacked us standing in front of me, wearing different clothes.

"We heard on the radio that something happened here last night," said one, whom I remembered running past on my way to the bush. I sipped my tea without offering them any—something that was rare for me—and I listened as they lied and offered to protect me. To them I was not a doctor who deserved respect but a stupid, rich woman that they could both cheat and rob. I didn't tell them that I knew they'd called strangers to help them break into the hospital and to attack my nurses. Instead I watched, in the broad daylight, as they lied to my face.

After they left, I called a meeting of the area's elders, who'd supported my work before the war and who did their best to support the displaced people as the need had grown. "I came here to help you—to assist your wives' labor, to treat your children, and your people are attacking me?" I said. "If you can't help protect us, I'll have to stop these things."

They acknowledged the problem and assembled fifteen young men—the oldest was thirty, the youngest, nineteen—who would live in our place and serve as our guards. They all brought with them their own weapons, which were the same heavy guns, the government guns, now in the hands of the different rebel groups. Since they were still young and undisciplined, about four of the elders began to stay with us as well, to direct the guards and prevent petty arguments from breaking out among them. I was relieved by the decision, although I insisted on one thing: "We will never allow guns in the hospital," I said.

When they left, I sat under the trees for a while, watching from afar as the children laughed and played. I thanked God for keeping us safe somehow, and for the blessing of memory, which dulls fear but not laughter. For me, the real blessing was remembering the warmth of eleven children gathered around me, whispering, nuzzling, or resting their heads on my aching knees. That was the reason why I had the strength to greet a morning just as unknown as that blackest of nights.

By the middle of 1992, most people who had the means to flee Somalia left, and we had with us just half the number that we'd cared for in the terrible early days. Now we had a total of 460 families—some were the original residents, and others were new, from Baidoa and Burr to the north and Mogadishu and Merca to the south. Among them was Sharif's sheikh, who had recently come to us from the south, in search of a home. Out of respect for my family, I gave him two rooms above our outpatient clinic. He brought his own cook and attracted a crowd of followers. I was amazed to see how people treated the sheikh as a small god, and how he encouraged this. "If you obey me, I will protect you," he would tell the people, and the people believed.

Aden also behaved sometimes as if this one person—"my beloved Sheikh"—could save us or destroy us. I reminded him sometimes that we'd met in a place where people didn't believe in God. "The people in the Soviet Union were living normally, in good condition," I said. But I was no match for the friends who flocked to him, exclaiming how lucky he was to have the big sheikh with him.

It was a chaotic time not just for us but for the whole area; thousands of other internally displaced people, or IDPs, as the aid organizations called them, lived in neighboring camps along the Afgoye Road. Many of our new neighbors came to us each morning—280 families from one side, 300 from another—to line up with our residents for food distribution. Managing the crowds was difficult, but with our new guards keeping order, people mostly respected one another. We still had some troubles, of course—when the sun was hot, and water was especially scarce, people grew impatient, wanting to be first, to take everything.

Clan hatred and suspicion were on the lips of many from the moment they signed our camp's registry. "She is caring for Darod people," a son would say to a mother, which caused suspicion, then arguments, then attacks. To change people's attitudes, we created a rule with no exceptions: In our place, we are all Somali. If you want to identify by your clan, you can't stay.

One troublemaking family was given three warnings, but when

they continued to fight with their neighbors, the guards gathered mother, father, and two children, and put them and their belongings outside the camp.

They apologized and protested, but I refused to hear them. "If I allowed you to continue fighting," I said, "then everyone would do it." They returned many more times to beg, until finally the elders agreed to hear their case. After some deliberation, they decided that the family could reenter the camp on the condition that the parents apologized to their own children, to the neighbor family they'd offended, and finally, to the elders. The family moved back in, and after that, they made no trouble.

We were skeptical when we turned on the radio and heard the BBC Somali service broadcast news of a cease-fire between the clans in March 1992, although for a little while, aid organizations that had been unable to unload supplies in Mogadishu were rerouted to Merca, where shipments could land and eventually reach us. Since everything from a box of bandages to a 50-kilo sack of rice had to be locked up, we set up two new storage areas—one for food donations, and another, in a place that was once meant to be a reception area, for medicine. At first, Deqo was in charge of the medicine; although she was just seventeen years old, we trusted her to meet the trucks that came in, keep track of the donations, and give out the proper supplies to the nurses or midwives who needed something. In time, that storage area would become a small pharmacy run by Aden and Khadija, which patients could visit with prescriptions written by me or by some of the other doctors.

Aden worked in the other storage area, supervising the committee of two storekeepers and twelve cooks, who were stirring in the big oil drums twice a day—early in the morning and at night. The cooks had to register how many sacks of rice they'd cooked by bringing the empty bags to Aden or the other storekeepers. Some of the people we hired cheated us, saying that they were cooking but really taking the rice to feed their own families. When that happened, we had another group of workers investigate; if the person was found guilty, he was relieved of his job.

I tried to reassure people that things would improve, but looking back, I know that I was exhausted and depressed. We were awake around the clock; the only difference between day and night was that, by day, aid workers and journalists flooded my place. While I knew it was important to talk with them, to make the world aware of what was happening, sometimes I had no words. "I have to rest," I would apologize. "I have many surgeries tomorrow."

The sheikh came to me one morning when I was eating a small bit of porridge among the others. "Ai-Hawa, you know, I have everything for you," he told me, using the term of endearment for aunt. "When you die, I can provide you paradise. Now, while you're alive, I can give you everything you want."

"That is true?" I asked, running my finger along the bottom of the bowl. "So what do you want?"

"I want you to give me half of your land," he said. He explained to me that he had as many as a hundred people wanting to stay with him, and I saw, at that moment, about twenty-five of those hundred standing nearby, watching and waiting.

I put down the container, which one of my helpers took to give to someone else. "I have given you your share, but the people living here are my guests, as you are my guest," I said. "I cannot give you the land."

He did not argue with me, but his followers appealed to my husband: "Aden, you are great. God has given you the pleasure of the sheikh. We will provide the building material for the sheikh's house, if you will provide us the land." Against my knowledge, they began assembling their supplies for the sheikh's house—one man provided stones, another cement, another wood.

Khadija came to me when she heard what I had told the sheikh, afraid that God would punish us for my defiance. "Take a look at all of this here," she sobbed. "All of it, it will be burned."

"You are just destroying yourself," said another one of my relatives, who came with Khadija.

"This is crazy," I said. "Nothing will happen to us."

I'd just left for Mogadishu a few days later when I noticed a group of pickup trucks coming in the other direction. When I looked behind me and saw them turning into my place, I asked my driver to turn around. We gained speed and passed them, and I was standing at the gate by the time the cars pulled over. "Tell those cars to stop," I told the guards, who went ahead of me to meet them.

The first car was driven by a man who'd come to deliver stones. "Those stones belong to the sheikh," he argued when he was turned away. But since the land belonged to me, I had the final say.

Aden came to me that night, furious. "Hawa, do you want the sheikh to destroy us?"

The bones of my legs were aching, and I could barely open my eyes. "I gave him money and food," I told Aden. "Did this man raise you? Your father is more powerful—he can bless you and curse you, not this man."

I didn't understand what had changed for Aden—how he could follow with such devotion, after living, for years, as I did. "He is not a small god," I told Aden. "If God is seeing everything, then there is no fear that we'll suffer." Aden didn't return to our bed that night, and soon after, the sheikh took his wives, children, and helpers to another place, in Mogadishu. Aden began to spend more and more time in Mogadishu rather than in the camp; he began staying some nights in Mogadishu as well. While I felt his absence as much as the children did, I refused to discuss the matter with anyone. The only explanation I could give my children was the truth: There was a 6 p.m. curfew in Mogadishu, and important business was keeping their father from coming home at night.

CHAPTER FIFTEEN

Today We Are Happy

Sleep was impossible, as all the pillars holding up our world were collapsing. I battled the exhaustion, drinking tea, my stomach like an angry fist. My body felt so heavy I didn't think much about losing weight, and although Faduma Duale and the other nurses often had to help me to my feet, I insisted that I was strong enough to make rounds on my own.

One afternoon I went to ask the cook to put aside a portion of the cow we'd slaughtered, so I could give it to a Saudi Arabian delegation that had come to the camp. Then I staggered back to my room to lie down for a while, worried that I wouldn't be able to join them for the meeting. My mind told my legs to move, and I was able to swing them over to the side of the bed; with Faduma Duale behind me, I was able to walk. I came in to the hospital meeting room, welcoming the men and thanking them for coming.

"Oh, the doctor's situation is like this?" asked the head of the delegation. "She's the worst of the starving people!" Embarrassed, I greeted them, sinking down into a chair. We talked about the situation in my country and about how help from others had saved so many lives. The man distributed a little bit of money to each of the cooks who were serving the meal, and later, after I returned to my bed, he gave the elders enough money to help us buy some more meat, some milk, some medicine.

Aden returned to our room a few nights later, wanting to talk. "I'm going to Saudi Arabia," he said.

He has gone mad, I thought. All around us, people were falling down, dying of starvation. I myself had spent the day in bed again, relying on the other doctors to handle emergencies. They'd come into my room to update me on the situation. "Aden," I said, "I'm sick now. You can't leave me. Who will see after the children?"

"The sheikh will go to Saudi Arabia, and I have to go after him," he said.

"What about your children?" Though I was shocked, I felt too weak to try to argue or to try to convince him to stay. He left me lying in that bed, feeling more helpless than I had in years. I knew that the pressure on him was great and that the deep fear we felt when he was kidnapped years earlier was still just as real. Still, when I heard his footsteps going down the stairs to where Deqo was working in the storage area, I got to my feet to try to stop him. What would he tell Deqo? He would need money to travel; maybe he would go after the suitcase that we kept in the back of the storage closet. Deqo had the only key.

I felt a shooting pain in my back as I rushed down the stairs. "Give me the money," I told Deqo when I saw them both there together.

"I already gave him two thousand dollars," she said, confused, concerned. For a moment we stood there, the three of us, while Aden was silent. Finally I went back up the stairs to my bed. I suppose Aden left sometime soon after.

I later found out that as Aden drove to the small airport in Wanlaweyn accompanied by one of our relatives and Kahiye, our eldest nephew, the car had been shot at by a group of men who'd heard Aden's accent and mistakenly identified him as part of a Darod subclan. Aden had immediately turned the car around, and everyone in the camp had come running when they saw the shattered window and bullet-pocked door, worried that someone had been hit. While Kahiye was safe, Aden and our relative, who had each been wounded in their legs, were admitted to the hospital immediately. No bones were broken. Our relative was discharged, and another hospital bed was brought into the room where I lay. For nine days, Aden lay in the bed beside me, saying little; I was so sick and so angry that I pretended to sleep. I did not ask him to reconsider his decision, and he did not offer.

How could a man leave his family like this, at a time like this? I could hear Deqo cry to him, "Father, don't go!" Amina and Ahmed did also; I don't know how he explained his decision to them.

By the time he left for a second time, I could no longer hold even small food in my stomach. I began vomiting, vomiting, vomiting continuously, and when my staff or aid workers came, they had to meet with me in my room, sometimes sitting down on the extra bed the staff had brought in for Aden. I finally agreed to an examination by old friend, a Burundian doctor who had been working with us. He shook his head when he saw me, calling to me in the comforting Italian of our earliest days at Digfer: "*Ah, dottora, dottora.*" While ICRC brought the blood, urine, and stool samples to Nairobi for analysis, I lay in my bed, imagining the people in the area laughing at me, thinking that since I had kicked out the big sheikh, I would never recover.

When the results came back a few weeks later, my friend diagnosed me with a gallbladder infection and severe anemia. He prescribed some medicine and vitamins and a diet with only boiled meat—nothing roasted. Looking back now, I think my sickness was not just malnutrition but a nervous depression. My country, my family, and now my body had failed, as I remained in that bed, on the second floor of my own hospital.

Since the room was above our two delivery rooms, I could often hear what was happening below through the open windows. One night we had with us three women in labor at the same time. The two nurses who were working—one who had received just on-the-job training and the other an American missionary—were together in one room when the third woman cried out: "Help me! I'm going to die!"

The only other person down there was Deqo, who ran in. "You have to wait," she said. "They are coming soon. I'm not a doctor."

The woman howled and screamed. "I don't care if you're a kid," she said. "Do something!"

So Deqo, who had watched me for so long, tried to examine the woman as I had, and she saw the baby's position. Around 4 a.m., she came to my bedside. "Mama, I did it," she said. "The woman downstairs delivered normally. The child is alive."

I rolled over in my bed. My daughter had been just thirteen when she'd witnessed her first surgery; she'd fainted when I opened that woman's abdomen and showed her the tumor. For years after, she would read my books, saying, "Let me help you!" Now she was a confident young woman, managing the medicine in the camp and the patients' treatment besides. While it was hard to imagine her standing on her own two feet when I could not, she had done so, and oh, how happy she was.

I insisted that a qualified midwife supervise her, but as long as that was the case, I was glad to know she was helping in the hospital. The work took her mind off her search for Aden. We knew that while he and the sheikh waited to travel to Saudi Arabia, they were in Nairobi. They had found an apartment in the neighborhood of Eastleigh, where the wealthy Somalis who had escaped the war had begun building up apartment buildings and their own sprawling markets. At night, she called every phone number we had. Most times she got no answer, or a woman responded, saying, "Aden is not in."

She called and called, always hearing the same thing: "He's not in."

"You have to stop searching," I told her. "Otherwise you will feel bad."

"Why did you refuse my father?" she asked. "What happened to make him go?"

"Please, Deqo, do you see around? There are children here whose fathers have died," I said. "They are still living, searching for some work, finding happiness. Please, forget your father."

She shook her head and walked out of the room. "I cannot forget."

God is great—the medicine, the vitamins, and the diet worked, and I became healthy, able again to stand to meet the demands of the camp and the hospital. As Deqo worked and Ahmed played with his cousins and the other children in the camp, Amina was my shadow, following me as I made my rounds and visited patients, or else sitting on an empty examining table in the outpatient clinic, watching people come and go. She was sitting there one day when we received a man who had been injured in a car accident. He was bleeding from the head and holding his gun. Faduma Duale met him at the door, along with another nurse. "Please, this is a hospital," said Faduma Duale calmly. "Please give the gun to your friend to hold."

The man, clearly in shock, kept the gun and waved it at them. "Will you treat me or not?" he asked. "I'm bleeding to death."

Amina stared at Faduma Duale, who said, "Okay, okay, we will treat you." The two nurses tried to be calm, to convince the man to sit, so they could examine his wound, but his mind was not normal. He started shooting off the gun in the hospital, blowing holes through the ceiling and sending everyone—patients, staff, and my daughter—running. Only one lady remained. Though she was able to walk, she was too scared to move! She just lay on the bed, pumping her arms up and down like she was running in place. "God help me," she repeated, "God help me."

By the time I came out, the guy had already left for the bush. We all walked back into the room to see the woman still pumping, still crying out. Finally, one of our nurses had to stand over her and shout: "Maria, you're okay, everyone is okay. Now shut up!"

Amina remembers that day as one of the funniest days in the

hospital, and you know, I can see why. These are the types of stories that we usually tell one another during darker times, to make each other laugh. They are stories of our lives, for while Somali poetry may be as lyrical as a flute, our humor is dark, blunt. We lived to see another day, so for Maria to cry and thrash, says Amina, is something silly indeed.

I stopped arguing with my sisters and tried to accept that my point of view was different than theirs. Asha became sick—weak and very thin—so I gave her money to go to Nairobi, to stay with Aden there and to search for treatment. Maybe eventually she could find some place to work, I thought.

For a while, our area was calm. "You see?" I said to my patients. "We don't have any bad relations with all these people who are fighting." Aidid and his men had control of about two-thirds of Somalia by this time, including most of Mogadishu and our area. Then came rumors that Siad Barre's men, the Somali National Front, were leaving their base in Kismayo, trying to recapture the capital city. One afternoon someone told me that we'd be attacked. How he knew this, I don't know. Was it true? If it was, where would we run?

"God, my God," I prayed, "I have nowhere to go." I didn't say anything to anyone else, although I locked every door of the hospital and put the guards on alert.

Around eight o'clock that night, a jeep full of armed men came into my camp from one side, and many other cars came racing in from the other direction. One of them crashed hard into the jeep. We heard the terrible noises from inside the hospital, and then we heard the voices of the people living in the camp: "Please bring stretchers!" "Take these people who cannot move!"

The man who had been in the first jeep, in the position to shoot, had been decapitated. People from the other car were also dead, and since gunfire had broken out after the accident, many, many were wounded.

The anesthetist was still with us at that time. Thinking of the many, many sutures the men would need, I began shouting orders. "I'm going into surgery!" I said. We would not have enough supplies, but we would do our best. "Bring everyone to us!" Soon all the victims, alive and dead, had been carried by stretcher to the clearing near the outpatient clinic. Some of the wounded people were screaming and moaning, but others kept quiet, just looking at me. "Deqo!" I shouted. "Find the most severe ones in there, and have the guards bring them in to me."

Deqo and Amina knew that during an accident, they should look for people who were too sick or too injured to yell—those were the ones in the worst condition, the ones who needed immediate treatment. Deqo walked up to the clearing, shocked by the sight of so much injury—heads almost severed, bullet holes in every place. One man with a wounded leg thrashed silently; as Deqo approached him to help, he grabbed her leg, digging his long, sharp nails through her skin. He died that way, hanging on.

There is a Somali superstition that if someone holds on to you while he is dying, that part of your body will be buried with him. If he catches your hand, for example, your hand will be cut off. "AAAAAAAAAAAAAAAAHHHHHH!" Deqo screamed as he clung to her, and she kept screaming until everyone came running. I rushed out of surgery even, and we held her together, in a big group, as her screams turned to sobs.

"Mama Hawa, I cannot keep running like this all the time," said Kahiye a few days later. "I can defend myself like the other boys my age. I can get a gun. I can drive a car."

I told Kahiye that a gun was not a solution, but I knew then that I could no longer keep my children in such a dangerous situation. Kenya had opened its doors to refugees, so we made arrangements with ICRC to fly all the children to Nairobi. While Aden had left for Saudi Arabia by this point, Asha could meet us at the apartment he'd rented in Eastleigh. I contacted a local school that would accept them, and we prepared to leave.

"Work as I work," I told Faduma Duale. "You know the hospital and the camp. You know the farm, so you can see how they are producing." While we could not communicate by telephone, Bakara Market had a CB radio, and I could find another in Nairobi somehow.

The children and I landed at the Nairobi airport in April 1992 and we took a taxi to the Eastleigh apartment. Asha was inside the bathroom when we arrived, and when she walked out and saw us, her face did not change. "Asha, you have to see after these children," I said. "I have to go back to the camp in four days. If something happens to me, please stay with them, and make sure they get a good education." I had brought with me, in my dress, a small bit of gold tied up in one section and a wad of U.S. dollars tied up in another. "Buy the clothes and the books so they could go to school."

"Okay," she said. With Asha, it was always, "Okay," and no more. I felt unsettled—she had left me before, and I didn't like the way she had treated my children in the camp—but she was my sister. I didn't have anyone else.

How I dreaded the moment when I had to say good-bye to my children. How I worried: Deqo was very humble; she never raised her voice. Amina understood everything, but she had a hot temper, and Ahmed was still just nine years old. "Amina, you are my daughter," I told her, my arms around her skinny, twelve-year-old body. "Your name is the same as my beloved sister. Please protect yourself, your sister, and your brother." When I walked away, she cried as she had when she was small.

When photographs of starving Somali children were finally broadcast by all the international news networks in 1992, the world woke up to the fact that hundreds of thousands of people were dying. While more aid shipments were making landfall, we still could not count on anything reaching us. I began a new routine with the camp's elders, similar to the morning meetings that I was

Hawa with President George H.W. Bush and delegation, December 1992. (©Larry Downing/Sygma/Corbis)

President George H.W. Bush is greeted by schoolchildren in Hawa Abdi Village, December 1992. (©David Ake/AFP/Getty Images)

Aden and Hawa, early 1990.

Deqo and Ahmed,
September, 2000.

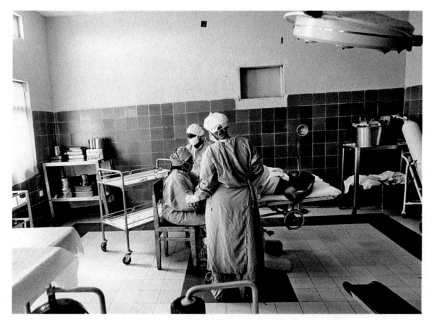

Hawa (seated) and her team perform a gynecological procedure in the surgical department, January 2007. (©Seamus Murphy/VII Network/Corbis)

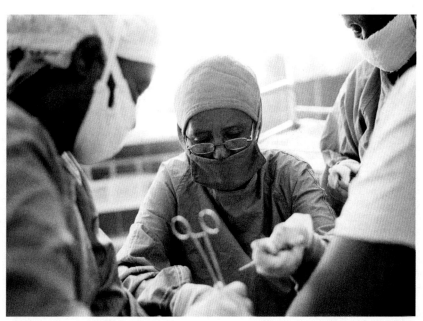

Hawa (center) operates on a patient in the surgical department, January 2007. (©Seamus Murphy/VII Network/Corbis)

Hawa (center) and her surgical team, January 2007. (©Seamus Murphy/VII Network/ Corbis)

Hawa in the camp, October 2007. (©Kuni Takahashi/Getty Images)

An armed security guard patrols the camp, January 2007. [After the May 2010 attack, camp guards no longer carried guns.] (*©Seamus Murphy/ VII Network/Corbis*)

View of Hawa Abdi Village from Hawa's "Camp David," January 2007. (*©Seamus Murphy/VII Network/Corbis*)

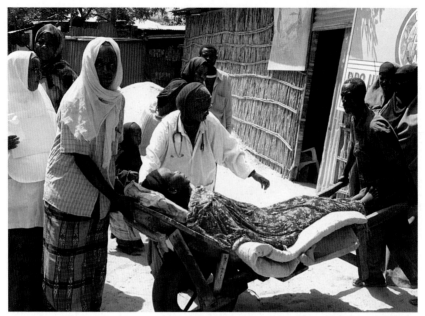

Amina (center) guiding a patient into the hospital's outpatient clinic, October 2010. (©*Farah Abdi Warsameh/AP Photo*)

The Hawa Abdi Hospital, October 2010. The building in the foreground houses the surgery department (lower level) and the gynecology department (upper level). The white building in the background (left) is the general hospital. (©*Farah Abdi Warsameh/AP Photo*)

Fifth- and sixth-grade students at the camp's school, July 2011. (©*Mohammed Ibrahim/The New York Times*)

Teacher (left) and student at the Women's Education Center, October 2010. (©*Farah Abdi Warsameh/AP Photo*)

Two women bring firewood, water, and food for cooking to the Women's Education Center, July 2011. (©*Mohammed Ibrahim/The New York Times*)

Two displaced children walk from the well through Hawa's "Camp David" toward their temporary homes, May 2007. (©*Sahal Abdulle/ Sipa Press*)

At the *Glamour* magazine Women of the Year Awards, November 2010. From left to right: Katie Couric, Deqo, Hawa, and Amina. (©*Dimitrios Kambouris/Getty Images*)

accustomed to as a member of a hospital staff: Each morning the elders and I discussed the situation in the camp the night before— I found out who was sick and who was starving, and together we determined the best ways to settle disputes. This small sense of order helped me, even as the number of wounded continued to flood our hospital hallways, and our cleaners struggled to keep up with the sand and blood tracked over the floors. Now we had a system: The people went to the guards, who went to the elders, who came to me.

As I worked, I tried to imagine my children in school at the same moment. Seeing their life in Nairobi had helped me to feel calm, even when we were far apart. On my second visit, I was able to stay for fifteen days—long enough to take the children to see some of the sights of the big, colorful city, like the zoo and the beautiful, green Uhuru Park. That time with them under the trees inspired another new routine: I spent part of every Friday afternoon away from the hospital, so I could write my children letters and meet some of my friends for sweets and tea under the big mango trees. It was my oasis; I had begun to call it my Camp David, after the American retreat where Russian president Boris Yeltsin had recently met U.S. president George H. W. Bush.

As more people came to our Camp David, we received more support, and my worry lessened. Most of the aid workers I met were Somali, although some were from Ireland, Switzerland, Turkey, China—all over the world. They gave of themselves freely, and I tried to find small ways to reward them, with fresh fruits or small bottles of Coca-Cola or Fanta or just an afternoon under our trees. Finally, I was living among people who understood what we needed to survive.

One beautiful September day, a journalist from Nairobi came to me there. "How are you?" he asked, surprised to see me relaxed. "How is the situation today?"

I remembered a book that I had read when I was living in the Soviet Union—the diary of a young girl who had survived the siege on Leningrad and who kept a log of the horror that her family suffered: *Today, Mama died*, she wrote. *Today, Papa died.*

I looked at the journalist, with his sunglasses and his wrinkled oxford shirt, and remembered the next thing she wrote in her diary. "Today we are happy," I said. "Nobody died." He scribbled in his notebook, and the next day, his article appeared in a newspaper with that as the huge headline.

CHAPTER SIXTEEN

Operation Restore Hope

My lifeline to my children, in those days, was a CB radio—mine in Bakara Market and theirs in an Eastleigh office—and the goodwill of the international organizations such as ICRC and the UN, which generously shuttled me back and forth free of charge on their flights to Nairobi's Jomo Kenyatta Airport. I thought of them constantly. As more and more refugees flooded Eastleigh, Kenyan president Daniel arap Moi began cracking down, filling the streets with gun-toting soldiers. I heard on the radio from Amina that the police came into our place one night, terrifying the children and demanding to see their documents.

I went to the Ugandan Embassy the next time I was in Nairobi. Uganda had a better relationship with Somali refugees than Kenya and a better infrastructure—even after surviving their own terrible civil war. Someone at the embassy office suggested that we send the children to a program at Makerere University in Uganda's capital city, Kampala; they gave us thirteen visas—for all the children, and for Asha and me.

The bus ride from Nairobi to Kampala was eleven hours long, and we all went together. I enrolled the children in school and found some tutors to help fill in some of the gaps in their knowledge. I remember a conversation I had with one of the professors at Makerere University, who marveled that after just two or three years of civil war, we Somalis had no wires, no pipes, no phone lines. "Your people are not patriotic," he said. "We are fighting for twenty years and everything is the same. You? When you open your water, you either get nothing or a dark, poison stream."

I didn't debate with him or dwell on how far our country had fallen; I just enjoyed the relief I felt to walk with my children in that place, where the people were beautiful, dressing well, and sitting together in cafeterias and restaurants. I said good-bye, blessing the children and praying for their safety. I threw myself back into work, seeing patients and talking with visitors, but when a month passed with no word, I worried. Our personal savings were almost gone, so I couldn't afford a flight to Kampala. I learned of a UN plane going from Mogadishu to Nairobi, though, and with a bit of negotiation, I got a seat the next day. I bought a round-trip bus ticket from Nairobi to Kampala, driving across the border town of Busia, which straddled Kenya and Uganda.

By the time we finally crossed into Uganda, I was exhausted. I hadn't slept the night before, as I was performing surgeries that I knew could not wait for my return. I hadn't been able to sleep during the eleven-hour ride, as we were jostled along the way. The official who met us at the border saw my Somali passport and demanded money to let me cross; I'd tied up in my dress only $200 U.S., which was to buy supplies for the children. Deliriously tired and anxious, I burst into tears, fearing that I would be held up at the border for so long that I wouldn't be able to see my children. After hours of negotiation, the official settled on a $100 bribe, and I eventually arrived in Kampala, head pounding, at eleven o'clock in the morning.

First I saw Ahmed playing outside with Khadija's youngest daughter; they ran to hug me, and I felt so relieved.

"Where is Mama Asha?" I asked, stroking my son's hair.

"She hasn't been here for two weeks," said Ahmed as he searched through my bag for the sweets he knew were there. He was just a child—eleven years old. "She went to Nairobi."

"Who is with you?" I asked.

"Only we are here." When Deqo and Amina came home later,

I learned that Asha had gone back to Nairobi. She'd simply left. "I am going to sleep for a while," I told the children. "When I wake up, we will make dinner and have a long talk."

I was trapped, forced to control my anger. Again my sister, like my husband, had chosen to follow her own fortune. I had saved her life and the lives of her children, but she was not able to do the same for me. I was frantic, knowing that I could not stay long in Kampala, and knowing that the danger at home prevented me from bringing the children back. We talked the next morning, as I had promised, and afterward I took Deqo to a branch of the Standard Chartered Bank and opened up an account for us. "I will sell some of our property," I told her calmly, "and I'll put money there so that if you need it, you can take it." She acted as an adult, nodding and taking the papers from me.

That afternoon, as the children rested, I went to see one of the few Somali men I knew in Kampala—a middle-aged man who had opened a hotel. "Please," I said to him, handing him the remaining $100. "Watch over my children and give them anything they need. I will come back in a few weeks."

While I was in Kampala, the first American Marines arrived in Mogadishu, bringing with them television crews and tons of food and more money than we'd ever seen. The day they landed was December 9, 1992, and their mission was called Operation Restore Hope—to disarm the warlords and their militias and to clear a path so that the aid could reach us. I first saw the American Marines when I landed at that small airport in Wanlaweyn, and I was afraid.

"No, no, no," said one lady who had been on my flight. "Somalia has changed—the Americans have come!" I could see a change in people's faces, which was surprising but hopeful. We had been waiting, for so many years, for peace.

By then we were high profile, one of the largest camps along the Afgoye Road served by ICRC. One of the heads of the U.S. mission, Lieutenant General Robert B. Johnson, came to my place, and a group of soldiers followed soon after, surveying our camp and offering to help in many ways. I admit that when the American soldiers first came to my camp, I was as wary as I was at the airpõrt, fearing that their presence would bring more violence to our area. They actually did bring peace. They brought a huge convoy of food into Baidoa, where the relief organizations were burying even more people than we were—at one point, as many as three hundred people per day.

The Navy came to our camp following the Marines, although it was hard to keep track of so many faces and titles. They built another big kitchen, this one with three huge stovetops where we could cook at once three big drums' worth of rice. Out of plywood, they built a big hall near the opearting room with an additional thirty-five beds for soldiers—and eventually for patients. They also decided that they would build a primary school. While they worked to dig a big hole in the ground for the foundation, they threw candy to the curious children who came by to watch.

All I could offer in exchange for their work was some very small hospitality, and like the staff of the international organizations, they seemed to enjoy it, delighting in our sweet fruits and resting under our trees, as Wim had. While I tried to give them more, they'd brought their own soda and water and other supplies—so much food, including fruits we didn't have and peanut butter and chocolate, which we gave to the children whenever we could.

A rumor spread that President George Bush would make a trip to Somalia; it was big news, to hear that a U.S. president would come to Africa, let alone to our suffering country. We knew that the two big warlords in the area, Aidid and Ali Mahdi, wanted to meet with President Bush, so I was shocked when General Johnson returned to me to say that the president would pass through my camp on the thirty-first of December, at 2:10 p.m. I couldn't believe it. A U.S. president in our place? It was a top-secret mission and a lot of preparation: A different official group came to me each day, asking me to show them where I would take the president on his visit.

"Here," I said, walking along my property to ICRC's outdoor kitchens, which each had orderly lines stretching out behind. "Here," along the path between the tents we'd set up outside the hospital, where the most severely malnourished lay on carpets or else right on the ground. And then "here," beyond the hospital, to the people's huts, where many mothers and children sat inside—six, seven, eight at a time—to avoid the strongest heat of the day.

As we repeated the drill, American troops assessed the security situation, and our committee of elders planned ways for our society to welcome the president and his delegation. At times it felt almost as though we were preparing for a party, bringing out art supplies and straightening up the tents as best we could. I was happy to see everyone working well, but I wished my children were with me to see the camp running so smoothly, full of food and people wanting to help.

Around one o'clock on December 31, hundreds of American soldiers came to surround my property—more than we'd ever seen. At 2:10 p.m. exactly, they sent up a flare, and a helicopter came flying in from the direction of the ocean. It landed in a clearing we had designated, near the displaced people's homes. President Bush walked out, wearing military dress, and at first I didn't recognize him—I was thinking that he'd be wearing a suit and a tie. Just as the senior officers had said, he came over to greet me. I thanked him for coming, and together we walked the path that I'd set out.

Earlier that day, ICRC had delivered maize and beans, so we saw at the kitchens our usual staff feeding and distributing, and many people waiting. Every person held a plate and some held containers to bring back extra dry food for their families. President Bush stopped to take a few photos with a group of people waiting in line, and he joked with them, trying to make them forget their pain and hunger. When the president entered the tents sheltering our severest cases, the mothers who had the strength stood up, saying "hello." Some of them also had legs swollen with edema.

"Hello, how are you?" he asked, trying to make them happy, to get their attention; he spoke loudly to the men whose faces were so swollen that their vision was obscured. He even shook some of their hands.

The elders and I had decided we'd show off the construction of our new school by gathering a group of the camp's children to stand inside the foundation. When President Bush and I passed that way, the children stood up and said in English, "Welcome, President, welcome." They held some of our signs: WE SOMALIS NEVER FORGET GEORGE BUSH. WELCOME PRESIDENT BUSH. He smiled, and some of them applauded; he then walked over to the group of soldiers, to talk with them and wish them a Happy New Year.

When news of the president's arrival spread, people lined the streets of Mogadishu and the Afgoye Road to welcome him. They had different requests, depending on who controlled their area: In some neighborhoods, the crowds carried photos of Aidid in one hand and of President Bush in the other; in other areas, they carried Ali Mahdi and the president. But President Bush walked back to the helicopter and flew directly to Baidoa, to meet the people suffering there, while the demonstrations were still happening on the streets.

"He's already come!" said some of the people who had been in my place as they returned to Mogadishu. "He visited in the Hawa Abdi place, and he has flown south. It's too late."

Oh, you can imagine, the warlords didn't like to hear that, and neither did many of their supporters. "The world's biggest Christian came to you?" hissed one man when I remarked that the hand he was shaking had also shaken the hand of the American president.

"Yes, that was a pleasure," I said. "And you will never get that pleasure."

On January 3, 1993, UN Secretary-General Boutros Boutros-Ghali came to the camp, taking a photo with me and Aden's father, who was living with us at the time; Colin Powell, chairman of the U.S. Joint Chiefs of Staff, also made a stop that year, greeting the leaders of our religious community and saluting the entire group before climbing back aboard his helicopter. While most people in the camp were happy for the attention, some began to fear reprisals from the warlords. "They say that President Bush gave you a suitcase full of millions of U.S. dollars," said one man, who came back from Mogadishu. "They say that Hawa will never be poor, now that the Americans are supporting her."

How could I make them understand that a single visit didn't change anything? The truth is that delegations come, they see you, they write a report, and then, after much time and bureaucracy, maybe you get a small donation. Without understanding this logic, many people talked behind my back.

"These people protesting may hurt your feelings," said my father-in-law, "but they will never reach your level." I decided to believe him. It was a new year, 1993, and with so much goodwill coming to us, anything was possible.

I spent almost all of our family's savings to fly to Kampala and then, from there, to buy eleven more airline tickets for the children's return to Nairobi. A Somali businessman who had a private plane planned to meet us there and fly us all back to the camp. While we waited for him in the airport, we watched the inauguration of U.S. President Bill Clinton on the television there. The children returned to a home where food was more plentiful and people were living peacefully. Although the suffering was everywhere, for the children, it was paradise: No matter where you have been, your home is the best.

The American soldiers came every morning, in their heavy dress and heavy boots, marching in together in groups of four or eight or ten. We all celebrated the opening of the school they'd built, with its seven classrooms and a big hall where the students could get their lunch. Deqo began teaching mathematics there and spending the late afternoons talking and laughing with the troops—many of whom were around her age.

Khadija came back to us around this time, carrying news that the sheikh and Aden had left Saudi Arabia and were now living in Djibouti, a part of northern Somalia long before colonized by the French. I didn't have many feelings about the matter, I told her, and I was too busy with the people who needed me, and the people who wanted to help. I tried to close my mind to the idea of him: I did not want to talk or to think about someone who had left me at one of the worst moments of my life.

Around that time, the United Nations Operation in Somalia (UNOSOM) collected a group of prominent Somali people to draft a new constitution; since I had a law degree, they invited me to join. For more than a month we sat, from about 8 a.m. to 2 p.m., taking some language from our 1960 constitution and some from the best of Siad Barre's, and writing new provisions based on what we saw during this dark, lawless time. Each of the members of this constitutional committee received threatening letters from the warlords—from Aidid, the strongest one, but from the other ones, too. "You will die if you come back here," read one paper, tacked up in the hall where we met. While we mourned one peace activist we knew, the owner of an electronics store who was shot and killed by Aidid's men, we continued our job. We handed in a draft constitution, thankful that most of us had come through the experience safely.

We had no choice but to look past the danger and try to move ahead, knowing that finding some common ground with the warlords was a matter of survival. The American troops, however, saw these complicated relationships as barriers to their mission. Since the militiamen representing the warlords' interests felt similarly about the U.S. presence, I feared we would never know peace.

*   *   *

In March, UNOSOM organized a conference on humanitarian assistance in Somalia; I was invited to attend on behalf of my hospital, and they paid my way to Addis Ababa, Ethiopia. There, a large group of intellectuals, organizers, executives, and representatives from donor countries assembled to hear from the people like me, who were working on the ground. I felt disoriented and weak as I walked into the hotel with a delegation of Somali women. As we sat together and talked, I was sorry to hear so many people quarreling over politics and jumping to their own clan's defense.

In one session, each person in attendance was given four minutes to talk on the subject of peace and reconciliation—the theme for another conference happening in Addis Ababa, which the leaders of fifteen different factions in Somalia would attend. When it was my turn, I shook my head. "I'm not going to talk for four minutes," I said. "I'll just keep quiet."

"Please give the lady the time to say whatever she wants," said one woman who helped organize the conference.

I took their microphone, looked out at the audience, and said, "No one of you is any better than another. You have all destroyed Somalia." I took a deep breath. "First, you government representatives brought your trucks to the national bank and took all the money, every car, every engine, everything good. I witnessed it—I live beside that road.

"Then, after you left, this other group of you came, and you raped all of the mothers and the daughters; you took the small money they were hiding underneath their pillows and stole their future. This is the way you support your country, going after one another? You're all bandits—you're not real Somalis."

I described the children suffering and the mothers who came, wanting something, when I had nothing to give. "The poor people who sent me here are waiting for you—they need peace," I said. "I will go back. What will I say when I go? Will you decide something to make Somalia a better place?"

I sat back down among my old friends from Kiev and my

colleagues from Mogadishu. As they hugged me, the anger that powered that speech still felt hot in my face. I remembered everything—I couldn't stand sitting there, among these people who were all pretending to do something good. Later, as I spoke directly with representatives from some of the donor countries, I felt relieved that I had told the truth. I feared God only, not these corrupt people; I would not praise them, and I would not keep quiet.

In the next few days, several journalists came to me, asking me questions about the situation in Somalia. One afternoon I spoke with a television reporter from Djibouti, and that night, the phone in my room rang. Aden had seen the speech on television, and he'd called to tell me that he and the sheikh were coming back to Mogadishu. "When you finish the conference, meet me in Djibouti," he said. "We will return together."

It was the first time I'd heard his voice in a year. I felt a mix of love and hatred for this man, who I had decided could not have loved me, if he left me when I was so sick. "No," I told him. "I will go straight home."

When you're hit the same way again and again, your body learns how to defend itself. If you hit me in the arm while I am relaxed, the blow will cause me pain. The next time, my muscle will be tight and ready. "What can I do, Aden?" I said. "I have to go back and do my job. You do what you want."

The donors at the conference pledged more than $130 million toward the rebuilding of Somalia; at a different conference, held just days later, the warlords signed an agreement on disarmament and the establishment of a transitional government. I returned home hopeful, thinking that, finally, we could move forward. We had not been able to find peace among the warlords with each one saying, "I'm powerful, I can do everything." Everyone wants to be president, but there is just one chair. It is impossible for everyone to sit in it.

A few weeks later, I was back at the camp, praying in my bedroom, when Khadija ran in, sweating. I told her to leave, to wait until

I had finished, and when I opened my door, she was still there, breathing heavily. "Aden has come!" she said. "Aden has come!"

I walked downstairs, and we met on the veranda. His face hadn't changed, but he had gained weight—I knew that in Saudi Arabia, where there are few jobs, people often sit around all day, drinking fruit smoothies. He carried with him a stack of papers, and as he shuffled through them, he explained that he had been trying to connect the camp with several rich men. Nothing had come of his meetings, he said, but he was optimistic.

He didn't act as though he had been far away for long, and he didn't apologize for leaving me.

"Okay, Aden, I have no problem," I said. We didn't discuss what had happened between us; I would accept him only because I didn't want our children to suffer without a family intact. I wouldn't fight him or beg for an apology. Somali people, you know, are very proud.

Some of the relief workers saw this pride when they tried to throw food from their cars to starving children, and to their shock, many of the starving children refused it. A similar thing happened in our camp once, when a delegation from Bangladesh was visiting. When they asked me how such desperate people could leave food on the ground, I tried to explain that we were still strong in our hearts, even if our bodies and our clothes told a different story.

"You know," I said, "if you want to give these people something, give it from your hand to their hand."

We wanted so badly to feel human, we were grateful to those who recognized our work. In April, ICRC financed the drilling of a well on our property by an American man working with a Somali engineer. They brought over a drill from a local businessman, and within three days, they'd gone 220 meters deep to get us plenty of sweet water, which would go into a 250-drum water tank for the camp and a 40-drum tank for the hospital. They built pipes out to the camp, so people could bring their jerrycans, and they also ran piping into the hospital, so we could scrub up before operations.

But while the humanitarian situation improved somewhat in 1993, politically we were unraveling. The ceasefire that the warlords signed didn't bring a moment of peace, and they now used foreign peacekeepers as targets. Aidid broadcast his hatred of Western intervention on Radio Mogadishu, accusing the UN of coming to colonialize Somalia. In early June, a group of Aidid's militiamen ambushed and killed twenty-four Pakistani UN troops, and wounded many, many others, during an inspection of one of Aidid's storehouses. The news was disturbing, shameful. We whispered among one another, wondering what would come of it. I sat down one evening, when I couldn't sleep, to write a letter to an American diplomat, trying to explain our position. "Please, we are sorry, but I am begging you not to seek revenge," I wrote. "We have suffered enough, we've seen enough death. Retaliation is not good." I sent another to the UNOSOM office.

While I hesitated to turn on the radio for the latest news, we did need to be informed. That's how we learned how the UN fought back: passing an emergency resolution that authorized "all necessary measures" to stop such violence against UNOSOM staff. Then they issued a warrant for Aidid's arrest and showered Bakara Market with flyers that offered a $25,000 reward for information about him.

"Dr. Hawa, we came here to help you, and now we can't even go outside our base," said a U.S. official one afternoon, when a group of them came to meet with me. They, too, were searching for some information about Aidid. "Why are your people terrorizing us?"

"You are just going after Aidid, and Somalis don't like one-sided people," I said. "We have fifteen warlords. If you stood up and said, 'We want all the warlords,' the people would capture them for you. But if you leave fourteen and search for just one, they will stand up and fight you."

"So what are we supposed to do?" he asked.

"Please," I said, stirring my tea. "Take them all, together."

CHAPTER SEVENTEEN

One Wrong Decision

Deqo thrived in the camp, teaching in the school and assisting in the hospital. While she learned a lot doing this, it was not what I had envisioned for my daughter. I had spoken with some people about university for her and for my sister Amina's eldest daughter, Su'ado, who was, like Deqo, nearing age twenty. I knew it would be expensive, so I brought another 500 grams of my gold from my hiding place inside my room; the women who sold it returned to me with about $9,000 U.S. Convinced that this would be enough, I bought plane tickets to Nairobi for the two girls and for me, so we could find a way for them to study. Leaving the rest of the children behind, I checked us into a cheap hotel in Eastleigh and called every number our friends had given us.

Since I had not paid for my own studies, I was shocked to learn the price of sending our children away. I was told that a year of tuition at one British university was about $38,000—similar to the cost of some private universities in America, where Deqo had wanted to go from the start. At the University of Nairobi Medical School, the cost of one year was about $11,000 for each girl, plus housing. Even that was too much for us to sustain.

I found a Russian charity organization that offered scholarships, and finally, I saw a way. Tuition and housing for the two girls at I.M. Sechenov First Moscow State Medical University, through their program, would be about $6,000 U.S. a year, plus an additional $2,400 for food. Remembering the Russian books in my home library and my tough professors, I sent the charity a fax, listing Deqo and Su'ado's birth dates and academic information, and explaining why they wanted to study. When we received word that the girls were accepted, I asked that they'd also send a visa for Aden, who could enroll them before classes started at the beginning of September.

The Moscow my children would enter in 1993 was a far different place than the one I had known. Since the collapse of the Soviet Union, there was deep economic trouble, social unrest, and political turmoil. "Please, Hawa," cried my cousin. "Don't send your children to that place!"

I called Aden at the camp. While he agreed that it was dangerous for the girls to go there, we both believed it was right. I left the girls with my cousin and returned to the camp to work and to ask for financial help from family members, friends, and even some of the ICRC staff. Once all the arrangements had been made, I began to worry.

I tried listening to my inner voice, as my mother had advised, but I found that instead of giving me comfort, the noise kept me up late into the night. What was I doing, I wondered, sending these girls so far away, to a place that was so violent and cold? The Russians I knew had advised me, and they'd cared for me as if I were their child. Would my girls have the same experience? Would they come home well educated and unspoiled, as I had?

The questions were not answered by the time Aden had to leave to take them. He stopped first in Nairobi to meet them, and they went together to Cairo, to get their plane to Moscow—the same route that we took in the 1960s. I went to the airport to see him off. While we were waiting, he saw two young women he knew and stopped to talk with them. I was too distracted to talk, so I excused myself and went to sit in an empty row of seats with my eyes closed. I stood for a while after saying good-bye, watching through the window as his bus drove out to the airplane.

For the next month, I suffered. We had no way of communicating, and the radio broadcast the frightening news that the Russian president, Boris Yeltsin, had dissolved the parliament. What to do, other than to pray and wait? Finally, Aden called me from Nairobi, where he had landed and where he was planning to stay. "Our daughters are okay," he told me. When he saw me next, he would give me their photo. I could call the school from the Mogadishu post office and ask to speak with Deqo directly.

When I asked about the security in the school, Aden said that he hadn't seen any guards, but that it didn't seem to be a problem. He'd asked a taxi driver about the political situation. "We don't care," the driver had said. "We are not part of the government. We are ordinary people—if they fight, if they make peace for us, it's the same."

Our food supplies became very low that September, and on October 3, I took the bus to Mogadishu for a meeting with the ICRC office. I got off at my usual stop, near Banadir hospital, when I saw, from across the street, a man wearing a white kameez, waving in his left hand a hunk of cow meat, about the size of an outstretched hand. Dozens of young boys shouted and jumped after him, cheering and repeating his terrible words: "They come to our place to bother us? We will eat their meat!" he screamed to the children, waving the hunk in their direction. "Like this! Like *this!*"

I was so shocked by the sound and the sight, the tone of his voice, that I couldn't move. I stood, my legs shaking, as the children screamed after him, a sound of *"Weeee-weeee-weeee-weeeee-weeeee!"* The oldest, I think, was ten years old.

"Go out!" the man screamed, and the children echoed, "Go out! Go out!"

"Go from our country!" said the man. "We will eat you like this! Like this! We will eat!"

I was shaken by the time I arrived at the ICRC office, and I stood as we discussed the rice and the oil that would come on the trucks, *insha'Allah*, in three days' time.

"Please add something," I begged. "People are coming, more and more."

"We will try our best," they said.

I waited for the very next bus home, and when I arrived, the radio in the hospital was on: The BBC Somali service reported that two American Black Hawk helicopters had been shot down nearby Bakara Market, and since it was the afternoon, the busiest time of day, hundreds or maybe thousands of Somali people, business owners and innocent women and children, had been killed. Some Americans had been killed as well, although no one knew how many.

The chaos was far away—we couldn't hear the shouting or the sound of bullets—but we still felt helpless and trapped. I began visiting patients anyway, but after about twenty minutes, I called Faduma Duale and another nurse into an empty examining room. I handed Faduma my clipboard and took off my glasses. "Please see after the rest of this," I said. I took two sedative tablets from the pharmacy, walked into my room, and slept.

When I awoke the next morning, I requested to have my breakfast in my Camp David, and some of the people living in the camp came over to talk. Most hadn't slept the night before, awaiting word from their families. Their tired eyes were wide as they told me that a thousand Somalis had been killed in the crash and the fighting, and at least five American soldiers. Someone had heard from a relative inside Mogadishu that a group had captured the dead American soldiers, dragging their bodies through the streets. "That is inhuman," I said. When the rumor was confirmed by the news, I would refuse to look at the photos, insisting, as I do now, that for a doctor, the human body is sacred.

In time, a crowd gathered around us. A man I knew well pushed through, sitting down near me. "You know, Hawa," he said, "I was in Bakara Market earlier this morning. When I entered one of the shops there, I saw a woman sitting with her husband and her two sons.

"On the floor, near where the mother was preparing tea, were two dead bodies, but no one was looking at them. The men were chewing *qat*, and no one said anything to me.

"'Who are these people?' I asked them.

"'These are my two boys,' said the mother. 'I had four, and now I have two remaining.'

"I was shocked," the man said, and then stopped talking for a moment, his head down, swaying from side to side, as though he were chanting. Then he continued. "They spoke normally, they ate normally. They had no feeling. They had no sadness. The mother was not crying."

When he lifted his head, I looked at him for a moment—his raised eyebrows, his sad, open mouth. "You know," I told him finally, "the world is very complicated."

For the next several months, until early 1994, the American soldiers stayed in their compound, and Aidid's men tried to attack them night and day. One day, a group of the Americans returned to our place, carrying supplies to clean the hospital—mops and brooms and buckets. We'd been waiting for things to calm down before we could return to Mogadishu for supplies, so I thanked their supervisor, a tall, handsome, bald man, about thirty-five years old. "I came to say good-bye," he said.

"I'm sorry to see you go, but I'm happy you've finished your tour," I said. "Will you give me your address? I would like to send your wife a present."

"Please, don't do that," he said, and went back to work. The rest of his team was particularly quiet, unloading their supplies and saying either nothing or their usual "Bye."

The next day, I took the bus to the Mogadishu post office for my scheduled phone call with Deqo. I climbed the stairs to the top of the six-story building, one of the city's tallest; since I was early for the appointment, I walked over to the big windows, to look out at the ocean.

I saw on the horizon many, too many, military ships, moving

out straight, away from the coast, and then turning south, in the direction of Kenya. I stared for as long as I could, watching as, one by one, they passed out of my sight. Then I walked away from the window with a heavy heart, understanding finally what the American soldier was saying to me. I knew they would not return.

I waited and waited to hear Deqo's voice, and when I finally did, I felt relieved that she was far away. She cried as I told her about the visit from the American soldiers, and about the ships, which had carried away her new friends—one had even confessed his love for her before she left for Moscow. She had felt such confidence in the Americans, for whom she translated, with whom she taught. We wouldn't survive without their help, she said. "Please, Mama," she said, "go to Nairobi, or come to me here."

"I can't leave these people," I said. "I'm praying to my God that we will all be safe." I hung up the phone and walked back up the stairs to search the horizon. I stayed, stayed, stayed, until I couldn't see the ships anymore.

There is a Somali saying that one wrong decision is worse than seven years of dry season. In what seemed like a moment, there were no more jobs in Mogadishu, no visitors to ask me what I needed, no one to appreciate what I was doing. The Americans had given me a paper recognizing what I had done for my country, but they were no longer interested in helping. Even the journalists turned their heads, traveling out with the aid convoys toward Rwanda, to cover the genocide. The people left inside Somalia knew only how to destroy it.

Some mornings, Aidid came out in a technical car, with two or three others following; he'd stop at the rival militia's checkpoint and shoot all the people standing there. Anti-American, anti-Western demonstrations continued, and many of the people in the area turned against me, burning tires along the Afgoye Road, shouting, "We don't want Americans, we don't want Bush, we don't want Hawa Abdi!"

"Say that!" they told their children. "Say it!"

One day, when a few of my guards were in Mogadishu, they saw Aidid's men shoot a car that looked just like mine, killing a woman inside. When I returned to the camp from a meeting, I saw people crying, saying, "Oh, Hawa died, Hawa died." I ran to Amina and some of the other children, who were in shock, to tell them that it was a mistake.

God is great. These hooligans never harassed me, and the warlords never entered my camp, never told me anything bad. I continued to make my own rules and to sit outside with the elders, discussing the situation in the camp and making decisions by consensus. Our own security was qualified to defend the area and settle small arguments that would otherwise grow into the same violent clashes happening on the outside.

In some ways, life improved: The rain returned, and we were able to once again cultivate the land. The UN-organized Somalia Aid Coordination Body developed an agriculture plan, instructing each farm in the area to grow maize, beans, and sesame. The river rose, which helped all of us, especially the farmers in the low-lying areas. As the crops grew, so did our optimism.

An Italian fruit company came to me and to some of the other farms in the area, offering to invest in us, paying for fuel, fertilizer, and even some of our labor so we could produce bananas. In exchange, we would sell our yield at $3 per 14-kilo carton, they said. An American fruit company followed close behind, for bananas grow dramatically. The opportunity was clear.

While I was wary of taking too much from any one organization, I did welcome the chance to hire more people; we began to produce between 200 and 300 cartons, and sometimes even 500 cartons a month. It was nothing when compared to some of our neighbors, who were producing as many as 100,000 cartons a month. The ships were coming twice a month, the farms were thriving, and the income allowed us to cultivate the crops we really needed to eat, like maize and beans. Aidid's men caught on, demanding three cents for each carton; this was a small enough fee, compared to what we were earning. People were receiving salaries; they had money to buy food and some, even, to pay for medical treatment. It was a small taste of the good life again.

But by this time, Aidid's group had once again divided in two. One of his top officials united with a rival clan, becoming a new, powerful group that wanted the contracts. They threatened the fruit companies; if the companies wouldn't pay, the warlords shot at their ships from the port, sending them back. The Somali farmers kept growing, growing, growing—enough to fill about 200,000 cartons a month—but we had to watch our harvest rot when the ships couldn't come.

Our group of farmers all wrote letters to the warlords. We were ready to pay them more, we said; we needed the ships to return, so we could sell what we had already grown. We had expected to sell these bananas, we said.

"Then eat them yourself," said the warlords.

Oh, the waste. The farmers who had produced the most became the most despairing; many lost the means to produce maize and other essential crops, and one ran mad and died. Again the United Nations World Food Programme intervened, transporting sacks of grain from the other side of the world and giving it away for free. While the aid did help to ensure that people would not starve, it devastated our economy. There was no market for the farmers' few remaining crops, people became poor once more, and many did whatever they could to find cash.

We heard more and more stories of bandits shooting at buses that were passing in the road as a way to rob all the people inside. People died every day from the indiscriminate shootings, and many travelers lost all they had. It was the same story every time: When the driver would stop, these evil men would lay a cloth in the sand and tell everyone, "Put whatever you have right here." They took money, watches, and jewelry. If they discovered you'd left something in your clothes, they would kill you on the spot and take what they'd demanded in the first place.

These broken families came to us, including one young widow who'd lost her husband that way. She'd brought six young children to care for—the oldest was about thirteen. Since there was no one else to watch her children, she often left them all together in their hut while she took the bus to Mogadishu in search of some small meat—some protein—to feed them. On her way back one day, her bus was shot and the bullet went straight through her heart. Someone stole her food, and someone else brought her dead body to me. We dressed her wounds and kept her in a room, hoping that we could find her sisters and brothers before we were forced to bury her.

Late that afternoon, one of my assistants came in to say that there was a thirteen-year-old girl waiting outside for me. I walked out to meet her, and I saw immediately that she was the child of the poor woman. She carried one of her younger siblings; another two were with her, by her side. "We are searching for our mother," she told me. "They said that you would know." I asked her to describe her mother to me, and when she did, I had no choice but to tell her the truth. I said I would bring her to see, if that was what she wanted.

When the girl saw her mother's face, she stepped back, putting her hands over her ears and squeezing her eyes shut. The younger daughters came forward, nudging and shaking the body. "Mama, we are hungry," said one as I hid my tears. "Mama." We brought together food to give them, but they refused it. How could they eat?

Our poor Somalia continued to bleed, mostly from the wounds we inflicted on one another. On my way from the hospital to the farm one day, I passed the Ministry of Agriculture, remembering the beautiful building, the state-of-the-art laboratory that experimented with crossing genes. When I was young, people came here from all over the world, meeting with Somali farming experts to figure out how to increase maize production, or how to make new fruits—crosses between grapefruits and lemons, or lemons and limes. Aden had gone there to rent our tractor, in the farm's earliest days.

Looters had long ago taken the Ministry of Agriculture's windows, doors, and pipes; for years, the grounds had been empty. So I was surprised to see the figure of a strong, well-nourished woman standing in the clearing, and next to her two strong, young men carrying saws. I asked the driver to pull over. "Why are you cutting there?" I asked one of the men.

"This lady ordered us," he said. "We are cutting them for her."

I called to the lady, who was walking over to the car. "My sister, why are you cutting these trees? It took many years for them to grow this long and straight. Why?"

"I will use them to build my home," she said.

"Please," I said, "are these your trees?"

"They're *our* trees."

"But the beautiful view here is yours and mine, please don't cut it down."

"I'm cutting," she said. "If you don't like it, do whatever you want."

To argue was foolish—maybe her clan was more powerful than I was. Without law and order, she could not be arrested, could not even be stopped. The next time I came back, all the trees in the area were gone; they had been loaded up in the men's waiting donkey carts to take to her home.

Such behavior began from the day Siad Barre fled, when people were so angry they destroyed the chairs, the tables—entire sitting rooms. In their narrow minds was only the thought of punishing one person—not about the rights of the Somali people, or the idea that another president might one day sit in his chair. With no education, this destruction was our country's only philosophy. If it's public, people think, it's ours, which means that everyone has a right to destroy it.

*   *   *

When I was a child, Faduma Ali and I once argued over the last *chapati*, and Ayeyo ordered us to clean up the food quickly and to follow her into the clearing near our house. She gave us a rope. "You take this end," she'd told Faduma Ali, "and Hawa, you take this end. Then tug! Tug! It is yours!"

Confused and frustrated, we'd pulled with our small hands, the grass-made rope rough and slippery. Faduma Ali would tire, and I would yank, and then, as I had to adjust my feet in the dirt, she would yank, sending me stumbling forward. We'd tugged and tugged, both thinking, I have the advantage.

"Hawa, drop it!" Ayeyo yelled suddenly.

I did, confused, and Faduma Ali staggered back and fell down, laughing, thank goodness.

"If you are two people fighting because of something you both want, it is best to leave," Ayeyo had said. "Fighting with all your force only means that someday you will fall down. You will never succeed. God is great—if you want something, he will give it to you."

This is our family's way. There is no proving "I'm right, I'm right, I have to have." Ayeyo taught my mother, my mother taught me, and now I struggled to teach my children in a world that had run mad. When I saw someone in Bakara Market selling material from the roofs he had pulled from other people's homes, I knew that I had made a mistake about bringing my children back.

I reached out to our friends for help, and Swedish Church Relief provided a flight to Nairobi. We found another small apartment in Eastleigh, where we could have, in one room, two triple bunk beds and a mattress on the floor for Asha. "Please, sister," I begged her. "Stay here." Now I can see how naïve I was, but I had no choice, and I had my natural weaknesses: Even now, when someone says okay, I trust her. I trusted that my family would be together, to study together, to be in a safe place, as I was risking my life in Somalia.

I stayed for just five days, knowing that at the camp people were lined up, waiting to tell me, "I want food," "I want money," "I want a job," "I want clothes," "Someone died—give me a *kar-fan*." Maybe I should have stayed in Nairobi, protecting my children instead of risking my life and leaving in my place some small money for safety and comfort. When I think of it now, I sometimes regret it. I went back, knowing that when I could help someone, I was happy. But what about my children's lives—and my own?

CHAPTER EIGHTEEN

The Fourth Container

We received any bit of news about the political situation with doubt at best, and at worst, with suspicion and anger. Aidid was killed in August 1996, but his son took over, and our land remained under their clan's control. While people came to me with hot, hot tempers, I insisted on keeping a politically neutral position: What was most important was that no person inside our place stole, fought, or killed. So long as that was true, I treated the wives and daughters of every warlord. Most people recognized me for this, and we were left alone.

From time to time the political and economic situation improved, and some women were able to pay for my consultations. That money covered some of the hospital expenses, including a small salary for some of our dedicated staff, who worked most often for food or for education—learning how to handle a normal delivery, how to do injections, how to draw blood. We also used the money to order medicine for the hospital and distribute it in our small pharmacy; Aden, who had returned to the camp, was overseeing the project. With him there, I was able to travel back and forth to Nairobi every month or two, to see after the children.

When a local telephone company installed a line and donated a phone, it opened up a new world for our family. This way, I could hear everything: Amina was reaching the end of secondary school, and Ahmed, the last year of primary school, Standard 8. By this time, Khadija had left the camp and had moved in with

Asha and the children, hoping to find some work in Nairobi. Each time I went to see my sisters there, I dreamed that they would be polite, that we would sit together and drink tea and talk about what we had seen and what we wanted to reach. Reality was different, however, so I never stayed long.

Thanks to the phone, I knew whenever one of the children was sick; I also knew that their money was almost gone. When two women who sold gold in India came to the camp, I reached back into my store. I divided their profit in two—half for the rent for the apartment in Eastleigh, and half for our own stall at a market nearby, where Khadija could sell fabrics to pay for the children's food and clothing.

More than a thousand kilometers away, in Somalia, all I could do for my children was make sure that the situation in the camp was peaceful, so I'd be able to bring them back. We tried to give struggling families—men and women—small jobs on the farm. Thanks to their hard work, we yielded about six hundred sacks of maize each harvest. When it was time to reap, the laborers and the hospital's patients were the first to benefit.

I didn't often stop and think about how much time had passed since we began living this way, but every once in a while, when someone who had been away for years returned, I could hear their shock, fear, and pity. They did not believe me when I said that I still felt as I did when my sister Amina and I strolled through Mogadishu twenty-five years earlier, back when Somalia was thriving. I knew that other places had safety and order, I said, but for me, home was still the best.

I answered the phone one day and heard Amina's tearful voice. "My daughter!" I said, surprised. "What is the problem?"

"Mama Asha slapped me," she moaned.

"Why?" I hated the distance between us, hated my sister.

Amina confessed that she had taken money from Asha. "I want Ahmed to go to school, Mama," she said. Although some of the other cousins had failed Standard 8, Ahmed had passed and was ready to begin secondary school. Fearing that Asha would not enroll Ahmed without the others, Amina took money from Asha's hiding place, sold her own small gold earrings, and brought the money to our cousin. "Please, please, Uncle," she had said, addressing him with our term of endearment. "We have to go today to bring Ahmed to school. Mama Asha doesn't have time."

Amina called me from that cousin's house now. She had been successful—they'd enrolled Ahmed in school—but when she'd come back to the apartment that night, the children had warned her that Asha had been shouting. She'd run away in fear.

My cousin took the phone, his angry voice loud against my ear. "I told Asha, 'How can you touch her? She's our daughter, too, and this house is rented by her parents, not by you.'" He had fed Amina, he said, and when she'd return home, she'd carry food back to Ahmed as well. The way he talked, I feared that the children were not getting enough to eat.

Before I hung up the phone, I spoke with Amina once more. "You have to be strong," I said. "Your father will come to you soon." For the next several days, I thought only about what could have happened when my cousin had brought Amina back to the apartment. Somali elders—parents, aunts, cousins—never apologize to children, even when they know they themselves are in the wrong.

Aden returned to Nairobi to see after the children, and Asha returned to the camp. I sold a piece of land that would pay for Amina's university preparatory course in Moscow; she and Deqo could protect each other there. When I was next able to return to Nairobi, to prepare Amina for her journey, it was the end of the rainy season there. While the children greeted me as usual, something seemed different: The small place was crowded and tense, and Amina and Ahmed seemed very thin.

I was lying in the small sitting room, trying to sleep, when around ten o'clock that evening, Aden and Khadija came home. They turned on the overhead light. "I'm here," I called from the floor. "Please turn it off. I'm so tired."

"Sleep if you want," said Aden. "It's up to you." I was surprised when he didn't turn off the light and didn't walk over to greet me, but after a while, I pretended that he was not there.

The next morning the children and I went to the market, buying a goat to cook along with rice. Later that afternoon, they invited all their friends to come eat, and I lay down plastic sheets and a carpet in the courtyard to accommodate everyone. The children ate well, and the breeze was on my shoulders, cool and welcoming. I enjoyed the day, even if Aden and Khadija were not with us to share in any of it.

The next day, I asked Khadija about the shop—about how much profit she had, how much she lost, how much she had been able to give to the children. "I don't have time now," she said. Later, Aden told me that he had also tried to discuss the business, and how the money was divided, with Khadija. "I tried to argue with her once," he said, "but when I came into the store, she wouldn't talk." We shook our heads together, laughing uncomfortably, as we had when Khadija was a teenager.

But when I finally confronted her, she refused to hear my side. "You have your own land, your own farm—you are rich," she said. "This shop is *mine*. I don't owe you anything."

The next day, I took the children to Uhuru Park for a picnic. As we ate, they told me that they wanted to go to the zoo park, to see some of the wild animals. I promised that we'd go during my next visit. "Can't you stay?" asked Ahmed.

"I'm very busy in the camp," I said. "You know that someone is always waiting for me. They're sick, or they need to tell me about a problem in their house." My children said they understood, but my words sounded hollow, even to me. I left for the airport, my heart full of regret. Maybe I should have stayed in Nairobi, protecting my children, rather than risking my life and leaving them gold and U.S. dollars for food and emergencies.

I took the flight anyway, and forty minutes after we took off, the pilot came on the loudspeaker to say that there was a problem with the engine and we'd have to return to the airport. I turned to one of my friends. "I cannot stay here—maybe we won't leave until tomorrow," I said. "I have to go to my children tonight, to stay with them." So I took a taxi back to the apartment.

The next morning, Khadija came into the kitchen to ask if she could keep my soap, which I had left out in the bathroom.

"It's the soap you're thinking of? Take it," I snapped. "You've already taken everything else."

By the end of the 1990s, Somalia was dry in every way: I could not earn enough from the hospital to keep it open and support my children. I spoke with a Somali nurse I knew, who worked for a doctor at Kilimanjaro hospital in Eastleigh. She told him about me, explaining how many women knew me, trusted me, and liked my treatment. He invited me to join his practice, and went to the Minister of Health to apply for my work visa. While I felt conflicted about my decision, my job—and my paycheck—was set. I left Asha in the camp and returned to Nairobi to celebrate the millennium with my husband and son.

At that time, Khadija was living with her children in another part of Nairobi, so we three, after years of distance, fell into a familiar routine: breakfast together, then I prepared for work, Ahmed for school, and Aden for meetings with his friends and powerful people in his clan. While some people ask if I was bothered by the fact that I was earning the income for our family, for us, it had always been this way. We were both students when we first met, and then he was an officer, a position that didn't pay much. I had decided at an early age that I would work and earn my own money, so I never needed to ask anyone for anything.

When I wasn't working in Kilimanjaro hospital, women came to our apartment, as they had in the earliest days of my clinic. I divided our downstairs sitting room in half, with a waiting room on one side and the other side closed off for examinations. I called one of my nurses from the camp to come assist me; sometimes, when women were delivering at night, she would stay up so I could get some sleep. Soon I was able to send about $1,500 U.S. a month to the camp, to keep the water pumps running and the electricity on.

That April, I was invited to Arta, Djibouti, to participate in another Somali reconciliation conference. While I knew that the last several had been ineffective, including the most recent, in Cairo, I accepted anyway. Deqo would be a doctor in May, and I wanted her to work with me in a peaceful country.

A few days before I left, Aden told me that he wanted to see his relatives near Hargeisa—it would be his first trip back to the north of Somalia since he was young. That meant that Ahmed, who was in his last year of secondary school in Nairobi, would be left alone, but he was a responsible young man. He looked forward to taking Deqo's place in Moscow, but he didn't want to be a doctor, like his sisters. He wanted to be a pilot.

"Oh, my child, it's too dangerous in the sky," I told him. "You have to stay down here with me!"

People traveled to Djibouti from all over—from the diaspora as well as from within Somalia—but many of the warlords, including Aidid's son, refused to come. I was at the reconciliation conference for weeks, restless and uncomfortable, frustrated by the oppressively hot weather and the same old arguments of clan, clan, clan. "We want only peace to rebuild our beautiful country," I said in a session one day. "We can't all sit in the president's chair, but if we select someone suitable to bring us peace, that, for us, is enough." When I finished my speech, some of the women from the diaspora hugged me.

Deqo called me one night at my hotel, and I told her that I would come to her graduation in Moscow. "I don't need to stay here and talk with these people who don't understand anything," I said. I tried to reach Aden, but I couldn't; we hadn't spoken since he'd gone to Hargeisa.

When I got to the Djibouti airport, I learned that in order to get to Moscow, I would have to fly through Paris. Since the French Embassy in Djibouti had a photo of a Somali passport with a red line through it, I could not get a visa. Instead I had to return to Nairobi so I could fly through Cairo. "I'm sorry," I said, leaving a message. "I'll be a day late."

Deqo and Amina were there to greet me when I finally arrived, and although they looked thin and tired, they were happy to see me. I was happy, too, seeing my daughters and my second motherland, where I had spent some of the most beautiful days of my life. Many of the tall buildings were gone, replaced by even taller structures without any design or character, and I immediately noticed that people looked at the ground instead of in one another's eyes. They were especially suspicious of foreigners—no longer welcoming and curious.

I slept in Deqo's bed as she prepared for her graduation party, cooking beets and eggs for salads, preparing meat, bread, everything. That night they had music and dancing for hours, and we all took turns making speeches. The students applauded when I said that Somalia was waiting for them, but not as loudly as they cheered for Deqo's speech: "My life is my friends and music, so always, I will be with you," she said.

For ten days I lived as though I were young again, sitting in beautiful green parks, visiting cafés, taking photos. One night Aden called to speak with Deqo. After she was finished talking with him, she handed the phone to me. "How are you?" he asked.

"I'm enjoying the beauty of Moscow with my daughters," I said without emotion.

"Congratulations," he said.

Later that day I told Deqo that I had spoken with my supervisor in Nairobi, and that he had prepared for her a specialization at Kilimanjaro hospital. "No, Mama," she said. She had begun working for the United Nations High Commissioner for Refugees while in Moscow, and she wanted to continue. "I want to have my specialization here," she said. "UNHCR will pay all my expenses."

"I want you to come work with me—to specialize at a university in Nairobi," I said.

"UNHCR has already accepted me," she said, "and I've told them I will stay." The words stunned me—while I knew that my daughter had enjoyed her life on the outside, I had assumed that she wanted to return home as soon as she could.

"Deqo," said Amina, "you will be cursed if you don't go with Mama." But Deqo had made up her mind, and if my children say something, they say it. They can't be convinced otherwise.

When I returned to our apartment in Nairobi, Ahmed was there. He hugged me and then looked over my shoulder. "Where's Deqo?"

I sighed. "Not now," I said. I was suddenly very tired. "I need to come inside and rest."

Aden said that he had enjoyed his trip to the north, and I could tell by his face that he was happy. "I saw many men who asked for my advice," he said. He thanked me for supporting our daughter, and he told me that he agreed with her decision to remain in Moscow. Together we watched the graduation video: Each child took a diploma, threw his hat in the air, and hugged his parents. Deqo, the only Somali student, tossed her hat and hugged her friends.

"You made a mistake," I told Aden. "You should have been there."

I returned to my daily routine: my shift at Kilimanjaro hospital, my home practice, and then long hours on the telephone with Faduma Duale, who was running our hospital at the camp. The UN's World Food Programme was still working in the region, so people were no longer starving, and some had been able to find work. In those days, the hospital at the camp was able to receive some payment from about 60 percent of our Somali clients.

Two weeks after Aden returned, I came home from Kilimanjaro hospital to find him in the downstairs sitting room, a large bag at his feet. "I have a job to do in the north, so I'm going to live there," he said. "I hope you'll forgive me if I die there. And I'll forgive you if you die."

I could tell by the way he spoke that something had changed. "Do you have another wife there? Please tell me." I'd had my suspicions for so many years—the rumors and gossip, the time we spent apart, the strange women answering the telephone in Nairobi or in Saudi Arabia or, I was sure, in Hargeisa.

"Never," he said, and he said it again when he kissed me goodbye. "I would never have another wife."

I told my children that their father had left us. When Ahmed called, Aden said, "Your mother is disturbing me—she says I have another wife but I do not, I swear."

One of Aden's relatives came to the apartment with his wife, who needed a consultation. I finished the examination and wrote her a prescription, and then he asked her to leave the room while we talked privately. "Hawa, I have to tell you," he said. "Aden has a wife and a daughter who is five years old." Now, he said, the wife was five months pregnant.

I wanted to scream so he would stop talking, but from the simple way he spoke, I knew that he was telling me something true. I had refused to believe it for so long, even when I was accusing Aden. He had lied to me and to his children, and he'd continued that lie for seven years. All the time he had been living with us, his relatives and the members of his clan were talking to him, telling him, "You are ours." They'd insisted that he take a wife that was one of their daughters—not someone like me, from a different clan, from the south.

Like their mother, my children refused to believe. Then one day Ahmed received a call from his father. "You must congratulate me," his father said, "for today, you have another brother, and I have another son."

So many women in our society run after men—asking where they went, what relations they had—fearing that they will be abandoned, left with nothing. "Sometimes we are more power-ful than men," said one of my closest friends, a talented midwife named Maimona, who was strong, well educated, and successful, and who still treated her husband like a small god. "We just have to know the right way to approach them." I could not imagine liv-ing as she did, working all day in the hospital but having another top priority: to please her husband, preparing food for him her-self, laying out his clothes, running his bath. She treated him as a child in some ways, but even more delicately. If she had a group of friends over, she would say after a while, "Please go. My husband and I have to have time to talk."

"I'm not his laborer," I had told Maimona then. "I love him, he loves me. We are equals." I knew that after the government's collapse, Aden and I had no time for each other. We struggled together, working and planning as we always had, even as the situ-ation grew more and more difficult. I always had my own targets, my own point of view; it turned out that while my mind had been busy, he had been busy in other ways. Somali men want to be powerful, and Aden was no exception.

We have a saying that comes from the time when we used to walk with camels, balancing two heavy containers on each side. In this world, we say, you never have four containers. It means that although you may make a plan, it's never fulfilled in the way that you think. Something is missing; that is the fourth container. I think of it now, remembering that Ayeyo never blessed me for a happy marriage.

While Deqo tried to make peace between us, Ahmed refused to talk with his father. "Mama, I am with you—you'll never have regrets," said Amina, comforting me. "I'm your daughter, I will give you everything you want."

As a lawyer, I knew how to end a marriage. Some friends advised me to wait awhile, to try to talk with him, to see if we could make peace. But he had hurt me so, so deeply. I could think only of all the years when I was struggling everywhere to save my family, and he was thinking how to cheat me, how to lie to me.

Other friends thought that he would give me a divorce if I asked him, but I knew that wasn't true. "I will bury you," he'd told me, the first time I'd accused him of having another wife. "And you will bury me."

CHAPTER NINETEEN

Vice Minister of Labor and Sports

Somalia's newly appointed president, Abdiqasim Salad Hassan, was inaugurated in August 2000, bringing crowds of thousands to Mogadishu and celebrations among the Somali people in the streets of Eastleigh. There, someone rented a bus that drove through Nairobi, filled with people who shouted out the windows, "We're going back!" Though I was working in Kilimanjaro hospital, I sent some of my nurses to buy cases of Fanta and Sprite, so we could celebrate with our many Somali patients. For so many reasons, I thought Abdiqasim would be a good choice. He had also studied in the Soviet Union, and I remember hearing about him when I was in medical school in Ukraine. Even then, he was known to be kind, well spoken, well liked—an active student and a leader.

One evening, when I was upstairs reading a medical journal and Ahmed was downstairs watching television, my niece Su'ado's husband came to the apartment, and my son brought him in to see me. "Did you hear the news on the radio?" asked my nephew. "You're a member of the government today."

"I didn't hear," I said. I hadn't been among the women and men running after Abdiqasim, asking for a position in the new Transitional National Government. My nephew was surprised that no one had told me, but I continued working as normal. Then, about a week later, I received a call from a man who introduced himself as the minister of labor and sports. I had been named his vice minister, he said. "We will be waiting for you on Friday." It was already Wednesday.

The other vice minister of labor and sports, he said, was a woman who had moved to Ohio as a refugee and was on her way back to Somalia. Like most members of the new government, she would live in the hotel where the government meetings would be held. The minister suggested I share the room with her, behind the tall walls and layers of armed guards of the hotel, where he knew I'd be safe. I thanked him but insisted on staying in my camp, so I could continue my work.

"Someone may recognize that you are representing this government and hurt you," said the minister.

"They'll never hurt me," I said, and I was right.

I had never wanted to be anything but a doctor. Even while studying law, I was thinking only about defending my rights and securing my family's own property—not about legislating. But I believed that peace was possible for my country, and I knew that many of the people who formed the new government would not have the interests of the most vulnerable groups in mind.

I quickly made arrangements to return to Mogadishu. Ahmed would remain in Nairobi, where he could finish his last year of secondary school and rent out the downstairs part of our apartment, where my small clinic had been. Ahmed laughed when I told him my position and that someone else from a stronger clan had received the vice minister of health appointment. "Mama," he said, "I think you should stick to labor—you don't know anything about sports."

I took the next flight from Nairobi to Mogadishu and arrived at the camp that evening. Being home, I felt a relief I hadn't experienced in months; while the hour was late, some of the staff stayed in the hospital to greet me. I gave instructions to my driver, who would bring me the next morning, at eleven o'clock, to a hotel in the center of Mogadishu. The council would meet every day from 11 a.m. to 1 p.m., and he would wait outside to bring me back immediately.

The TNG, as this transitional government was called, used a 4.5 principle—the ministers were divided into four parties, for each of the strong clans, and another party that was half the size represented all the rest. I saw that on my name tag, I was identified by my name, my position, and my clan. When members of the Hawiye clan heard the news about me, they came with their stories, their requests. "You are representing us," they told me. "You have to protect us."

"No," I said, "you are Somali, like the rest of the people living in my place. I will defend your equal rights, as I do there."

"So you like other people more than you like us?"

"I like all of you," I said.

The beginning of any new project, from a garden to a government, is filled with promise. Inside the hotel was a big hall with many long tables, where the ministers and vice ministers, about ninety people in all, would meet every day. The prime minister didn't know me, so on the first day I introduced myself: "My name is Dr. Hawa and I live between Afgoye and Mogadishu." I didn't mention my clan.

By the second day, it was clear how few of the representatives truly understood what was happening with the people in their country. "The society that welcomed you here is waiting for you," I said when it was my turn to talk. "Each person here should go back to their region, back to their people, to help them settle, to make peace."

Many people applauded, including the prime minister. "What she's saying is right," he said. "We have to do it and we have to begin now."

But the idea of returning to the streets of Mogadishu, to the needy people and the primitive villages, was not so popular among the representatives from the diaspora, most of whom preferred to stay inside the safety of the hotel, smoking and talking. I left them there each afternoon, returning to the hospital, where I worked for as long as I could. I went to sleep around nine o'clock and was back to work by five in the morning, going first to the farm to start the generators and see the crops and then to the hospital, where I consulted with my staff.

The TNG had no budget for any new programs, so we representatives had little power. Nevertheless, some of the strongest clans began to argue, each side wanting his clan to have more—more control, more soldiers, more business opportunities. The airport and the seaport were still under the command of warlords, whose militias surrounded the places, refusing people entry. Some people believed this was the right way; others supported businessmen who had opened another, private port that was supposedly earning tens of millions of dollars.

I arranged a private meeting with President Abdiqasim to discuss the gridlock. "Hawa," he said, "we don't want to create problems among the strong clans." He believed in dialogue, he said, reconciliation. "We don't want to kill anyone during our stay here, and we don't want to call in outside forces. We will talk only."

As much as he tried to reason with the warlords, they never accepted. Part of our job was to try to negotiate from our own positions. One man that I spoke with offered a piece of advice. "You know," he said, "if you want peace, Abdiqasim has to come to me and step down."

Frustrated, I stopped going to meetings, preferring to focus on my responsibilities in the hospital and on the farm. No one said anything about it until one day Abdiqasim called me to his office. My position had been transferred, he said; I was now vice minister of health.

"Why?" I asked.

"We want you to reopen Banadir hospital," he said.

"But that's as big a job as opening the airport!" Banadir, like so many other hospitals and institutions in Mogadishu, was itself a casualty of civil war—its once-rich resources all in the hands of thieves and bandits, its windows stolen or shattered. As far as I knew, people were squatting in the patients' rooms and the staff offices.

"Try," he said.

People laughed when they heard the idea, knowing that the government could give me no money to build and no guards for protection. "You will die there," they said. "The people are wild—killing everyone."

Still, how could people argue with opening a hospital? I made an appointment to meet Osman Ali Atto, the warlord who had control of Banadir, whose office was in front of the hospital. Since my driver was a relative of Atto's, he made the introduction. "How are you?" asked Osman Atto. "You are welcome."

"I'm here because I want to open Banadir hospital," I said.

"Oh, I have no problem, I'm ready," he said. "We can't control all these militiamen, you know, but we will do everything within possibility."

So as Abdiqasim had asked, we began to try. The next day, on my way to Banadir with my driver and three of my own guards, I thought about how I used to enjoy working there, next to the friends who had helped me in my clinic's earliest days, or with fifteen or twenty students by my side, showing them how to deliver, how to operate. But when I walked through the door and saw the unsanitary conditions, I returned to the present day. My friends and colleagues had either fled or died, and any instrument or fixture of value in the hospital had been stripped away long before. Families squatted in the patient rooms; we saw one in which the tile floor was shattered by someone pounding maize directly onto it. I saw remnants of fires in the surgery departments and of weddings and dances in the big wards.

People began to approach me, asking questions, and as I walked through the halls, I realized that the hospital, lacking in every possible way, was still full of *staff*—nurses, assistants, cleaners—who had been coming in the early morning, every day, just as they used to. Even though they were getting nothing, not even five cents, they'd remained there, waiting, someday, for their beautiful Somalia to return.

When I called a meeting, they all came, wanting to protect their positions. "We're going to open this hospital," I told them. We would ask of each patient about 15,000 Somali shillings, I said, which was the equivalent of a half-dollar.

"Oh, we bless you, Dr. Hawa," said one of the nurses. "Don't leave."

We had few supplies in the beginning, and at first I was the only doctor, but we adapted as best we could, relying on some donated instruments and some medicine that I brought from my own hospital. The local media covered the story on the radio, and we began seeing on average about thirty patients a day—more if there had been an accident or an explosion.

The small amount of money that the needy patients could offer was barely enough to pay for the staff's transportation home, but it was a start. A few other doctors joined us, and it seemed that, each day, the faces of the staff became more and more alive.

Then a man working under Atto came to me one day. "What are you doing?" he asked.

"I'm examining patients," I said, "and I'm giving these hard-working nurses their transportation home."

"Not anymore," he said. "From now on, the staff will collect the money, and then they'll give it to me. I'll distribute it."

"How will you distribute it?"

"Every Thursday," he said.

I was helpless to argue—the place was as much his as it was mine—but I called after him: "That is not government money, that is not your money. I work for that money and I want them to have it!"

The next day, when my driver entered Banadir's front gate, a boy with an AK-47 began to fire in the air. Our car stopped suddenly, and everyone in front of the hospital ran! "Do you want this lady to die here?" said that boy to my driver. "Don't bring us this lady. Go back."

Without our lives, we'd be useless to the people we were trying to help. We told Abdiqasim what had happened, and he called a meeting of all the doctors to address the situation. We were all responsible for the health of our country and for Banadir hospital, said Abdiqasim.

One man stood up to offer a suggestion, "Okay, Mr. President. Hawa is vice minister, but if you want to send her to Banadir, let's change the positions. Have her stay in the hospital, and make me vice minister."

"We request that every hospital in Mogadishu return to its original aim," said another doctor. Since Banadir was once a women's and children's hospital, he preferred to work somewhere else.

I returned to Banadir a few days later, and my staff and I tried our best to speak nicely to everyone we encountered. While we were able to make a bit of progress, it wasn't long before the same young, armed boy met us at the hospital gate. "Go," he said, clutching his gun. "Go, go." Some of the hospital staff saw what was happening, and one young assistant begged me not to leave.

"I'm sorry," I said, but I had to get back in the car. I spoke with Abdiqasim that afternoon. "If you can convince your children not to kill or terrorize anyone, then I can work as your minister," I said. "Otherwise I will not."

There is an old story from this time about a father who bought a gun so his boy could go to work. With no government, however, their definition of work was to earn money by killing someone or robbing someone. On the boy's first day of work, he was successful; he brought back all the money to his father. The next day, the boy tried to rob someone, but the man had a gun and killed him first. "Oh," said the father when he saw his son. "Yesterday he was worth a million and today he is a dead body."

This violence was still the true law of our land, so I decided to end my time in the government. The best thing for me, I learned, was to stay and work in my own place, my clinic. When Somalia once again tried to form another new government at the end of 2004, I turned down the invitation to attend the meeting. People who are fighting will never be able to build.

CHAPTER TWENTY

We Can Remember

When Ahmed flew from Nairobi to Moscow to enroll in university in August 2001, all of my children were together again, in one place, for the first time in many years. I was relieved that they were far away from the inhuman people in their own country, but Moscow was full of a different type of suspicion and intolerance. One night a group of young neo-Nazis beat a group of Somali students waiting for a bus; Deqo and Amina were with them, and one Somali boy was injured. I moaned when Amina told me the news on the phone, unable to accept that a place that had once welcomed me so generously had become so closed—that my children could face such danger simply by walking down the street. "Do not argue with anyone who threatens you," I told her. "Keep quiet and give these evil people whatever they want."

Another time a group of ten or fifteen neo-Nazis came to an apartment owned by an old Somali woman, where many of the Somali students came to get their dinner. When these evil men entered to fight, the Somali students stood to defend themselves with knives and forks, and the men ran away.

"Before I was shocked," Ahmed told me over the phone one day. "Now I'm adjusting."

In 2002, we learned that Deqo had been granted refugee status by the United States. She had worked so hard through UNHCR on behalf of other Somali refugees, sending away her friends and even her cousins; now her new home would be Grand Forks,

North Dakota. I had never heard of such a place, and while I kept quiet, I worried about her travel and the people she would meet when she arrived. Ahmed reassured me. He promised that he would take her shopping in Moscow and see her to the airport, and he called me after her flight took off. Once she had arrived in North Dakota, he called me again with her phone number there. "Mama," he said, "she is so happy."

When I finally heard her voice, I knew he was right. "I have good people here," said Deqo. "They prepared a house for me, and they're looking for a secondhand car." When I imagined her there, I saw her as I had been as a young student, among a sea of white faces. Remembering that part of my past gave me confidence, however: She would work as a teacher and a translator, and she would find her way.

Ahmed finished his preparatory course and decided that he would go on to medical school after all. I was proud to hear the news, thinking that he would become a surgeon, but still I worried, hearing his tired voice from so far away. The cold weather had affected his asthma and gave him chronic bronchitis; I knew that his depression affected his health as well. "Mama, when I was in Nairobi, I was powerful," he said. "People were running after me, respecting me. I had friends. But you sent me to a place where they call me *monkey*."

Ahmed's health still hadn't improved by the time he came home with Amina for a short vacation in February 2003. When I saw him, I decided that he would stay with me until he recovered. The political situation at the time was relatively calm: Abdiqasim's government was still in power, but they controlled just a small corner in Mogadishu. Our area was controlled by a group of Sharia courts, and while I knew that their schools had extreme teachings, they were also generous, offering goats, pasta, rice, and dates to people in need. They did not disturb us, and the surrounding area was peaceful.

That season, our mangos and papayas were plentiful, and Ahmed was able to relax, get well, and grow into a leader. Among the boys—now young men—who'd grown up in the camp, he organized a soccer team, planning matches with some of the neighboring camps and even finding a coach who could run with the team in the mornings. We believe, as you know, that a boy is your protection—he guards your property, your life, your daughter's life. While I'd been raised by only women, and we'd all found our way somehow, I felt happy and relieved just watching Ahmed sleep. I admired my grown son so much that I began to question the importance of education: Why should Ahmed be so far away from me, if life for him there was so difficult? Maybe he was like me, needing a simple life, close to home.

I remembered a time when Ahmed was just fourteen years old. We'd walked together through the camp one day, stopping for a minute to see how one of the newest families had built their home.

"It's very difficult for them," I had told Ahmed then. "You must be grateful for all you have in your life."

"But they are happy," Ahmed had told me. "As long as there's happiness, then maybe to live under the trees is the best."

Now that my son was becoming an adult, I wanted him to stay close. One day I showed him a magazine article about a successful American farmer who owned 3,000 acres of land. "That could be you," I said, and as he flipped the pages, I thought proudly of the land that spread out around us, below the homes of so many. We would not always have the difficult life we have now, I thought. Maybe it was Ahmed's destiny, I thought, to marry, to have children, to take over the farm. When a family came to me to offer their daughter's hand to Ahmed, I asked him to consider it.

"Mama," he said, "that girl is not well educated. I didn't select her."

"But son, I want a grandchild," I said. "If you want, you can go to study, and I'll take the grandchild." He was surprised by what I said, laughing and shaking his head, but I was serious. Why couldn't I have the happiness that other people enjoyed, with big, strong families and many children?

Ahmed insisted that I would have all of it, but he first had his own ideas about his future. He and his friends organized a youth group called the United Somali Patriotic Party, which organized events and looked out for one another. They wrote slogans and encouraged one another to volunteer. Likewise, when some of the people in their group ran out of food, they told the Party, and Ahmed told me; together we worked to find something extra.

Deqo heard the way I was talking and grew concerned: "Do you want my brother to be an uneducated man from the bush?" she asked. While I protested, I knew that she was right. Ahmed would return to Moscow in August, but until then, he would enjoy his time at home in the camp. His soccer team was busy preparing for the final game of an all-Afgoye tournament in our place, on a field that the Americans had cleared with a bulldozer in 1993. They arranged for more than a hundred chairs for the spectators and bought a trophy that I would present to the winner. The day of the match, a huge crowd of people came to our place, picnicking on the lawn and cheering for their favorite players. I think I may have cheered the loudest: When our team won, I handed back the trophy to my son, hugging him.

Amina returned to us for her summer vacation in June, and we celebrated together. We had a big cake for Ahmed's twentieth birthday, and then, about a month later, Amina and Ahmed organized a twentieth anniversary party for the clinic. They asked a group of young boys to distribute invitations across town: Our friends, my colleagues, the prime minister, and many other members of the government were all invited—about two hundred people, not counting all of the people who lived with us in the camp. The day before the party, my children and their friends swept up the area under the mango trees and set it up like a beautiful open-air restaurant, with different carpets serving as different sitting rooms. A well-known Mogadishu cook came to us to prepare a big cow and several goats, working all night by the light of the fire and a big, generator-powered lamp.

The first guests arrived at eight o'clock the next morning to find many, many carpets scattered with beautiful red flowers and green leaves. As people walked around, amazed, they found old friends and sat down with them, remembering the old days in Mogadishu. The young men, wearing white shirts and black suspenders, came out to serve the food, which the cook had divided into individual dishes, three for each person—meat, rice, and fruit. Ahmed and a few members of the soccer team had collected some drums in the camp to form a band: As people ate and drank, they played on and on, singing popular songs as well as an original song they wrote about the hospital. When they stopped to rest, there was a performance by a troupe of African dancers that Amina had hired.

We'd arranged just a few speeches. The prime minister stood up, calling our work courageous. "I didn't know that inside Somalia, something like this was going on," he said. I shook his hand, but when it was my turn to talk, I didn't feel right about thanking everyone. Our successes were before our eyes now, but I also saw all the difficult times. I decided to remember the women we'd lost and those we had protected somehow. I mentioned one woman whose husband and children had been tied up and killed in front of her. She had survived that unimaginable pain, and she still came to me, to talk about her children and mine. "How many people have we buried here because of hunger and gunshots?" I asked the crowd. "Can you remember with me? We cannot count, but we can remember."

When I asked people to help us continue our work, Amina stood up to join me, saying that she would follow in my footsteps. Many of the older people were confused, wondering if that meant I would retire. "Oh, Mama, do you hear them talk?" said Amina. "Don't say that I will take your place—don't say that."

"I will work beside her," I told the crowd. "To have my children beside me is the ultimate happiness." It was true, really, even in the shadow of so much suffering. We would rebuild our society, I thought, watching Amina and Ahmed dance with the rest of the camp's grown children. They would lead, and I would have my golden time, sitting with the people of my generation, offering advice, and enjoying what I had built.

A few days later, we arranged for a minibus to bring a group of Ahmed's friends to the airport, to see him off to Moscow. When his flight was called, the team made a huddle, and Amina and I joined in. Our shoulders fit under the arms of the big boys. "My brothers, my friends, I want you to care for Mama," Ahmed said. "You're still a unit."

I was well known by the airline, so they let me go with my son aboard the plane, before it took off. "Don't worry," Ahmed said as we walked to the bus that would take us there. I was surprised to see at the foot of the stairs a Russian pilot that I recognized. We'd just started to talk when the line began to move and Ahmed walked up the stairs and into the plane. I'd wanted to hug my son, to kiss him one last time, but I didn't get the chance.

After so much activity, the next several months were lonely for me, but Amina kept her promise: In 2004, she brought her diploma directly to Mogadishu, as I had done in my time. And from that moment on, she did not sleep. A new doctor goes through a rigorous training regardless of where she specializes; while Amina's first job in our hospital was in some ways very difficult, she was, in other ways, very fortunate: She had her own hospital to learn in, and her own mother as a teacher. "Oh, how you are lucky," I told her, pushing her to trust her instincts. After a few months of Cesarean sections, she grew comfortable with surgery, and she worked well with the rest of the staff—some who had known her since she was a child.

Now in the early mornings we went side by side to the farm to start the generators and to inspect the fields. We returned through the hospital's side door, removed our old clothes and sandy shoes, and took showers while the nurses organized the day's plan. Then we walked into the consultation room together, to start our work.

One night around this time, we received a woman who had

been transferred to us from another hospital with heavy bleeding. Her husband was already preparing to bury her; he was amazed when Amina treated her well and she recovered. He was so grateful that he offered us money and food from his farm, but since Amina knew that he had big tractors, she asked to borrow them instead, so we could dig our own farm. "Please," Amina told him. "It's the people living here who need the money."

As she found her way as a doctor, my daughter also tried to address the problems and the needs in the camp, asking help of anyone who would listen. Another woman lent us a bulldozer; we collected money to buy fuel for the water pumps and the irrigation systems and to pay more staff. When the man who lent his tractors brought his wife back for a follow-up visit, he was amazed to see how his happiness had turned into food for hundreds. "You must be very proud," he told me.

Like me, like all my children, Amina's heart is open. When she sees something, she reacts immediately, wanting to do everything! When Amina wants to operate, she operates today; once she makes a decision, she will not turn to another thing. But she is warmer than I am, and more active with the patients—taking their hands, welcoming them, talking with them. If we received a wounded child and we had no blood, Amina would say, "Take my blood." She'd give him her arm.

CHAPTER TWENTY-ONE

Ahmed

In the last days of June 2005, Ahmed called me from Moscow and told me that he was preparing to travel. "*Hooyo*, I'm sorry," he said. "I don't know how I can see you and Amina this time."

"Where are you going?" I asked.

"I'm leaving tomorrow for my father's place," he said. "I'm going through Dubai, but I won't have time to see you."

"If you are in Dubai, then I will send you a ticket from Dubai to Mogadishu," I said. "Please don't go there." I could not think of him there, among strangers, living with his father's new wife and his new children. I would not believe it.

"No, no, no, Mama," he said. "Don't send me a ticket. I have a ticket already."

"But there isn't anything there for you, Ahmed. Amina and I are waiting for you here."

"I don't want to come to you. I want to go to my father."

I hung up, angry that he would defy my wishes. Had his father called to him? What did he want with the boy all of the sudden? When I called Deqo to discuss the matter, she supported Ahmed's choice. "He has to go to his father," she said, which made me furious.

"Why?" I asked. "To see someone who lies and cheats?" I slammed my phone on the table. Amina sympathized with me; she was the one who told me that Ahmed had landed, first in Dubai, and then, the next day, in Hargeisa. After that, many days passed when Ahmed didn't call me. I didn't call him either.

Amina tried to make peace between us. "Why are you not calling Mama?" she asked Ahmed.

"She told me that if I go to Hargeisa and something happens to me, she will die," he said. "So I'm not going to tell her that I'm here."

When she told me that, I closed my eyes, seeing a lifetime of sacrifices. "Beginning today," I told Amina, "I have no son."

I couldn't close him out of my mind or my heart, though, even as he'd hurt me. He finally called one day, around the first of August. "How are you, Mama?"

"Ahmed, how are you?" Though I had taken a strong position, I was relieved to hear his voice, to feel the big, exaggerated love I felt for him. Still, I wouldn't ask him to come to me, even though I wanted to see him so much. "Where are you now?" I asked.

"I'm in a hotel," he said. He told me that he had spent some time in Burao, his father's ancestral home, where two opposing clans lived. "I don't trust these people," I told him. "I think they forced your father to go with another woman, and we don't know this woman's family."

"Don't worry, Mama," he said, "I'm going with my two friends." He mentioned one boy who'd lived for a short time in our Nairobi apartment, and another who had grown up in the camp. "I'm driving a car—bringing my father to his office in the morning and home in the evening."

"My children," I said. For a moment, I tried not to worry. "I have three children. They're all doctors, and they're all drivers."

"That's right," said Ahmed. "Deqo is driving in America, Amina is driving you, and I'm driving my father." The end of our conversation was relaxed, and he told me that he loved me. He promised, too, that we would talk again soon, and I began to look at a calendar to see when he would return to Russia for school. Maybe he would come to me first. Maybe he would come to me that Sunday.

Three days later I heard a loud cry coming from Amina's room.

When I came in to find out what happened, she was hysterical, clutching her phone. It was Asha's son, she said, calling from Canada. "Have you talked with Papa Aden?" he'd asked. "The boy died."

Ahmed. In my mind, so clearly, I can still hear Amina's cry. Half her life, she raised him in Nairobi. The other half, they were in the camp together. "I called," she said, "and Father said it was true."

I preferred to die than to believe what she told me. A car accident. Two broken legs, two broken arms. The two other children in the car—the son and the daughter of Aden—were barely wounded.

When news of a death first spreads, people drop everything they are doing and run to you or call you, to tell you their stories. I didn't want to talk to anyone—to hear about my extraordinary boy, about the pain that my husband was feeling to lose his son. "Poor Aden," people would say. He was already nearly sixty years old, and his other son was just four years old. "He won't have the pleasure of seeing that boy as a man."

Ahmed had been searching for his father, but his father did not protect him. Now, because Aden had brought our boy to the north, I had no son. My mind raced with suspicion: That clan— perhaps they saw how Aden loved his son, how Ahmed loved his father. Sometimes the two spoke in Russian, so other people wouldn't understand what they were saying. Maybe this clan saw how Ahmed was clever and worried that he would take Aden back. Every person has an enemy, I knew.

By the time I finally spoke with Aden, the news had spread in the camp, and people were carrying food to us. "I'm sorry," he said, and I could hear in his voice deep pain. I refused to cry or to console him. I knew that Aden loved his son, but he had chosen to leave us and go there, to a place where such a thing could happen.

"Did you bring him to the hospital?" I asked.

Ahmed had died immediately, Aden said. The man who had first seen him knew that he was dead, but that man hadn't known my Ahmed, hadn't known Aden. He was searching all the wrong houses, while my son's body was still lying in that strange place, either dead or alive.

There was no refrigeration system in Hargeisa; they wanted to bury Ahmed the next morning, Saturday. "Please," I begged. "Send me his body."

"No," Aden said. "I cannot send it to you."

"What really happened?" I asked. "Who killed my son?"

"Maybe you can come on Sunday," said Aden.

All that remained for me was deep, deep pain, hot tears soaking my pillowcase every morning. "Don't go there," I'd told Ahmed, but he'd refused me. I'd loved him so much, but he'd wanted the people who didn't love him instead. I continued to search for an explanation. Maybe someone had been hired to drive the other car. Maybe that person had suffocated him first, by pillow, and then put him into a car and crashed another into it.

One of Aden's coworkers called me. "Oh, Hawa, I am sorry to hear what has happened," she said.

"Don't tell me that," I said. "Did you kill my son?" Although I knew in my heart that she had not, nothing was beyond my imagination. I could never have believed that I would live to see a day when a mother could kill her twenty-two-year-old daughter, but I had seen it with my own eyes.

"Hawa, don't say that," she said. "All of Hargeisa is crying for you."

"I raised and educated that handsome boy," I said, unable to control my anger. "You people eliminated him and now you're calling to tell me you're sorry?" I threw down the phone.

I considered going on the Sunday flight from Mogadishu to Hargeisa, but it was canceled somehow. After that, I refused to leave my bed, pulling the blankets tighter, thinking too much: They had told me that Ahmed woke up early that morning, put his brother and sister in a car, borrowed a camera, and went to take photos with them. I had never seen Hargeisa, but I had heard the place was just white sand and stone—no trees. Ahmed wouldn't have done that—he wouldn't have wanted photos when his home was filled with big, beautiful trees.

Since we'd both lost our son, I had thought that Aden would act with humanity, that he'd come to us and say that he was sorry. "Father, are you coming to us?" asked Amina.

"Not now," he said. I knew that Aden had served as the Minister of the Interior for the north of Somalia, and Amina had told me that some people wanted to make him the Minister of Defense. I realized that if he came to the southern part, to his old wife, then maybe they would not give him the position they were preparing for him.

My life stopped. I lay in bed for weeks, then months, unable to sleep; the small rains came in October, but the farm lay fallow. Amina saw my beloved patients, and saw over all the rest, while I thought only of my son. "Don't be a pilot!" I'd said. Let him stay in the sand as is normal, I'd thought. But death comes from everywhere. I couldn't stop it.

In the beginning, Amina gave me sedative tablets to calm me. When I'd cry, she'd say, "Mama, I'm here. We need you—we are your children. What, you have only Ahmed? Do not leave us!"

I wanted to leave them, I admit. I preferred to die rather than to feel the pain I was feeling.

Amina began to think like me, and to search for answers. One of Amina's friends still living in Moscow went to the university office to get Ahmed's papers, but someone had already taken them. Who would want that file, with all of his preparatory course information, his grades from his first years of school? I did not sleep for seven days, as my mind raced to find other clues, other signs. "Amina, tell me he's alive," I begged her late one night when she came back from the hospital to see me.

It was too dark to see her face, but I could hear her weary voice struggling to tell me something untrue, something we both wished to believe: "Ahmed's alive! Ahmed's alive!" That night, I slept immediately: The human body, it is very strange.

CHAPTER TWENTY-TWO

"A Doctor Bound by Humanity"

Another endless dry season spread across the land—the worst we'd seen in ten years or more. Food and medicine disappeared; water catchments dried up; and children began dying of the diseases that always spread easily with poor sanitation, such as cholera or watery diarrhea. A new generation of starving, suffering people began their long journey to our place. Sometimes we received twenty or thirty families in one day, with little to give them, and little space to share. We had no choice but to make the children comfortable, even when we had no infusions to replace the water they were losing. Some days we lost five children, some days ten.

Although I was still in my bed, I heard Amina's tired voice every night when she came in to sleep with me. "I need your help, Mama," she said, growing more and more desperate. Eventually I had no choice but to get up and continue my life, even if I still did not want to live. When so many people are searching for your help, you have to try—to run after them, to see, to do something! Some mornings I entered the hospital at five, without even one cup of coffee or tea. We could not rest anyway, knowing the line of people waiting downstairs.

Amina had met a reporter from the BBC, who was now calling me every day: "How are you? How is the situation?" One evening, he connected me with a head of UNHCR, but the woman there told me that they could not help in our place because the people in the area were killing expatriates.

"If you don't help us now, it'll be a repetition of 1992," I said. I asked her to call on the local organizations that Somali people were forming, which could work with the international organizations and bring food to where the people were most vulnerable.

Thank God, the UN responded quickly; we all worked together—my guards, the guards of the transporters, the guards from the UN's World Food Programme. The food arrived in big shipments; the local organizations picked them up and brought their trucks to our camp, where they stayed overnight, standing guard, making sure that the food was protected. The next morning, early, they would leave our portion and travel on to other camps. Our volunteers would distribute the maize, beans, oil, and porridge—most were dry rations, although two young women, Nura and Hodan, managed a kitchen to feed eight hundred children who were moderately malnourished. As all the children lined up, Nura and Hodan sang songs to keep the people calm and happy.

I can't remember the exact words, though I can imagine them there, smiling, even as people pushed and shoved. *We have to bless the people who are giving us this food. We are grateful that they came and knocked on our door, brought food to our home, cared for us. We have to understand, to be honest. In the future, there will be peace. Amen, Amen.*

Somali people say that when you solve one problem, another problem arises. Though we began to see less watery diarrhea and cholera, violence broke out like another disease, just as deadly. This time the violence was caused by religion, something I believe is private. When religions become political, they wind up disturbing and even killing in the name of God. The United States had declared a war on terror after the September 11, 2001 attacks, searching for people they believed supported Islamist fundamentalist groups. On their list of most dangerous suspects was a leader of one of Somalia's Sharia courts, Sheikh Hassan Dahir Aweys, who had been linked to al-Qaeda. As the world's suspicion of the courts grew, so did the tension in our country. Still, many Somali people preferred the courts—which promoted Islamic law, not clan warfare—thinking that anything would be better than the warlords who had oppressed us for so long. The other power in Somalia at the time was the ineffective transitional government, which had elected a new president and for security reasons had moved to Baidoa under the protection of Ethiopian troops.

One of the courts' leaders brought his wife to us for an examination one day. The man seemed uneducated, inexperienced; he alone had five armed guards running after him. While I was visiting another patient, one of the guards came to me. "Our leader wants to see you," he said.

"Okay," I said, "I cannot go out to see him, but I can meet with him in my sitting room. Tell me when he is ready."

"But you cannot wear that!" the guard protested. He wanted me to cover myself as more and more women were covering themselves in those days—head to foot, as Catholic nuns. In areas outside of the camp, the more fundamentalist leaders were insisting that women dress this way, and they were also trying to ban music, movies, sports, and *qat*, punishing people with harsh fines or violence.

I still made the rules in my place, so I did not change out of my doctor's coat or cover my neck. The leader came to me anyhow, proudly telling of how his group was running all of the warlords back to their own places. "Injustice," he said. "We want to fight this injustice."

"Okay, my child," I said, "but please, no more fighting. I miss peace."

In 2006, the Sharia courts in and around Mogadishu came together to form the Islamic Courts Union, or the ICU. By the end of the year, the ICU called for the Ethiopian troops' withdrawal from Somalia. The Ethiopians remained, and the ICU declared war, attacking their troops protecting the government in Baidoa.

Oh, it was a disaster. With aid from the United States, Ethiopian troops backed the Somali government troops to fight many heavy battles, killing hundreds, and advancing north toward Mogadishu. One day, nine big trucks came into our camp, carrying people who were not speaking Somali. "These cars have Ethiopian military inside," said one of our guards. "Be careful." They left without bothering us, although as they drove south, they left total destruction.

At night, I lay in the dark, thinking too much, scratching my head. One night as I scratched, I felt something very hard, up against the bone near my right temple. Maybe a tumor? I was not bothered by the idea after spending so much time feeling desperate, crying day and night for my son. In many ways, I still felt as though I were just waiting to die.

I showed Amina the growth and told her that I had decided not to treat myself. I called Deqo, who had moved from North Dakota to Georgia. "Deqo, please come see me," I said.

"*Hooyo*, I can't come," she said. "I only have a green card."

"You will come when I pass away to bury me," I said. "You don't want to come when I'm still alive?"

So Deqo took her green card, and she came to us. The day she arrived, I remember, it was raining—beautiful weather, cool and calm. I called some of my most senior staff, including Faduma Duale, and told them she was coming. We prepared a big lunch and set the big table in the hospital meeting room, telling everyone else only that we had a special guest coming.

Amina went with our driver to Mogadishu, and when she brought Deqo to me, I didn't recognize her. The last time we were together, at her graduation ceremony in 2000, she was skinny, wearing shirts and trousers, her beautiful hair open. But now, she was covered totally—from her head to her long sleeves and long skirt—and the way she stood was completely different. She had closed off her entire body. "No, no, don't touch me," she said to Ahmed's friends, who had come to hug her. "It isn't a Muslim way."

While I was confused by the change in Deqo, I was no less happy to see her. Still, there was little time to celebrate her return to the camp: We had so many people coming to us that we all worked together until nine or ten o'clock every night. After that, if there were an emergency, the duty nurse would come to our gate, sending the guard to knock on our door, saying, "Something happened, Doctor, get up!"

Amina and I adapted to working with another doctor—one who had come of age outside. We'd always known that Deqo was quieter than Amina or me, but now we saw her stubborn streak in a new way: While Amina and I say whatever we want immediately, whether we need help or know the answer, Deqo has to observe, analyze, understand, and only then will she respond. Amina's impulsiveness meant that she was always calling me if she didn't understand a case, saying, "Mama, I saw this and this symptom, and the patients said that, that, and that—what to do?" Together we could find solutions. Deqo sometimes preferred to do a job alone, instead of asking her sister or me for advice.

One day there was an explosion in the area—a bomb loaded with bits of iron, nails, and stones was set off in a nearby camp. While I knew that a few of the wounded people had been brought to us, I didn't know of their conditions until a nurse came to me and said, "Dr. Deqo wants to operate—to open the stomach!"

"Is the anesthetist here?" I asked. "She can't do this with just a local injection—no!"

I came down to her and said, "Deqo, stop. Put the guy in a bed and we'll call the anesthetist. You can operate tomorrow." Oh, how we argue, my eldest daughter and I, until she realizes that it's no use. As her mother *and* her supervisor, I say what is best.

When we finally had the right people to assist, Deqo made the incision, taking many nails and stones from the man's stomach and reconnecting the places that had been cut. I was very proud of the way she worked—especially her ability to remain calm. That man survived, and when another man came to us with a huge stab wound in his stomach, we operated together.

Amina had been right: My beloved son was gone, but at least I had my two daughters together, alive.

My head had first troubled me almost thirty years earlier, when my children were still small. One day I'd felt a sort of knot, about the width of two fingers, right below the skin near my right temple. I'd waited until 1988, and then, I biopsied it myself: I put the piece in a small bottle of formaldehyde and had sent it to a pathologist friend. It turned out to be a meningioma—a benign tumor on the cover of the brain.

I was devastated by the news; at the time, Deqo was almost a teenager, Amina was just eight, and Ahmed still small. Mohamed Ali Nur insisted that I have the operation at a clinic in Freiburg, Germany, where they specialized in such things.

"My only advice is to do whatever you want now," he joked. "You know surgeons—you may die during the operation."

My friend's husband was the Minister of the Interior at the time; he offset the cost of the procedure and a round-trip plane ticket: Mogadishu to Rome, Rome to Frankfurt, and back. After speaking to his cousin, who was also a government minister, Aden was given the same amount of money and his own plane ticket. I sent a telegram to my cousin Asli, who had married a German man and was living in a small town called Lörrach. We greeted one another as long-lost sisters. "You," Asli said, hugging me, "you look the same! And Aden, hey, you are still with Hawa? How many years are you still together?"

During the 70-kilometer bus ride to Freiburg, I sat next to Aden, fearing that I had somehow brought the health problem to myself, with so much worrying. "You are so serious, Hawa," Asli had always said back when we were students in Odessa. Maybe she was right.

We arrived at the clinic, where a nurse shaved off all my hair. I cried, refusing to look in the mirror: If I could not see myself, I could not see my own life ahead. If I died, I thought, my body would be brought to Mogadishu, and my children and relatives would want to see my face. Was this what they would remember?

The next morning Aden stood in the elevator with my stretcher as the nurse took us to the operating room. "I wrote you a letter," he said stiffly. I read it as they wheeled me into the room: *Don't worry about anything. You're not going to die. I'm sorry that you're sick, but I'm praying to God that you will be safe.* Reading it, I felt calm and happy, as though for a moment my whole life was in order.

I opened my eyes to see only a little white point and a little black point. I fluttered my eyes again and again, until I understood: The white point was the doctor who had performed the operation, and the black point was my husband. I wasn't in any pain. I felt for my head, still enclosed in gauze, as the doctor explained what had happened: When they'd removed the formation on the right side, they'd removed the skin as well, so they had to move some skin from the left side to compensate.

Aden and I stayed in Germany for close to two months, while I recovered. Asli bought me a wig, but I'd decided I would rather cover my head in a scarf than pretend to be someone I was not. We sat up late into the night with Asli and her husband, discussing Somali politics. "That country is empty," Asli said. "There is nothing for you there."

She wanted me to extend our visa and bring the children over. While Aden considered the possibility, I refused immediately, reminding her what I had said when we were students visiting London in the summer of 1969. "I still prefer the smell of Ceelgaab to the beauty of Oxford Street," I'd told Asli, referencing one of Mogadishu's low-lying villages. "Your country is beautiful, but mine is the best."

"You are stubborn, Hawa," Asli had said, shaking her head.

"I don't see it that way." I had the words of Ayeyo, blessing me: *You will stay in this place, my child, and no one will bother you here.*

By the end of 2006, the two sides struggled inside Mogadishu; innocent people fled the fighting, coming once again down the Afgoye Road, although this time in numbers we could never have imagined. In addition to the violence, it seemed that the Ethiopians brought some kind of poison with them. While I don't know if it was in the bullets or the shells they used, I suspect it was white phosphorous—so many pregnant women came to us in those days, miscarrying. The weakest ones came to us caked in blood, horrified—we must have seen close to two thousand cases before the fighting stopped. Amina and I were doing D & Cs every night to stop the bleeding, and in the morning, our guards searched the road for the bodies of the women who didn't make it to us.

On the ICU's side, their powerful militia, al-Shabab, which means "The Youth," came into area schools with their cars, saying, "Oh, you young Muslim guys, do you want to go to paradise? Today you have a chance! Come fight the unbelievers—the *gallo*."

All the children ran: "I want paradise! I want paradise!" Secondary school children! The men wouldn't train them, they'd just hand out guns: AK-47, AK-47, AK-47. "Let's go to fight with *gallo*!" they said. One group of children was loaded into a car to kill Ethiopian generals, and during the fighting, every single so-called soldier was massacred. No one came back.

News of war brought the journalists to us. They often stayed at hotels in Mogadishu like the Shamo Hotel or the Peace Hotel; they wanted to see something, so the Somali people they hired often brought them to me. A young American journalist named Eliza Griswold visited us several times in those days. One day I gave her and a photographer, Seamus Murphy, a tour of the whole camp. That day, I remember, there were new displaced people coming, carrying sticks, bending them this way and that, in order to make their huts. I told Eliza and Seamus that when they were finished, they would cover the open spaces with plastic sheets, or whatever else they could find—cardboard boxes or empty sacks.

It was difficult for any Western journalist to stay with us for more than an hour or two, as we didn't want them or the camp to be targeted. As Eliza and I walked back to the hospital, many children ran after us. I told her about the ways we had tried to educate them: The school built by the American Marines lasted until 1997; as it was now ten years later, termites and other insects had eaten away at the plywood structure, which was only supposed to be temporary. We'd moved the school somewhere else for a while, but when we were no longer able to provide food for work, all the teachers had left. I left Deqo and Eliza sitting together, discussing plans for the school. Deqo, I knew, believed in the school more than any of us. I knew that she'd do anything to get it back.

After photographing some of the smaller camps in the Afgoye corridor, a Swiss photographer named Matthias Bruggmann came to our place. The heavy rains had finally returned, so when Amina took him on a tour of the camp, they were caught in a downpour and his camera flooded. Soaked, he came back to the hospital meeting room, where we sat and talked about what he had seen, about the impossible political situation, about his work and mine. Like Eliza, Matthias also returned to us several times during his stay in Somalia, and one of his photos from our camp appeared in *Time* magazine.

A reporter from the *Los Angeles Times* visited us as we were tending to the sickest children, whom we'd laid out together on a big veranda, each one on a blanket. It was the best we could do, with no beds to give them, and when the rains came, their mothers leaned over them, to protect them somehow. For two days that journalist stayed with me, writing down everything I did. He watched as I examined the abdomen of a child suffering from severe diarrhea. I showed him how I could tell how well hydrated the child was by pressing down on his skin.

"Why do you stay here?" he asked me.

"You see these people? How can I leave?" I told him that my son had been killed, and that I also wanted to die. Still, as these people suffering so much wanted so much to live, I knew I could help them in some way.

He published it all with a big headline, A DOCTOR BOUND BY HUMANITY.

When I first saw it, I felt sorry for myself, thinking of the growth on my head, of all that I had seen and suffered. As I read it, though, my attitude changed. The journalist had asked some of the people, "What do you think of Dr. Hawa?" "She's a queen," one woman said. "We don't have anyone else to protect us here."

An American man read the article in the *Los Angeles Times* and found my number somehow. Saying that he appreciated our work and wanted to support us, he sent us a check for $200. We later learned that fifty more people had contacted the journalist, wanting to help. Can you imagine? Fifty people from the other side of the world? That small money was the beginning of the Dr. Hawa Abdi Foundation, which Deqo had established in Georgia.

Eliza contacted Deqo with wonderful news: She'd raised enough money to begin building two rooms for the school. Other organizations had offered to help us set up makeshift schools in tents, but they had not been willing to build desks and tables, which I believed the children needed. "We have to make it look like schools all over the world," I'd told them. "Otherwise, how will the students write what they want?"

Finally, we were able to build something that we knew could last: Two rooms made from sticks, some wood to sit on, and some more wood that served as the children's desks. Two teachers from the area, who had been working privately, accepted some small money to come work for us. I laugh now to think about the opening of the school, which created so much interest that we couldn't fit every one of our eager students at the desks. In the end the teachers and the students sat outside anyway, studying together.

CHAPTER TWENTY-THREE

An Ocean of Need

Amina went into Mogadishu one day to see about opening an Internet connection in the camp. While she was there, in Bakara Market, she was stopped by a group of men who shoved into her hands a heavy, black *abaya*. "Put it on," they said, and although she became hotheaded, insulting them, in the end, she had no choice but to wear the cover and return home.

During the warlords' time, we often saw two groups fighting: One group would fail, and another group would overtake. These so-called religious people coming to power were different, attacking, pressuring, and controlling as I'd never before seen or read. In the name of God, they entered houses without permission—something that's prohibited by the Holy Qur'an. Then, if they saw a woman uncovered, even if she were just sitting in her room with her children, they would beat her. I can't understand how anyone could think that clothes can send them to paradise. The Qur'an says that God knows what's in your heart. Everything is from your heart.

As the religious people became more powerful, everyone and everything suspected as Western or Western-backed was under threat: If the person was military-trained or had government connections, he could be killed. Even schoolteachers risked punishment for teaching something other than to fight in the name of their God. This attitude is nonsense! God creates life—he doesn't want you to kill people unnecessarily. The religious people claim that faiths outside Islam are different, but every religion has the same commandments—do not kill, do not lie, do not steal. There is nothing written that says breaking these most important rules will send you to paradise.

These men tried to recruit one of our boys, Ismael, whose family had come to us at the height of the most recent cholera outbreak. He was well nourished and strong, and he was also very smart. When we heard the rumors, we offered him a job, which we hoped would keep him occupied inside our place. Ismael loved working as an assistant in the hospital; he came to us every day and boasted about the job to his friends. He was, I admit, difficult to supervise at first. I was the one to train him on infection control: "You," I said, "wash your hands here, with chlorine. Otherwise don't go into that room."

Deqo began working with Ismael and a group of his friends. It was a pleasure for her, as they were very eager, studying more intently than a regular student would. She trained them to administer IVs and to oversee a new room, with nine beds, that she'd designated for emergencies. While they were on duty, they wore white physician's coats, so they would feel very important.

One day a young girl was brought to us with a severe uterine rupture; when we opened her abdomen, we saw that she had lost too much blood. Our nurse's assistants heard the news, and they told their friends, who all lined up outside the hospital, wanting to donate their blood. We knew that the boys who had grown up in the camp were healthy; we knew that some had the right match. From those arms alone we received two liters for the girl; when she recovered, her father brought us a goat, which we slaughtered and ate together, with all of the blood donors.

"Drink the soup," said the man. "You, my children, made me very happy."

Since we didn't have proper storage, these boys became our blood bank. You know, they were all like Amina—wanting to help immediately. For example, one of the young men, about twenty-five years old, had A-negative blood, which is very rare. Every time he saw me, he put out his hand: "*Dottoressa*, I'm ready," he said.

"I don't want to kill you, my child," I said. "You just gave me your blood!"

They were among our leaders, for after fifteen years of civil war, the traditional dynamics of our society had changed completely: The women and the youth ran everything, while most of the grown men had either been killed or were away—out fighting or somewhere abroad, trying to make business deals. For those men left behind, there were very few opportunities. Home, for them, was their only source of control, and the sad result was that some lashed out at their wives and their families, wanting to own, to command. I can't explain the number of homes that were broken, consumed by this violence; when the brothers or uncles of a battered wife heard the news, they often brought their clan to fight with the husband, causing even more difficulty along the camp's dusty corridors.

We created a new rule: No man may beat his wife. I instructed the guards to break up domestic disputes and take the perpetrator to our storage room, which we used as a sort of jail. My guards were all young men, just the same as the men they arrested; the difference was that they knew how to treat people. "Why are you doing this?" they would say to the men they caught. "She's not a small child, she's an adult. She knows what's good and bad, so let her talk."

One man they caught had lived in our place from the beginning. He had four wives, and the youngest was jealous, often talking back to him. All of their neighbors heard their arguments, and heard how they escalated until he knocked her down, taking a big stick and beating her with it. Someone heard the cries and told me what was happening, so I sent one of my guards to capture him.

"*Dottoressa*," he said with angry eyes. "What do you want between me and my wife?"

"I don't want you to beat her," I said. "You know that she's very weak. Are you showing her that you're strong? We already know you're stronger than she is."

The man stayed closed up in the storage room the whole afternoon, and he fought me every moment. "This is our personal affair," he said. "You shouldn't be involved."

"I will be involved," I said. "As long as you're here in our place, I'll be involved in everything happening."

The guy, God bless him, God forgive him. When he had been hungry, when his children were dying, I'd fed him nutritious porridge. He was, at that time, one of my biggest supporters. He had stood up the day President Bush came, when all of the other people were lying helpless, waiting for food. "Good day, President!" he had said. "We are happy! You're welcome!"

Now he was struggling against me, saying: "Hawa is like the police. Every time you need Hawa, it will be as if you're going to the grave."

After he had spent some time in jail, though, he had time to cool down. Then I appealed to him, as I had to many others: "If you insist on beating your wife," I said, "go to the rural area, or go back to where you came from. But we cannot support you here." Violence cannot straighten anyone out, I said, not even children.

Over the years, we have seen many types of conflicts, many arguments that seemed to have no solution. Still, if you use reason and explain in a way that people can understand, they will, over time, begin to accept.

The fighting between the Islamic Courts Union and the Ethiopian-backed Somali government continued, with frequent suicide bombings and other attacks. By May 2007, at least 365,000 people had fled the latest fighting in Mogadishu; the number of people on our 1,300 acres alone had reached at least 50,000 people—a number that we could never have imagined. There were so many people with me that the United Nations named the surrounding area the Hawa Abdi area, which also included the other camps in the area.

What had once shocked us in the early 1990s, when we lived with 460 families, seemed relatively calm now as we sometimes received 90 families per day, all fleeing the fighting. They occupied every inch of land, even where we buried our dead. "We have to live," said one man, who agreed to build his hut there. And it was true, really. Still, overwhelmed by need and by other people's suffering, people became agitated, restless; when they felt the committee had made a wrong decision, they staged protests outside my bedroom.

The elders and I decided to divide the land into seven areas, according to water distribution; we expanded our committee into seven groups, each group reflecting the makeup of the area, with at least one woman, one elderly person, and one boy or girl under the age of eighteen. That way the camp's residents could know and relate to their leaders, and each person could bring to the committee an important point of view. The young people, for example, were the most committed—when they believed in something, they would defend it! The women's sense of justice was often sharper than that of the men, who were more interested in taking sides than in settling a problem. I found, too, that the women on the committee tended to be more honest and hardworking than some of the men. They weren't chewing *qat*, for example, or trying to cheat me by telling me something untrue.

One day, a young man named Faysal came to visit; he was a representative from Médecins Sans Frontières (MSF), or Doctors Without Borders, in Switzerland. He returned with a truck full of plastic sheets, enough to cover the children lying outside in our intensive care unit, and he was able to find us some cases of hydrating solution to give those suffering from watery diarrhea as well. In time he brought to us the head of health care for MSF Switzerland, to assess our situation. They were looking for a place to work in Afgoye, said Faysal, but it was clear just how much help we needed.

A group of them opened an outpatient clinic in one of our

existing rooms. We didn't have much to offer for their help, but we could give them a secure, clean place to sleep, clean water, and as much food as we had. I prepared for them two apartments, each with beds, a small refrigerator, and a table to write. Amina hired a cook to prepare whatever they wanted: lobster, fish, eggs, beefsteaks, pasta, rice.

It was a beautiful partnership. MSF gave a salary to both Deqo and Amina; they employed our hospital staff, some of our guards, and about twenty-five young people who worked as community health workers. The difference was remarkable: Suddenly, people in our area were living well, having money for food, clothes, and even to pay for health care.

The job of these community health care workers was to get into four cars and to drive through our camp and the camps in the surrounding areas, looking for children who were the most malnourished. Since some of the other camps' owners were resistant to this, we advised our group to be kind, to talk nicely, to say, "Oh, my uncle, we want to see here, we want to help."

Still, the owners sometimes said no: "If this organization wants to help the camp, they will come here." In those cases, our team had to pay the leader of the camp in order to make the rounds and to find the most serious cases.

With the help of MSF, we were able to meet the huge need. They built an administrative office in one of my first rooms— a beautiful place, with a garden and many flowers outside. They also made two consultation rooms, and one pharmacy. We opened another porridge kitchen to fight moderate malnutrition, for the children who were able to still eat something, but the number of severely malnourished children was too great.

So along with a big cholera treatment center, with more than a hundred beds, MSF opened a separate internal therapeutic feeding center to help suffering, starving children. I remember that we lost the first two patients immediately. They were a boy and a girl, each about three years old and each weighing under five pounds—less than a healthy, newborn infant. We tried to feed slowly, through small, small gastric tubes, but there was only so much we could do.

That December, Deqo and I were invited to Geneva, to partici-pate in an event that focused on international aid after the Sep-tember 11, 2001, attacks. We had just arrived and were checking in at the Hotel Cristal when we saw our photographer friend Mat-thias coming to us, bringing Swiss chocolate! He had stopped by MSF's office coincidentally, and they had told him we were com-ing. I hugged him, happy to see him in his own country; the next day, he took us to a very nice restaurant in the center of Geneva.

After so many years inside Somalia, I was overwhelmed to walk through a big, clean city. The cars had changed so much, and I didn't understand the streetlights. "You people—you came from the U.S., Deqo, and you are Swiss, Matthias, but I was in the bush for twenty years," I said. "I have never seen this!" They laughed at me and took me by the hands, trying to explain the colors.

The meeting involved many people from many different coun-tries, all discussing and debating how to go and help in places like Somalia, where people were killing one another. "What is your strategy?" one person asked. "These people are killing the expatri-ates who are coming to work."

"First, I have to negotiate with the society," I told them. "These bandits aren't coming from other countries, you know. Solve the problem within the society, get those people to respect and trust you, and they'll never bother you."

When we were all out to dinner that night, Deqo and I dis-cussed our travel plans. I'd decided that I wanted to go to Dubai, where I knew a doctor who could examine the growth on my head. One of the men sitting with us, an Ethiopian doctor who worked with MSF, overheard part of our conversation and asked if he could help.

"A visa to the Emirates is very difficult with a Somali passport," I told him.

"Why are you going there?" he asked.

"I had brain surgery many years ago," I said, "and I feel another formation in my head."

By the next day that kind doctor had made all the arrangements for me to have a CT scan; a Swiss doctor he knew, who had worked in Somalia, identified a tumor. I was upset to see the scan, and Deqo cried. Our new friends were very straightforward. In order to determine whether or not the growth was cancerous, they needed to operate, and since the best surgeon would not be available for another six weeks, I would have to come back.

The news was unsettling; on our way back to the hotel, I questioned whether I'd made the right decision by agreeing to an examination in the first place. "For me, to die is simple," I told Deqo. Although years had passed, part of me still did not want to live without my son.

But Deqo could not hear such talk—she protested, as my daughters often do. Soon after we learned that MSF had made a generous offer: Since I was a humanitarian, the operation would be free. God is great, I thought. The answer has come in time.

CHAPTER TWENTY-FOUR

A New Generation

News of my condition had spread by the time Deqo and I returned to the camp in December 2007. People had begun to talk. "If Hawa dies," one man told Amina, "this camp will belong to her male relatives."

Amina, by this time, was starting her own family. She and Faysal had married; we found out, when I was in Geneva, that she was expecting a child of her own. "Mama, how can they say these things?" Amina asked. "What is this religion? How is it fair?" She was, you see, raised by a strong mother and educated outside the country. She had no idea about the harsh Sharia property laws that had almost destroyed my own family.

I called my lawyer, and together we wrote my will—something I had been thinking about for years. Deqo was my witness; she cried as I wrote my name and looked up to a camera, which was recording the moment. "All of this land," I said, "and all of this property, belongs to my daughters."

The next month I returned to Geneva for the procedure, Deqo by my side, while Amina stayed on the ground with MSF, overseeing the camp's security. I drifted off in the hospital to the sound of Deqo reading the Qur'an. When I awoke, the tumor was gone.

"*Hooyo*, I'm okay," I told Amina later as Deqo held the phone to my mouth. "I'm not feeling any pain." I could hear her tired voice, saying that in the camp that afternoon, hundreds of people came together, in a big clearing, to pray for me. I was relieved to think of my daughter there, with her growing belly and her eyes full of tears, bringing the people sweets and milk, thanking them.

But not everyone was praying for me. There was a man that we knew, who had begun to write MSF's main office in Geneva, saying, "Do not support Hawa Abdi." His clan had adapted to doing business with the international aid organizations; he wanted MSF's money for himself, so he accused me of cheating the organization and using the money for myself. I was still recovering from surgery when representatives from MSF came to ask me about the letters. "It's a lie," I said. "The people who are saying this want to be employed." The man who wrote this letter had once come to me, looking for a job, I said; since I knew he was neither educated nor honest, I'd refused to hire him.

I sent a message back through the committee: "If you can't find a way to stop these letters within 24 hours, I will never come back, and you will all lose your jobs." When the committee went to the man, threatening him, he immediately wrote another letter to me and to MSF: "Mama Hawa, we know you are the mother of Somalia; we know that you sold your gold during a difficult time. MSF and Doctor Hawa are doing a good job."

The people in MSF's office were surprised. "Dr. Hawa, one phone call, and you change everything!" one man laughed. "The people who said you were taking the poor people's things are now calling you Mama Hawa."

The results of my tests came back, and the pathologist called a meeting with my surgeon and an oncologist. Although the tumor was not cancerous, it was an aggressive meningioma with atypical cells. They suggested that I undergo an experimental dose of radiation—10 percent more than the recommended amount—to help ensure that it would not return. They would send a piece of my tumor on to a lab, to study it in more detail, and monitor my progress after the radiation.

Lying in the hotel room that night, I turned toward Deqo. I had suffered so much, and this proposition meant three months away from my home, my work, and my pregnant daughter. There was also my own health to think of: Although the doctors had promised me from the beginning that my mental capacity would remain intact after the surgery, there could be complications from the treatment—especially an experimental treatment. I was in agony, trying to reason it out in my head, but this time, I was not alone: "Deqo, if I leave here and go home now, I'll still be alive, helping the people in need," I said. "But if they experiment on me and find a new way to treat a disease, I'll be helping far more people into the future."

Deqo sighed. "It's a difficult decision," she said, so I returned to the debate in my own head, thinking of my own work over the years. I had given my land and my time to other people—my whole life. It made sense now that I would give my body as well.

The next day I signed the documents, and MSF booked a room near the oncoradiology center where Deqo and I would stay. For the next three months, Deqo and I walked from that hotel to the center for my dose of radiation. Although the treatment itself was not painful, my face became very swollen; sometimes you couldn't see my eyes. Matthias came to us, to visit and to help, and so did many, many members of the Somali diaspora, who told me that they were praying for me. While I was weak, I was still happy to see them; to talk about our country's beautiful past and my goals gave me strength, even if I woke up in the morning with a pillow full of hair.

My sister Khadija called our room one day, saying, "Sister, I'm so worried about you!"

"Khadija," I said, "I've done my job—I raised you and raised your children. I wanted your respect and your help, and I didn't get it. You care for yourself, not for me."

Khadija cried when she heard that, saying, "Forgive me, sister, forgive me." I knew that someday we would continue the conversation, and I was happy that she called. But from my bed at that moment, I didn't have any answer.

Around this time I was invited to receive an award at a Somali community event in Geneva; since the group had a particular clan affiliation, I declined to attend. The organizer cried when she heard that, but I was firm. "Fighting by clan is low class," I said. "These beautiful buildings—these clean roads and lights— are not yours. Someone else owns them. They have built them for their country, not for their clan. You have to do the same, for your country."

Deqo and Matthias went without me to the reception, where they delivered a presentation about our work. There they saw a Swiss woman named Claire-Lise Dreifuss whom I'd met a few days earlier; she and her friends had come to our hotel, wanting to meet me, because they'd seen a documentary filmed in our place. I'd liked Claire-Lise immediately—she was a strong, committed woman, a bit older than I am, and very involved with the refugee committee in Geneva. That night she invited Deqo and me to join her for a visit to the Camarada center, which supports and educates women refugees—including many Somali women— living there.

When we walked through the door at Camarada, I felt a new energy in my blood. It was a perfect place! In many different rooms, they had different teachers working with the women on language, computer skills, and sewing. In another part of the cen- ter, there was a kitchen where women from different countries each brought their own national dishes. Three people—including one Somali woman—worked entirely on issues of integration, and regardless of their job or their focus, all their children played together and went to school together. I loved being there, seeing how, when you have good friends, you don't miss your home so much—I felt that way once, when I was a student. I had begun to feel that way again.

"Claire-Lise," I said, "we have to do this in our camp."

"We will try," she said.

*   *   *

Deqo did not want to tell me that Amina had been suffering under the strain of work, the dust, and the sickness in the air, so I learned about her condition while talking by phone with another man in the camp. "Do you know how your daughter is?" he said. "She's seriously sick!"

"Give me my daughter," I told him. When she came to the phone, I could hear her labored breathing.

"I don't know, Mama," she said. "They think it may be pneumonia." MSF made arrangements to fly Amina to a French hospital in Djibouti; when she landed there and I spoke with the doctor, we learned that she had the same strain of pneumonia that was plaguing the camp. The doctor also feared that she was at risk for a pulmonary embolism, which was very serious. And she was pregnant. I squirmed through my treatment session that day, wanting to jump off the table and run. She had been healthy when I left, and now, she could barely breathe without a big pain in her chest. I was shocked, thinking of the mistakes that I had made. I was still mourning my son, and now, my daughter's life was in danger. Without Amina, how would I live?

"I'm leaving," I told my doctor in Geneva. "My daughter is pregnant, and her doctor says she may have a pulmonary embolism."

"You are the more serious one," he said. "If they've already diagnosed the pulmonary embolism, she will recover. You must stay."

I argued with him, insisting that it was better for me to risk dying—I'd already had a long life. He convinced me to remain, and for another two weeks I sat and worried. Then, when I had just two treatments left, I learned about a flight from Geneva through Nairobi to Djibouti.

"Can I get two radiation treatments in one day, in the morning and the afternoon?" I asked my doctor. "Please allow me that?" He agreed, so I booked a flight leaving for Djibouti the day after.

That radiation burned my skin until it was red, red, red; it made my entire body smell bad. The hair on that side of my head never returned, and now, when I'm in the hot sun for too long, I feel weak and dizzy—I've even fallen unconscious, I think, because of the extra exposure to radiation caused by the sun. At the time, though, I didn't think of the risks or even the outcome. I just wanted to see my daughter.

The sight of her beautiful, full face at the airport filled me with joy, for what I had imagined and what was true were very different. We stayed for a while together in the hot, hot city, and finally, on July 12, she delivered a strong, healthy, baby boy. We call him Ahmed, to remember.

"How many hours, how many months have I been waiting for you?" I asked, looking down at my Ahmed. "You're late, but thank God you've come to me now."

I cared for Amina as I had cared for my own sister Amina, feeding her soup from the head of a goat and giving her, each day, a small cup of olive oil to drink. After carrying Ahmed for nine months, she needed to relax and to feel her own strength return. Unfortunately, she couldn't rest long. Two weeks before Amina had delivered, we'd learned that Deqo had been called to sit for her U.S. citizenship test. She couldn't miss the opportunity, so she'd immediately flown back from the camp to Atlanta. Since our agreement with MSF was that at least one member of our family had to be in the camp, Amina and I boarded a flight from Djibouti to Mogadishu when Ahmed was just fourteen days old.

I worried so much as that plane took off, thinking about the air pressure and the tiny new life in my hands. Still, we made it through. The short rains had returned to Mogadishu by that time, so we touched down to very cool, very nice weather. We went immediately to the third floor of the hospital, where we had a small guest room. All the people ran when they heard we had arrived, and a young woman named Fayeri was the first to scoop up the child.

"Don't touch!" I shouted. "Close the door!" How they laughed at me, the nervous grandmother, suddenly concerned, after so long in the bush, about whose hands had been where. I understood the irony and laughed, too, but still, in the beginning, I didn't permit any other woman to care for Ahmed. He was ours alone.

After about three weeks, Amina grew restless, and she got up to work. "I can't just sit down here, when there's so much to do," she told me. I protested, wanting her to have massages, to sleep well, and to continue eating the special, nutritious food that was part of the forty-day *umul*. When she insisted on working, I stayed with the child. Many journalists were coming at the time, about two or three times a week, so my Ahmed and I greeted them in our sitting room, offering them something to drink.

At the end of 2008, at a conference in Djibouti, the UN helped establish another new government, calling for the withdrawal of all remaining Ethiopian troops from Somalia. As the new president, Sharif Sheikh Ahmed, took office in January 2009, the Islamic courts split into two groups, al-Shabab and Hizbul Islam, the latter of which was headed by former ICU leader Sheikh Hassan Dahir Aweys. Hizbul Islam controlled our area, and we knew they disapproved of our leadership within our land. Some of them tried to order Amina around, and she clashed with them. "This is my place," she said. "I will be the one ordering people."

I encouraged Amina to be calm and even-tempered, but we were all, in our place, at the ends of our abilities. The number of people with us was still going up and up; a count at the end of 2009 showed that we had 90,000 people in our camp. What that meant for Amina and me was ceaseless work and very little sleep. While we were constantly alarmed by the difficult cases we saw, there were so many that we forgot them almost immediately—the details we'd just written down replaced in our minds by the sight of someone else's suffering. To see the children in need was the most difficult, especially when we didn't have much to give them, but when we could do something, they were also the ones who returned to health most quickly.

Deqo flew from Atlanta to meet me in Geneva, where I had a follow-up doctor's appointment. While we were there, I met Claire-Lise's husband, Jean-Jacques Dreifuss, and Deqo presented them with a proposal to expand the overcrowded school to twelve rooms. We also discussed a separate proposal, a Women's Education Center, which was based on the good work Claire-Lise brought me to see at Camarada. Agreeing to support our plans for the schools, Claire-Lise and Jean-Jacques established their own organization to help us raise money in Switzerland—Association Suisse Hawa Abdi. With the help of the association, we could guarantee that the school would stay open for the next four years, and that the teachers would earn a steady monthly salary.

We returned to the camp to oversee construction: Using the same strong sticks, our workers added another ten rooms onto Eliza's two in less than two weeks and built the Women's Education Center in another place, using the same materials. A huge crowd of boys and girls formed the day we reopened the school, and we had the difficult task of choosing which children would attend first. While many people argued, we tried to convince them to be patient. Having trusted in us to provide free medical treatment and free water, they believed that free education would be possible in time.

When the Women's Education Center opened, we had the same high demand—about 3,000 women wanted to join, although we could only take 100. We began with instruction about sewing and other handicrafts, so women could make something and earn a small income. Since most of the women in our camp didn't know how to write their own names, one of our schoolteachers came to teach them the Somali language. We set up a small kitchen at the center, as we had in the school, to guarantee that at least once a day, a small group of women and children would have enough to eat. I got my lunch with them on Wednesdays, and I talked with the mothers about the best ways to care for children: how to prevent, recognize, and treat illness; how to administer basic first aid; how to prepare balanced food.

We also tried to discuss the female circumcision ritual that by then had become widely known as female genital cutting. Although the brutal practice had caused me—as well as the women who sat around me, and more than 90 percent of the women in Somalia—so much pain, my daughters and I knew that telling people to stop the practice would never work. The beliefs of a society are often solid as stone, and most of the mothers in our center believed that their girls wouldn't marry if they weren't circumcised. They felt that they would be seen as unbelievers—as *gallo*—and shunned.

We tried to explain the difference between what was written in the Holy Qur'an and what was a Pharaonic custom, as old as Moses. The most straightforward way was to show them the many complications from circumcision. If the clitoral artery was cut, there would be too much bleeding, and the child could die. Others died of infections like tetanus, which were picked up in the sand, and as you know, many young women and children died during labor because the child could not pass through in the right way. Sometimes we even brought the women in our center to the hospital to see the complications like infection or birth defects. They were shocked, but they began to understand.

As conditions in the camp stabilized, my daughters were able to start thinking of their own lives, their own dreams. Deqo prepared to return to the U.S., and Amina made regular trips to Nairobi, where Faysal was now working and where she was required to attend certain meetings for MSF. After a while, Amina decided to resign from her position with MSF and stay in Nairobi, where she began working at Kenyatta Hospital with the hopes of opening her own clinic. I was happy to have her away from the tense situation in our place, as she'd had a few more run-ins with Hizbul Islam. Deqo, who had been away from her new home for so long, kissed me good-bye. "We will be together soon," she promised.

"*Insha'Allah*," I said.

CHAPTER TWENTY-FIVE

The Attack

There is a Somali saying that when you finish hard work, life gives you more hard work. People remarked that I had become the mayor of my own city, but I didn't think about power and influence—or even about the fact that 90,000 people were depending on me. I simply continued on my own, making rounds, meeting with the committees, fighting to support the people who were suffering.

When we began to hear rumors that Hizbul Islam was trying to brainwash young people in our camp, turning them against one another, we tried our best to protect our place. We recruited more young boys to work as nurse's aides, as we had done for Ismael; we took their photos, so that they would be proud of their jobs and defend their home. Otherwise our elders, our committee, our guards, and I tried to approach the rule of Hizbul Islam in the same way that we had all the other groups who had lost and gained control of the area for two decades—we gave them what they wanted, within reason, and we didn't ask for anything in return. Along the edges of our property, we hung white sheets to declare our neutrality.

Hizbul Islam pressured us anyway, harassing some of our staff, asking our guards to give them their guns. While it was a common menacing tactic among these groups, I told the guards I would never agree to it. My place was private, I said, and the guns belonged to the guards themselves. If they wanted to defend me, it was their choice.

A few of their men approached one of our young doctors, an MSF employee. "This lady is almost seventy years old," they said. "Since you are a man, we want to talk with you. What has happened? Why does the lady say, 'My guards, they are not giving you my guns'?" The doctor responded with my logic, which angered the men.

They began coming to our gate in the afternoons, wanting to see me, to negotiate. At first I refused to speak with them, but when they would not stop, I agreed to a meeting. I called for my guards and the elders, and we welcomed a few Hizbul Islam representatives in my sitting room, where I'd received so many guests over the years. But when we all sat down to talk, the men insulted us. "We want to take over this place," they said. They thought that since a woman was in control, it was their right.

No one on our side agreed with this proposal, and I argued with them, citing my professional, legal, and moral authority: "I built this myself, to care for these poor people. I am the only doctor here. With what qualifications would you run this place?"

"You people are not obedient," said one of their men. "You are not recognizing us."

But what had they done, besides killing? I tried to explain to the men of Hizbul Islam that the people in our camp had a different idea about leadership, although when I could see that they weren't listening, I stopped talking and returned to my crowded hospital, to work. I knew that after more than twenty years, the people in my place believed in themselves and in their own society. They would never recognize a leader whose only aim was to take.

The first call to prayer in Islam is before sunrise. Usually, I prayed in my room and asked for my breakfast after, while downstairs, the guards at the gate would pray together. On the morning of May 5, 2010, two of my guards were finishing their prayers. One of them, Macalin Hussein, was still reading the Holy Qur'an, and the other guard, Abdisalan, was walking back toward the gate with a big stick in one hand and prayer beads in the other. Suddenly another man they knew, who worked for Hizbul Islam, pushed through the gate without warning. About 50 meters away, I heard the sounds of gunshots and ran to my window. That man's name was Sharab, and he'd begun firing immediately.

"What's happened?" asked Abdisalan. "Sharab! What do you want? Whatever it is, take it!"

But the bullets didn't stop; one struck Macalin Hussein in the shoulder. Abdisalan had been military trained, so he dove under a nearby minibus. While Sharab sent more bullets, hitting the car, grazing the top of the guard's head, Macalin Hussein took his gun with the good hand and shot Sharab through the heart, killing him immediately.

"Sharab died!" I heard the scream, and someone came running to me. "Mama Hawa! Sharab died, Macalin Hussein is bleeding!" More Hizbul Islam men ran in after Sharab, capturing our guards. I had once seen them together, drinking tea in the afternoon, joking. What had happened today?

"Bring Macalin Hussein to the emergency room and stop the bleeding," I told the boy. "Give the first aid immediately." Who had provoked this? As I rushed to dress, my phone rang. It was one of Hizbul Islam's big bosses, telling me to prepare my guards and their guns.

I knew we were outnumbered. "Okay, my child," I said, "I will prepare them. But please, here I have women delivering, children sick—the most vulnerable groups. Don't attack me, we can't defend ourselves. Anything you want, we will do."

I called all the elders, who agreed with my decision to surrender our arms, but still, their eyes were fearful, their hands shaking. We were all like chickens sitting on a nest of fragile eggs, thinking of the suffering people in the hospital, the defenseless people in the camp. We hoped we could talk rationally, to reach an agreement.

When our thirty elders collected all the guns and came to the gate, they were met by a big crowd of militants. They'd come to take the camp by force. While gunfire came from every direction, their men forced the elders onto the ground, beating them with the backs of their guns and then taking them away.

Hizbul Islam's black flag hung inside our emergency ward while their mortar shells slammed into the cement walls and aluminum roofs of our hospital compound. A group of our staff was arrested and brought to another place, in another direction.

I learned all this while pacing inside my room, listening to the explosions. I called Amina to tell her what had happened, and to tell her that I didn't know if I would live or die. "You are now a doctor, you have your family, your child," I said. "I thank God you're not here."

"Mama, stay there," she said. "Don't run from them. You are stronger than they are." She told me that she and Deqo would call everyone they knew, to try to get some help.

She reached a BBC producer, who called me immediately, during some of the heaviest shelling. I told him what my guards had told me: Hizbul Islam's targets were the maternity ward, the surgical ward, and the pediatric malnutrition section. One woman recovering from a Cesarean section I'd performed earlier that day had stood up to run, her wound opening as she disappeared toward Mogadishu. Another shell had hit the cholera treatment center. Terrified mothers had detached feeding tubes and IV lines from their dehydrated children's noses and arms to flee into the bush. We knew those children would not survive.

Imagining my voice on the radio, I tried to appeal to all Somali people, begging them to stand up to defend their society: "You hear what's happening now? It's a disaster." When the next round of gunfire sounded, I said, "That is aimed at the house and the camps." Then I stopped talking, having heard a loud noise. I shouted for the people around me to close the doors, fearing that the soldiers would come in.

"There was no confrontation between the two of you?" asked the BBC producer.

"They came the other day and said they would take control." We heard more explosions in the camp, and then a heavy crash. "Pray for us," were my last words before hanging up. "Pray for us."

More staff members and friends pushed into my room, wanting to help me flee. I refused, begging them to save themselves. "These people want to kill me. I don't want you to be wounded here, or something to happen to you. Please leave me alone."

"Mama Hawa, if you're going to stay, then we are going to stay with you," said one young man, who had been with us since he was a child. I swallowed my fear, and we all huddled together and waited.

Around noon, about fifty Hizbul Islam men came to our apartments; they first broke the gate and shot through my iron door with a round of bullets, which shook the entire house, making a terrible sound. Then about twelve men stormed in and began beating our young men who were still inside. They were going through the different rooms and looting, hoping to find something—money, maybe, or gold. They destroyed a small container filled with grass and vegetable seed packets, which Amina had bought, and then they entered all the bedrooms, looking under the pillows and mattresses.

The men came into my room, shouting. "You've talked to the media outside?" Faduma Duale and several other nurses surrounded me for protection.

"Why?" I asked. "You did not tell me not to talk." I had to act strong. I couldn't be intimidated, with so many of my people watching me with terror.

He grabbed my phone and ordered the rest of the women to give theirs as well. "Dress up," he said. "We're taking you to our court."

"I am dressed," I said. "This is traditional Somali dress." I even managed a smile, saying, "My sons, I don't even know how to wear *hijab*." The frightened nurses covered my body with a large shawl, and together we walked silently down the stairs and outside, where about 150 people stood in large groups. As we were pushed toward a waiting minibus, one of the boys in the camp came to my side, saying, "I will go with my mama."

The militants refused him, shoving him aside.

"But she is my mama," the boy said.

They permitted the nurses to follow me inside the bus. As we drove away to an unknown place, I heard Macalin Hussein's screams. Hizbul Islam were holding the hospital staff hostage, refusing to allow them to help Macalin Hussein—to dress his bleeding wound or to even give him antipain medication.

A few days earlier, he'd brought his mother to me. She lived in nearby Merca, and she was skinny, her face hard from a lifetime of rearing cows, goats, and chickens. As we had talked for a few minutes before her examination, I could tell she was proud of her handsome, well-educated son. He was twenty-five, and married with two boys. Thank God his mother couldn't hear his screams.

After about fifteen minutes we pulled into a small compound and were ordered to get out of the minibus. As we had walked into one of the buildings, some of the young men who knew me from the area approached me, saying sincerely, "Oh, *Dottoressa*, you are welcome." We were led inside a big, open hall, furnished by only a carpet and two mattresses. We sat down on the mattresses, talking quietly to one another, for hours. We were interrupted from time to time by the men, who came in saying, "I am the administrative head," or "I am the security head," describing their position in the administration.

While we were listening, waiting, we worried so much about the situation in the camp—had our guards been returned? Did they all think that we were dead? One of the senior nurses, who had worked with me at Digfer and knew me well, was menstruating at that time. She went to one of the guards and told him that she was bleeding heavily. The guard came to me and said, "Doctor, what do we do with this nurse?"

"I don't know," I said, "it's your job—you treat!"

"I was pregnant!" the nurse lied, crying. "And now I lost my child, because of you!"

Not knowing what else to do, the men released her and another nurse to accompany her. They ran back to the camp to tell the worried people that we were okay. The men had given us food, they said, and although we'd at first refused to eat it, we finally accepted. Then the same nurse changed her clothes and came back to me, reporting that the camp was quiet.

At five o'clock, when the BBC Somali service came on, I heard my own terrified voice from the next room—it was a recording of the interview from the attack. A few minutes later, one soldier entered the room and handed me a mobile phone. "You have many supporters," he said. "Tell them that we didn't kill you or beat you." I talked and talked, reaching out first to my daughters.

"Stand! Don't give up!" said Amina, her voice strong and bright. "You're telling the truth."

When I called Deqo, she cried, "Mama, what can we do?" She had e-mailed Eliza Griswold, asking her to alert the international community. "We have to speak out," said Deqo. "It's the only power we have."

I continued to make phone calls as the guards stood outside. I asked the hospital's staff about Macalin Hussein's condition and then called as many supporters as I could, assuring them that I was unharmed and urging them to condemn the attack. Hizbul Islam, I said, didn't have an ounce of humanity. They'd done things far worse to others than what they'd done to me.

We'd been at the compound for ten hours when we heard, "Let's go." As we stood up, we were silent, fearing that they would take us farther away or even kill us. When I got on the minibus, the driver gave me his mobile phone. "Take this—your son-in-law has called me a hundred times."

"How are you, Mama?" asked Faysal.

"I am okay," I said, "but I don't know where they'll bring me."

"Do you want us to bring you home?" asked the driver. I hung up the phone. "We can also bring you to a hotel or the home of one of our bosses," he said.

I couldn't understand this kindness, after so much brutality. "Bring me to my place," I said.

"To sleep in your room today will be very difficult," he said. "All our soldiers are there."

"It's no problem," I said. "They're my people. I will be with them."

The camp was dark and quiet when we returned. I was told that when our staff took out the fuel to start the engines for power and water, they were beaten. The men in the camp had taunted the residents by shouting, "No Hawa, no water."

When the light and water came back on, people immediately knew that I had returned. As the word spread, they began to leave their homes and come to me, but the men now stationed outside immediately sent them away.

Inside, I walked from room to room, my eyes moving across my bookshelves, my desk, the walls: They'd destroyed every one of my family pictures, shredded my documents, shattered our CDs. My mattress was ripped open, my furniture slashed; though they went after my safe with a sledgehammer, they'd failed to open it. They'd even stomped on my daughters' framed college photos, which showed their friends from Moscow, boys and girls. "This family is *gallo*," they'd said.

Since my own room was destroyed, I walked into Amina's room trailed by forty people, who covered every inch of the floor to protect me. One of the guards sat and told me what had happened to Macalin Hussein. These evil men had taken him to another small city on the way to Mogadishu, where they said they would treat his condition. His sister, brother, and uncle ran after him and finally found him lying there with no nurse. So much blood had drained from his body that he was very weak. When the doctor came in to see him, the family went out, as is customary. When they came back inside, he was crying, clutching his neck. "They injected him with something, Mama Hawa," said the guard. "He took his neck, saying, 'They didn't treat me, they killed me!' He fell into a coma, and at one o'clock, he died."

I didn't know what to say. Instead I lay on the bed, listening to the shooting into the sky, *pah-pah-pah-pah*, terrifying people in the camp all night. Without our guards, we didn't even have protection from a regular thief.

When dawn finally came, it revealed a huge crowd gathered around the house. When I walked out onto the veranda, they began shouting, "We want to see Dr. Hawa!" It was like a protest, a rally with hundreds of people, maybe thousands. Since Hizbul Islam's guards could not overtake a group of that size, they had no choice but to ask me for advice. "If you want them to be orderly, you have to let them in," I said. I suggested they start with four hundred people at a time.

So although I was under house arrest, I was able to welcome visitors between the hours of 6 a.m. and 1 p.m. Eliza called me at night, to ask about the situation. I told her what was happening and what we needed in order to reopen the hospital; I trusted that she would bring the story to the outside world. I also gave a local reporter a short interview, reiterating that Hizbul Islam had entered my private property, and that the needy women and children they'd attacked were my guests. The area's safety, I said, depended on the intruders' removing their black flag and leaving. Since I didn't have a force to fight, I could only raise my voice. It was as Ayeyo had said—although my physical body was weak, my mouth could defend against a thousand.

Most of the Hizbul Islam men left immediately after the attack; just five soldiers remained in my house. "Dr. Hawa, you are stubborn," said one. "You're not listening to what we're telling you. Do not give any interview to any person outside."

"I'm not going to stop," I said.

"You are an old woman—you need to sit," he said. "We are men. We are in control."

"You are a man—you have two testes," I said. "A goat also has two testes. What have you done for your society?" They looked at me, shocked, and though I could see fear registering in the faces of the nurses, I continued. "I do something for my people and my country. You need to give something to these people in need."

They were angry, using harsh words, calling me an old woman and a murderer, responsible for the death of their Sharab. But they couldn't do anything about all the people who were still lining up to see me and share their concern. Although those people could only say, "We are with you. We support you. God is with you," their visits gave me strength. The hospital and the school remained closed, and the committee did not meet. We remained at a standstill, the camp's wreckage a reminder of unimaginable cruelty.

"What are you doing today?" a local journalist asked a group of students. "Why aren't you going to school?"

"We had a free school," they said, "but it's been closed since these people attacked."

One of the elders who had come back to the camp said, "You know, Hawa, this kind of demonstration is very powerful. They will be sorry about what they did to you." The interview with the students was published, along with many others, including one that Eliza wrote for an American website called The Daily Beast.

After that, the five soldiers returned to my room with a different demand: "We told the media that the place is open," they said. "You need to open it."

But nothing in this life is simple. I knew that if I accepted their request to open my facilities today, they'd have the power to return tomorrow, to tell me to close them. "I'm not going to open it until you write a letter of apology to me and to this international organization that is treating and helping our people," I said. "You have to say that you recognize your mistake."

"We are not writing any apology letter for *gallo*," one man said.

"This is private property—not the government's, not yours," I said. "Until you write it, the place will be closed."

My colleagues at MSF agreed with my decision, although it caused all of us great pain. I remained in my room, greeting my supporters and giving orders to staff in the ways that I could. The summons to Hizbul Islam's court arrived, saying that as a result of my disobedience, one of their men had died. The punishment was 100 camels.

The leader of the whole group, Sheikh Hassan Dahir Aweys, came to me to discuss the matter. "I'm your Somali brother," he said.

"What is this?" I said, showing him the paper. "That I will go to your court? Please cancel."

"If they call us to go to the court," he said, "we have to go."

By law, if two people are fighting, one of them can't go and charge the other of whatever crime he wants. A third, neutral party must decide. I would certainly be condemned if I went before Hizbul Islam's court. "I'm not leaving anywhere; this is my private property," I said. "People come to me, not to you. Go and form another place like this, and call me—I'll go work with you."

Hassan Dahir Aweys wrote something on a small piece of paper and stood up. "If you ever want to talk with me, this is my personal number," he said.

The standoff continued for days, with no hospital, no school. I barely slept, thinking only about the suffering people, the destruction of all my work. "My son," I asked their guard. "When will you stop killing the people? Will you tell me the time?"

"When our leader goes to New York or Washington, and Paris. He will capture the people who are living there and say, 'You have to be Muslim, the way I want.' When they accept, we will stop fighting. Before? No."

After a week, their second in command came to me. He was the head of relations between Hizbul Islam and the international community—a tall man in his early fifties, eloquent and articulate. I knew from the beginning, when we were sitting at the negotiating table, that he was more intelligent than the others. He'd urged them to speak reasonably, to show respect.

He handed me a signed letter of apology, written in Somali. He stood by me as I read it, and then he gave me another paper, with the letter written in English. It apologized first to me, Dr. Hawa, and then to the nongovernmental organizations helping in the camp, the camp's staff, and the Somali people around the area who had lost loved ones. When I looked up, our eyes met. "Thank you," I said. He offered me his own heartfelt apology, saying that nothing like this would ever happen again.

I shook my head, telling him he'd made a mistake. "I am Somali," I said. "I am a mother, I am a doctor, and I deserve to be respected. I care for so many people around you—this was a tragedy you could have prevented. Never do this again," I continued, but my voice caught on the words. With his recognition, I felt pity—how I'd worked, how I'd sacrificed, only to be attacked. But if this man could understand me? I began to cry for the first time. Tears streamed down my face as he left the letter with me, closing the door behind him.

It was my time to die that day, but my people saved me. I'd told them from the beginning that fighting was not a way to lead our society, our nation. "If you want to go with me," I'd said, "change your way." When all we'd built was under attack, they understood that they could speak out and stand up against evil. They could come into my house, and they could tell the world what had happened.

Hizbul Islam understood that they could not kill thousands of people coming to me, and I understand that I am alive because of my people. When I think of it now, it still gives me life.

CHAPTER TWENTY-SIX

Women of the Year

While the hospital and the school reopened, we no longer had our guards to protect us—just those five men who were sent from Hizbul Islam. After they worked with us for a while, they came over to our side, believing in our mission and becoming a part of our community. Nevertheless, they were few, and the only other weapons we had were four small pistols—a small fraction of the arsenal we'd had since 1992.

We began to focus our efforts on reconstruction, to talk with the people about the problems facing our work, and about why we needed their help. I was depressed and fearful, convinced that anyone could turn on me. While I was still closed up in the camp, my daughters convinced me to accept an invitation to Kampala, to attend an African Union summit on the invitation of an organization called Solidarity for African Women's Rights. When I landed at the Kampala airport, I was surprised by Amina and Ahmed, who'd come from Nairobi to see me!

We spent thirty-five beautiful days there; I slept and ate well and regained my strength. Still, Amina insisted that I follow them to Nairobi, rather than returning to the camp. She needed help with Ahmed, she said, for she was running her own clinic, which she'd named the Dr. Hawa Abdi Clinic, and she was earning a good salary. She'd rented a beautiful apartment in the Westlands section of Nairobi, and had a very good woman working with her, Felicta, who cooked nutritious meals for me. Amina wanted so much to care for me. "You are depressed," she said. "You have to relax."

I couldn't stop thinking, questioning a lifetime of actions. If you tell me something, I will trust 100 percent. I don't doubt that something you say will happen will actually happen; I don't question your character. If you tell me something is black, I will tell you it's black, for a thousand years. If you tell me it's white, it's white. I expect that people will do what they say, and for too long I even had an expectation that people could act a certain way in return for what I gave. There is a Somali saying that each human being is like the bush. If you go inside, you can meet snakes, lizards, and other harmful things—things you would never expect. My rational side could not live with the truth of such evil, such deceit.

Most nights, after dinner, I watched some television with Amina and then went into her spare bedroom to sleep. This routine made me feel useless—I didn't want to sit in a house, eat, and in the evening or afternoon just walk, then come back to bed, as old people do during their retirement. I wanted to be a little bit more active than that. I tried to conduct as much business as I could by telephone, but Amina said, "Relax. Don't talk with the camp—they may tell you something that will make you nervous."

I obeyed her at first, but I could not help myself, and Amina had no choice but to let me talk. We learned that MSF was leaving us, as they cannot work in a place that has been attacked, especially if their people were involved. I was devastated by the loss, heartbroken. Amina tried to do everything she could, calling a young doctor who had gone to medical school with Ahmed and a qualified nurse who'd been working before. They began to address the huge need left by MSF, doing what we could with the little money we had.

When people found out I had returned to Nairobi, they came to the apartment, welcoming me, telling me that they were shocked and sorry about what had happened in May. Some of them were so upset that they cried, but most days, I didn't want to talk. I wanted to go to my farm, to see how the farmers were digging, planting the seeds, harvesting.

"No! No more!" said Amina. She refused to give me the telephone. "You've worked enough. Now you have to rest."

A few days later, though, she came into my room and sat down hard on my bed. One of the elders called her to tell her that twenty Hizbul Islam soldiers had entered our place, capturing the five guards who had stayed with me and who had come over to our side. I was shocked, breathless even, to think that these evil men who had attacked me were back in my clinic. They remained in our place about ten days, with their heavy guns, and then, just as suddenly as they came, they left.

Those were the first days of Ramadan, a time when we waited until sunset to begin eating, and when the days seemed to stretch out forever. One night, after dinner, I called to Felicta so I could ask her for a glass of water. "Yes, Mama Hawa? Which water do you want? Hot water for the bathroom, or for drinking?" She asked me three times, but I couldn't get the words out. *"Principessa!"* Felicta called to Amina. They rushed into their clothes and carried me down the stairs to Amina's car.

I was dizzy and confused, trying to walk but letting Felicta carry me through the doors of the hospital, past the waiting area and into the emergency room. The doctors gave me oxygen immediately and rushed me to the intensive care unit; they tested my blood and ordered a CT scan. We waited together, Amina, Felicta, and I, until the doctor came in and told me that I'd had a minor stroke somehow. While he said he hoped for the best, he wanted to keep me there, in intensive care, for two days, telling me that my situation was critical. Amina refused to leave my side, even after visiting hours had passed.

"If you want your work to be easy, leave this lady to sleep with her mother," said Felicta. "If you want everything to be difficult, go ahead and kick her out."

"You have to be calm," said Amina when she brought me back to the apartment a week later. But how could I be calm as our people slept unprotected, without as much as a guard? How could we continue in a place that everyone, even our dearest MSF, had left behind? Still, when Deqo and I saw only little money and few supplies, Amina believed that we could run the camp ourselves. She insisted that if we continued asking for help, something would come through, and she proved to the people that we would not abandon them by hiring fifteen new employees—staff cleaners, administrators, secretaries—giving them a small salary, and saying, "Go to work."

Slowly by slowly, more help came in: The African Union Mission in Somalia contacted us about a donation from the Danish government, and Amina requested that all of the money go toward medicine. While I remained in Nairobi, resting, she traveled back and forth to the camp to survey the situation, to see how the new staff was working, and to give from her own pocket to buy the supplies we needed.

After a few months, I recovered, and I was able to travel back to Geneva to be checked by my doctor there. This time Amina accompanied me, and Deqo met us there. One afternoon, I met with the head of MSF in our hotel. "Did we work well together?" he asked.

"Yes," I said. "We worked well—we did an excellent job for the community."

He apologized that we were no longer working together, and I told him that I was also feeling sorry, and that I'd had a minor stroke. "You were very dear to me—I loved you," I said. "It hurt me to disconnect our relations." The problem, I knew, was that we were women with many enemies. Though we wanted to live peacefully, our enemies had made the decision for MSF.

While we were in Geneva, we received an invitation to come to the United States. *Glamour* magazine wanted to honor Deqo, Amina, and me as 2010 Women of the Year. Eliza would write an article in the magazine, and there would be a ceremony at a famous New York City concert hall called Carnegie Hall. We received the news while we were visiting the farm of Claire-Lise and Jean-Jacques, seeing how their tomatoes and grapes were growing. We were surprised and happy to be recognized, although we didn't know what to expect. We knew we were happy to see Deqo's life in America and her friends, whom she said were just like the Somali people we knew—shouting, greeting one another, and laughing.

For Somali citizens, travel to the United States is very difficult. While we had tried to get visas in the past, the situations were always too complicated. This time, though, we succeeded, and *Glamour* magazine booked us tickets in business class. Can you imagine? When you sat, your legs went up, and the chair became a bed. The flight attendants, who gave us food every five minutes, were always asking, "What can I get you? What can I give you? Can I help you?" When we landed in John F. Kennedy Airport, we were fresh and happy.

Amina Mohamed is a very common Somali name. Some-one who shares my daughter's name must have made a mistake because when we came through the airport, the immigration officials took Amina away from us and told us to wait. Little Ahmed ran to his mother, but they pushed him away. "No!" she shouted. "He is my son! He will stay with me."

After about an hour, some lady came to us, holding the *Glamour* magazine, open to the page where Eliza's story was written. I saw the beautiful photo that the photographer Martin Schoeller had taken of us in Geneva. "Is this you?" she asked. "This is your daughter?"

"Yes," I said, "this is my daughter, this is me, this is my other daughter." We waited and waited, and finally, they released us into the warm hug of Eliza and the women from *Glamour*.

We were in New York for seven days, staying in a beautiful hotel, the Empire, and meeting many people and many organizations— Human Rights Watch, the U.S. Mission to the UN, Women for

Women International. The city was too fast for me: Taxis carried us through Times Square, full of lights; elevators shot us into the sky; and when we stepped out, we looked through boardroom windows to see the huge, modern city in every direction.

Eliza and Matthias came to join us the night of the awards ceremony. Before we could take our seats, though, we walked into a big, white tent the length of the street and onto a red carpet. About thirty journalists took photos, lighting up the whole place! During the ceremony, a television journalist named Katie Couric presented the award to me and my daughters, and we walked up onto the big, bright stage, looking out into the crowd of beautifully dressed people watching us. I made a brief speech, thanking *Glamour* magazine and the U.S. government for allowing me to have the beautiful night. I thanked Eliza and all the journalists who came to my place, risking their lives.

"We are three women, and we are committed to change Somali women's lives," I said. "We can't do it alone—we need the help of the American people, and those all over the world."

At the dinner that night, many people came to me, saying, "We will help you." We met women from an organization called Vital Voices Global Partnership, which would work with *Glamour* to raise money and send it to us through Association Suisse Hawa Abdi. We met Susan Rice, the U.S. Ambassador to the UN; Ellen Johnson Sirleaf, the president of Liberia; and so many other powerful women—prime ministers, politicians, actresses, humanitarians. I could not believe that these famous women recognized and respected me. Although I hadn't done anything for them, they saw that I had done something for poor people. In that beautiful night, and the days surrounding it, I felt half of my depression— the feeling that Italians call *tristezza*—lift away.

From New York we went to Atlanta. I was proud to see Deqo's life there, although it was so different than what I knew: By the time I was her age, I was already married with children. Still, I was proud and happy to see how the Somali community in Atlanta respected her, coming to her home with their daughters, saying, "Deqo, advise them. We want them to imitate you."

I sat with these women in Deqo's living room, drinking tea. "You are lucky," they told me. "You are helping people, and your daughter—educated, honest, and hardworking—is helping people, too. God gave you this because of the work that you do." And that is true.

While we were in Atlanta, Asha called to congratulate me for the work that I've done. "It's wonderful what is happening to you," she said. "The biggest people are recognizing you, giving you prizes." I believe that she was telling the truth, and that she wanted to have good relations. Still, it was hard for me to forget the way I had felt for so long, how I had once told her what I had told Aden: "Someday you will search for Hawa, but you will never get her back."

When the Somali diaspora saw me on television in the United States, they all began to call, sending plane tickets. I visited Minneapolis and Dallas, Washington, D.C., and Boston, and many other cities; wherever we went, we were welcomed by a big crowd of Somali people, many of whom I hadn't seen since I was young. At one big community event, a friend of mine from medical school, Dr. Osman Ahmed, introduced me. When he walked up to me, I was so happy to see him! I hadn't seen him since the first days after the government collapse. His face was the same, while I had grown very old, drowning in an ocean of need.

"I want to tell you Hawa's history," he told the crowd. "Hawa came to us, and we were only boys. She was young and skinny, so we protected her as if she were a fragile, golden egg. She finished her medical degree, but do not think that she is only a doctor. She is also a lawyer." Everyone laughed when they heard that, and I laughed, too, able for the first time to reflect on my life and my accomplishments. The experience was so much sweeter because it was shared with someone who had known me from the beginning, and a crowd of people who had seen what I had seen.

Wherever I went, I spoke all that I had in my heart and my mind, asking, "Who will remember with me that time, how it was in Mogadishu, in the afternoon? Who will remember with me?"

The people from the diaspora sometimes cried, feeling homesick, when they heard about the young people passing on the roads, dressing well, the cappuccinos and the ice cream, the sound of the waves. In all my travels I didn't meet one person, even wealthy businessmen or college professors, who told me that he was so happy, he didn't want to go back. It doesn't matter how rich, how successful you are, or how complicated the situation is that you left: The best place, for you, is your home.

"Somalia is waiting for you," I said. "Let's die together, fighting to rebuild our country." The young people cried when they heard that. Although they had finished university and had high hopes to change the world, they were refugees and far from their homes. I knew that for them and for many of their parents—well-respected, economically independent people who were buying and building their own houses, voting for the government—it was still about "my clan, my clan." That was rubbish, I said.

"The person who protects the clan is cursed," I said. "Unless you can stand here and count back four generations that are all of one clan, you're fighting with the people who once loved you."

I worked out the logic with them, counting, *abtirsiinyo*: "Can you show on your fingers of one hand your grandfathers and grandmothers, all of one clan? Then why would you want to kill your uncle, your grandparents?" Wasn't killing your own relatives like cutting off one of your own hands—or removing one of your eyes?

"It is better to have one body," I said. "Let all of Somalia be one."

I returned to Nairobi at the end of December, but I would continue to travel back and forth to the United States, speaking before audiences of many kinds—doctors, aid workers, Muslim communities, women leaders. A prominent journalist named Nicholas

Kristof had written an article about the attack in the *New York Times,* and many people sent money through the *Glamour*–Vital Voices initiative. It helped to keep the maternity ward open, even while we struggled to rebuild the hospital. Although the travel was difficult, we understood that the more we talked, the more people we met would understand our aim and offer their help.

One of our trips was in March 2011, when we returned to New York to attend *Newsweek* and The Daily Beast's Women in the World Summit. There, I was honored to talk with some of the world's most respected people, including President Bill Clinton and Secretary of State Hillary Clinton. Secretary Clinton told me that she appreciated what I was doing. "You inspire *me*," I told her. "You are a very strong woman."

I think she knows that there were Somali people who could understand their friends and their enemies, even though many among us are uneducated or naive. While our situation is so complicated, I believe that, for the United States, freedom means trying to do what one believes is right.

CHAPTER TWENTY-SEVEN

Forgiveness

While we were honored all over the world, our phones continued to ring with unsettling news from home. We had still been
in New York City in December 2010 when, during a big battle
nearby Afgoye, Hizbul Islam merged with al-Shabab, which was
growing more and more powerful in the country. Hizbul Islam
hadn't bothered us in the camp for several months; since so many
men went from one evil group to another, we hoped we would
still be safe.

Our biggest concern, at the time, was the fact that two big
rainy seasons never came—the drought stretched on, into May
and June 2011; the wells ran dry, and illness spread once more.
In May, we received sixty families in one day; they'd walked from
Jowhar, 80 kilometers away, to reach us, and we had almost nothing to give them. Our staff did our best to administer to the most
serious cases, even as supplies were scarce. Still, the money we
had received from donations was reserved to keep our hospital
running. Most international organizations would not stay with
us or even give to us, fearing that since we were working in an
al-Shabab–controlled place, we would be looted and their money
would fall into the hands of terrorists.

In July, the United Nations officially declared a famine in
our region, and slowly by slowly, many of the international organizations who had been away for so long returned to work, in a
high-profile way, in Mogadishu. Still, because of the presence of

al-Shabab, they could not reach us. After so many years of relying on these organizations for aid—and in many cases, for good
salaries—people in our place understood that their return meant
big employment opportunities. When one group held interviews
in Mogadishu, our entire hospital staff left us in one day; the other
organization offered them good positions at a price that we could
not afford to pay.

Deqo knocked on every door, and with the help of our new
friends from abroad, we changed our plans to respond to the
emergency, calculating how much we could budget to keep a few
nurses, cleaners, and guards in the hospital and to buy some small
amount of food to help prevent so many people from dying. We
returned to North America—to Toronto and New York—to fund-
raise, and we were successful: For one month, we were able to
set up seven kitchens that fed 4,200 people each day. It was not
enough to help all, but our volunteers tried to give the rations to
the people who were the most serious. We kept going until, by
October, the money was gone.

The rains returned around this time, though, and when they
did, Amina cultivated six hectares of maize on our farm. We knew
that we had to push people to work with us, so that they could
become self-sustaining somehow. Our laborers watched the crops
carefully, and when it was time to harvest, they received half the
yield. The other half went to the hospital and to the poor people who didn't have the power to dig—the sick, the old, and the
children.

Amina and I remained in Nairobi, where each month we spent
several hundred dollars on phone bills alone; she worked at her
clinic, sending money every day to the camp by wire transfer, and
I began planning for farming and fishing projects that I hoped
would sustain our people in the long term. We spoke with the
committee every few hours, and we tried to offer advice about
serious medical cases and to solve problems as best we could.
The panic would be about a lack of fuel, a lack of medicine, or a

particular conflict inside; once a person whom we hired to help with the generator and the electricity for the hospital got so angry that he cut our power line.

It sounds like an impossible situation—especially to manage from so far away—and in many, many cases it is. Even when our job goes smoothly, we know that the people around us might see something good and attack. In the rare time I have to think about our situation, I wonder whether the origin of our difficult lives is the divided family. If a husband has two wives—or three or four— the children are born among some hatred or suspicion. A Somali proverb says that you don't deliver a child, you deliver a society. A child born among a big hatred will grow up to create the same. But the child born into a society that is patriotic, that is doing everything good—*that* child will go the same way the society is going.

Amina tries her best to make me calm—doing everything I want, sometimes thinking of something that she knows would be good for me, like some special food or even a massage, without my even knowing I wanted it. Still, sometimes, our situation seems too impossible to continue: "Deqo," I'll say, "let's sell the land and buy another place, where it is more calm."

"No," says Deqo. "This is the land where I grew up—where you grew up. It is for your descendants. We are not selling it."

While we were traveling, receiving honors, and telling the world about our work, Aden was in the north, suffering. Around the time that we received the *Glamour* award, my daughters sent money so that he could have hernia repair surgery; he recovered, but still he was calling Deqo and Amina, telling them that his condition was getting worse. When they learned that he was diagnosed with hepatitis, Amina wanted to transport him to Nairobi. Somehow his family wanted him to travel to Kuala Lumpur, in Malaysia.

"I will give my father the money and let him go where he prefers," Amina said when she told me the news.

For two or three months Aden was in that hospital, and they tried their best to treat him. By the first days of 2012, his condition had become very serious. Although Deqo had the information first, Amina was the one to tell me, "My father is now semiconscious—I have to see him."

"Okay," I told her, feeling sorry to see her pain and worry. "He will recover, *insha'Allah*."

While we brought Amina to the airport, on the other side of the world, Deqo prepared for her long journey, across the whole of the United States and all of the Pacific Ocean. Amina arrived first, and she called me from her hotel. "Mama, I have seen my father," she said, "but my hope is very little that he will recover from this situation." I could only reassure her in a small way, telling her that I was praying for his health and waiting to hear from her. Once I hung up the phone in Nairobi, I just sat on the apartment's balcony, looking out from the fourth floor into our parking lot, watching the children chase one another, shouting and laughing.

Two days later, on Monday, January 9, my phone rang at three o'clock in the morning. Amina. "My father's heart stopped," she said, crying, crying.

"I'm sorry," I told her. "Please don't cry. Everyone is dying. This was the end of his life."

A few hours after Aden passed away, Deqo arrived in Kuala Lumpur, and my two daughters sat together, their father's body lying before them. I could not bear to think of them standing there, so helpless in some ways, but also so strong. They arranged to send his body back to Somalia, to the north, as he and his family would have wanted.

My phone rang all day, all night, with thousands of condolence calls from people I hadn't heard from in years. According to law, I was still Aden's wife, expected to fulfill the promise that was made in the beginning of our relationship and the decree that he made at the end: "You will bury me."

What could I do? "Mama Hawa," said Noor, one of the boys who grew up in the camp and who was now working with our family in Nairobi, "it is indispensable that you go and participate in the burial time."

I know that there are moments when you have to act, even when every part of you wishes to keep still. Finally I understood that the most important parts of my life were my two daughters, and that I had to support them no matter what the complicated circumstance. Noor kept watch over little Ahmed, and the next day, on Tuesday, I traveled from Nairobi to Hargeisa. When we stopped in Mogadishu, I met a group from the camp—some of the people who loved Aden best—from many different clans. There were thirty-two of us who traveled together, and each one of them was mourning Papa Aden.

I'd told them not to come. "That is not my place," I'd said. "I can't support you there." They'd insisted, however, and Aden's brother prepared two homes, side by side, for the Mogadishu family to stay.

Unlike Mogadishu, Hargeisa has little green—mostly sand and hot, hot sun. One of Aden's sisters met me at the airport. In the 1970s she had lived with us, at our place by the seaside, in Secondo Lido. The last time I saw her was before the civil war, when she was still a young girl; now she was a woman with eleven children, smiling and greeting me. One of Aden's brothers whom I raised was there, too. "Are you going to the place where Aden lived?" they asked as we drove into the town.

"I'm very tired," I told her. Deqo and Amina would not arrive for two more days; I did not want to go to the home that my husband had shared with his other wife and his other children. So they brought me to another home, owned by a beautiful young woman with four boys. The people I knew followed me there, surrounding me.

"Ayeyo, someone has come to you, they want to see you," said my host. She took good care of me, offering the guests tea and sweets in her modern sitting room.

"Thank you for coming to us," the people said. "We are sorry."

"Please come live with us here," said others. "You are the elder of the family."

I thanked them in a strange voice, although I couldn't think of it. From the moment I landed, when the car had driven from the airport to the house where I stayed, until now, as I sat in the house greeting people, I thought only of my son.

Ahmed. In the Holy Qur'an is written a story about Joseph, Jacob's son, whose brothers left him in a well. They put blood on their shirts. "Father, we are sorry!" they said. "Joseph was eaten by some wild animals." Though Jacob became blind with grief, still he said, "He's alive—I know he is alive." They told him he was mad, but in the end, he found his son. Since those most terrible days of 2005, I had searched, too, wishing we had the money for private detectives, and even following the false hope of someone who had suggested she'd seen Ahmed passing by in Mogadishu.

Though it pained me, I'd asked whether Aden would be buried alongside his son. "The area is full," his brother told me.

Oh, how I struggled as I spoke with them, feeling only my own sharp hatred and my own suspicion infecting my mind, threatening my life. What good then was my own education and experience, if in the end I was reduced to these feelings? I sat among well-wishers and old friends who mourned the life of a man who had left me, who was still considered my husband, but I could not swallow the anger. I worried about my daughters: I raised them, I educated them; like their brother, they did not belong there. When they would finally come, I would insist that they stay with me. I would not allow them out of my sight.

One man came to me whom I'd last seen in 1993, in Addis Ababa. He was a part of the movement for independence in the north. "Why are you doing that?" I remember asking him at the time, hearing that he wanted to divide Somalia. "Do you want to cut our body in two?"

When I saw him again, he sat by my side. "I am responsible for taking Aden from you," he said. He explained that at a meeting in London, the powerful members of the Issaq clan decided to make Aden a part of the government. Like so many, Aden was a man who loved to be the boss; he had to leave his home to find a way.

I asked that man if he remembered our conversation in Addis Ababa. "You were creating and cultivating hate these twenty years," I told him. "What have you done?"

"We haven't done anything," said his wife, shaking her head. "Just, we suffered." They had only a few goats, she said. No river, no water catchment.

"You see how you changed?" I asked the man. "Then you were a very strong, smooth, and handsome man. But now, how do you look?"

By the time Aden's wife came to me, I was tired and overwhelmed. When I saw her face for the first time, I was shocked: She was a young, innocent woman, not at all what I had expected. "It is God's decision that we will meet today only," she said.

"There is no problem," I said. "I got my portion when we were still young, and we were playing together. You got yours when he became heavy, old, and sick."

Her mouth opened, her chest shrinking back, as I continued, "I loved him, and he loved me—it was love at first sight," I said. I felt every minute of those thirty-two years that Aden and I lived together, the beautiful days and the angry silences. I saw past his wife's shock into the twenty-four years that I was connected to our Ahmed. "So you took him. I have no problem—I didn't come after him," I said. "But what happened to my son? Don't you know that if he were still alive, he would be raising your children?"

She cried when she heard that, grabbing my leg in protest. "Don't cry," I said. "You now have a son. Ahmed was very strong, and his father loved him well. Did someone think that he could take his father back? Is that why they killed him?"

Many people came to see about the noise, and finally she spoke, "Excuse me! Why are you saying this?"

"I believe that his killing was planned," I said in an even tone. "But what can I do? I can do nothing." She ran from the room, and a silence settled into my heart. As we drove in a group to the airport, to meet my daughters who were accompanying their father's body, those ugly words rang in my ears, along with all the ugly things I had said to my children—"Your father is a liar," I'd told them again and again. "He lied to you, he lied to me."

For so long I had wanted to eradicate every thought of Aden because he had caused me so much pain, but I was here now, the reality of his death before me, and with it, all the facts of our lives.

My daughters had made all the funeral arrangements, insisting we go directly from the airport to the grave, which Aden's brother had prepared. They returned on a Thursday. When I saw Deqo and Amina before me once more, in their eyes was a deep sadness that they had never before known, and I knew that I had to stop fighting, to stop searching. I was always thinking about other people when I spoke about reconciliation—not about my own life. I saw now that although Aden was gone, my blood and his blood were mixed. I had for so long spoken for my country—now I had to act for myself. I had to let the north and the south come together in my children. It was the only way that we would survive.

By the time we arrived at the burial ground, I had let go of my anger. "He lived well in his life and reached a normal age," I said to the people who came to pay their respects.

My daughters brought me to the edge of the grave. "We want you to forgive our father, his body is lying there," said Deqo. I could not cry as they did, but I stood with them, agreeing to join them in the ritual of taking sand and placing it atop the body.

"Mama, we have no brother, our father died," said Amina. "We have no one else. You have to forgive."

We stood there together, three women, knowing everything that had happened, and knowing, too, that somehow, by the grace of God, we had survived. For the hope of what could come, with the thought of my Ahmed who died and my grandson Ahmed, my soul, who would continue our story, I opened my hand. "Aden, I forgive you," I said as I released the sand. "Go to paradise."

Somali tradition says that if you are a woman and your husband dies, you will dress all in white, wearing the mourning veil called *asaay* for four months and ten days. For the sake of our daughters, for the memory of our son, I wore the white, giving my daughters the possibility to say, "My mother is in *asaay*, my father died." That is Somali tradition, to say, "My mother doesn't have to move anyplace—we will work, to give her whatever she wants." As I tell you my story now, I am still wearing the shroud. To me, the *asaay* is a symbol of a bigger loss, one for all women and the whole of our society, as old as the canal nearby Afgoye, Kel Asaay, where many Somali slaves broke their backs at the hands of the Italian colonists.

Our lives have changed drastically since that time. Now as we prepare to mark the thirtieth anniversary of my clinic, the threat is just as great as it's always been: innocent people still suffering because of division, violence, and poverty. The young men controlling Somalia were, like my beloved late son Ahmed, only small children when our government collapsed. Having come of age without law and order, too many of them see no choice but to side with the evil that we pray will leave us.

Just one month after we buried Aden, a group of al-Shabab's men came into the camp with a fleet of buses, forcing at gunpoint seven hundred schoolchildren to board, and many other people as well. Deqo, Amina, and I were together in Nairobi when Deqo's phone rang with the news. It was Ismael: He told us that the mothers had run after the buses on foot, terrified that their children would be forced to pick up arms, or worse, that they would be killed. Then, for hours, the phones were silent, and we were helpless to do anything but alert the media and our other friends and partners, and to pray.

By the late afternoon, we learned that the children had been forced to attend a nearby rally to announce that al-Shabab had joined with al-Qaeda. We thank God that they had been returned unharmed, but it was a sign that the big hatred was only growing. Oh, if I had been there. "You didn't collect these children," I would say. "You didn't build a school, you didn't care for them. Why do you want them to support you? Support yourself!" I would have died of a heart attack, I know, saying these things.

Two weeks later, an al-Shabab-backed businessman took about 100 square meters of the land in front of the hospital—some of my very first property—falsely claiming that he had the deed. While we tried to argue, sending our lawyer to contest the claim, the only court in the region was an al-Shabab court; we were powerless to stop him. Soon after, when a bulldozer came to clear the land of the carefully built huts, four hundred of our people were again displaced and we again began appealing for help all over the world.

Every person in the world has an enemy, but I do believe that those enemies get what they have given. Although they have seen unimaginable difficulty, the people living in my place still call every day, telling me that they pray, just as we do, that these evil people will leave us.

"I know that God gave you power," one person told me recently. "If you pray, al-Shabab will be lost, as Hizbul Islam was lost."

"We know that you will succeed," they say, and after so many years, I believe it, too. I pray that I will return to my place, to speak to my people in person, to tell them that because we are alive, we can fight this biggest enemy, this ignorance. So long as people are ignorant, I will say, they can't see another person's value—what he was doing before and what he is doing now. Ignorance is the reason why people attack without any reason, as they have attacked me, as they have attacked countless innocent people in Somalia and all over the world.

Although I am proud of my daughters, I regret that my worries are now theirs: These days we stay up late into the night wondering when the next drought will hit or whether the people who have taken a portion of our land will return for our hospital. "You must relax," Amina says, but still, sometimes I become angry, insisting that I will fight with the stupid people. You gave these people your blood and your soul, your life, I think to myself, and all they are thinking about is how to disturb you.

My only expectation now is that God will reward me, but it does not mean that I don't feel pain when I remember. I risked my life for my own sisters, whom I carried in the name of our mother and father, and for my people, for whom I have tried my best in the name of our beloved Somalia. When you love so much, you are exposed to so much pain. I will try to forgive nonetheless, for while my daughters and I are only three, with my sisters' children, and with all the other families together, we make a small village. Children grow to love one another, you see, if they have a parent who is patient, who can guide them in the right way. Love is the only way to peace.

When I was eight years old, Ayeyo told me something that I will never forget: "You will be the big trees that everyone comes and relaxes under," she said. "On the road, people will say, 'I am going to Hawa.' 'Where did you come from?' they will ask. 'I come from Hawa,' they will say." Many people might think that it's a curse, but I say that I am happy, anyhow, with what Ayeyo gave me. I know that one day, the truth will come out; the bandits, the people who use our religion as a shield, will be destroyed totally, and the poor people will get back their rights.

In 2008, when my grandson Ahmed was just three months old, I brought him to the farm. "This farm is yours," I said. "You have to protect it, you have to see it and defend it." I know that he will, and I know that he will succeed. As you know, blessings last for fifty generations—as I have been blessed, so, too, will he be.

In my place are all different parts of Somalia—that rural area and the seaside, my mother and my father. It is paradise, so long as we have peace. I live for the hope that peace will come, so I can build a beautiful home for myself by the seaside, nearby the place where, long ago, Aden and I planted five hundred coconut trees. There, where the waves are roaring and the fruit from the trees provides water in the driest times, is where I will spend my happiest days. I will divide my time between the seaside and the farm, where, in the green space, I will walk slowly, enjoying time with my children and grandchildren.

Until that time, I can only give them my story. Seeing the mistakes that I've committed and the good things that I've done, they can build on what I have started. When peace seems impossible, I will tell them to remember so many other things that should have never happened—that I would be educated, that I would build something of my own, that I would survive. That is how I know they will grow into a future that we have dreamed for them, that we have all worked so hard to build. I cannot wait.

Glossary of Somali Terms

Abayo—term of endearment for an older sister
Abtirsiinyo—counting ancestors
Ai—term of endearment for "aunt"
Asaay—white garment worn by a widow
Ayeyo—grandmother
Bun—green coffee beans cooked in oil
Darod—Siad Barre's clan
Dugaal—fence around a typical Somali home, protecting your open courtyard from threat of wind or wild animals
Fakash—pejorative word for another clan
Gallo—unbelievers / people who are not Muslim
Garas—big tree with broad leaves
Guntiino—traditional one-shouldered Somali dress
Hawiye—Hawa's father's clan
Hooyo—term of endearment used in the mother / child relationship
Injera—flat pancake often served for breakfast
Insha'Allah—God willing
Isaaq—Aden Mohamed's clan
Karfan—white shroud used to cover the body in Muslim burial tradition
Jaaji—fishing community
Qat—a popular stimulant made from leaves
Umul—forty days of traditional rest following the birth of a child
Zakat—charity given to the poor; one of the pillars of Islam

Hawa's Family

Abdi Diblawe (Hawa's father)
Abdi Karim (Hawa's nephew)
Aden Mohamed (Hawa's husband)
Ahmed Aden Mohamed (Hawa's son)
Ahmed Faysal (Hawa's grandson)
Amina Abdi (Hawa's sister)
Asha Abdi (Hawa's sister)
Amina Aden Mohamed (Hawa's daughter)
Asli (Hawa's cousin)
Ayeyo / Salaho (Hawa's grandmother)
Dahabo (Hawa's niece, Amina Aden's daughter)
Deqo Aden Mohamed (Hawa's daughter)
Faysal (Amina Aden's husband)
Faduma Ali (Hawa's half-sister)
Faduma Mohamed Hussein (Hawa's daughter)
Kahiye (Hawa's nephew)
Khadija Abdi (Hawa's sister)
Mohamed Hussein (Hawa's first husband)
Sharif (husband of Amina Abdi and Khadija Abdi)
Su'ado (Hawa's niece)

Acknowledgments

Grateful acknowledgment to my daughters, Deqo Aden Mohamed and Amina Aden Mohamed. To Jean-Jacques and Claire Lise Dreifuss and the Association Suisse Hawa Abdi; Médecins Sans Frontières; Matthias Bruggmann; Aisha Ahmad and the team at the Dr. Hawa Abdi Foundation; Eliza Griswold; Sahal Abdulle; Melanne Verveer, Alyse Nelson, and Vital Voices Global Partnership; Cindi Leive, Susan Goodall, and *Glamour* magazine; Tina Brown, Kim Azzarelli, Kyle Gibson, Ellen Kampinsky, Anna Hall, and *Newsweek* and The Daily Beast's Women in the World Foundation; Angelina Jolie and the Jolie-Pitt Foundation; Raj Gandesha, Leslie Morioka, and White & Case LLP; Daniel Wordsworth, Said Sheikh-Abdi, and the American Refugee Committee; Ahmoud Foundation; Alalusi Foundation; Amanda Lindhout and the Global Enrichment Foundation; Chautauqua Institution; the Somali diaspora community of North America; Saint Louis University; the Virtue Foundation; and the countless individuals who have sustained our lives and our work.

To Sarah J. Robbins, for telling my story, and to all who have brought it to light: Jamie Raab, Karen Murgolo, Linda Duggins, Karen Andrews, Claire Brown, Joan Matthews, and Grand Central Publishing; Lennie Goodings and Virago; David Kuhn, Billy Kingsland, Becky Sweren and Kuhn Projects. To Nadifo Farah, Terrence Finneran, Bashir Goth, Osman Harare, Abdi Issak, Erika

Iverson, Safia Jama, Imam Hassan Mohamud, Omar Mohamed, Mohamed Ali Nur, Dan Salemson, Abdi Samatar, and Elisa Slattery. To David Anderson, Nicole Francis, Lindsay Goldwert, Tim Heffernan, Noelle Howey, Mike Wipfler Kim, Brian Marcus, and Amanda Grooms West; to Lawrence and Terry Robbins, and to Craig Holland.

About the Authors

Dr. Hawa Abdi is a Nobel Peace Prize–nominated Somali human rights activist, one of the country's first female gynecologists, and a lawyer. She is also the founder of the Doctor Hawa Abdi Foundation, which runs a hospital and school in one of the largest internally displaced persons camps in the country and which has, for more than twenty years, offered sanctuary to as many as 90,000 people at any one time. In 2010, *Glamour* magazine named her and her daughters, Deqo and Amina Mohamed (who are also doctors) "Women of the Year," dubbing the trio "the Saints of Somalia," and calling her "equal parts Mother Teresa and Rambo." Dr. Abdi was named one of *Newsweek*'s "150 Women Who Shake the World" in 2011 and received the 2012 John Jay Medal for Justice and the Vital Voices' Global Leadership Award in 2013. She and her daughters have saved tens of thousands of lives in their hospital in Somalia.

For more information on Dr. Abdi or to donate to her foundation, go to dhaf.org.

Sarah J. Robbins is an independent journalist whose work has appeared in *Glamour, Newsweek, Marie Claire, Real Simple*, and *Publishers Weekly* magazines, among others, as well as in the anthology *The Unfinished Revolution: Voices from the Global Fight for Women's Rights*. She is a professor with the Bard Prison Initiative, and lives with her husband in Brooklyn.

2023764